5 STEPS TO A 5™

AP U.S. Government & Politics

2016

5 STEPS TO A 5

AP U.S. Government & Politics

2016

Pamela K. Lamb
Revised by Stephen Armstrong

Mc
Graw
Hill
Education

New York   Chicago   San Francisco   Athens   London   Madrid
Mexico City   Milan   New Delhi   Singapore   Sydney   Toronto

1 2 3 4 5 6 7 8 9 0   RHR/RHR   1 2 1 0 9 8 7 6 5 (book alone)
1 2 3 4 5 6 7 8 9 0   RHR/RHR   1 2 1 0 9 8 7 6 5 (Cross-Platform edition)

ISBN   978-0-07-185054-4 (book alone)
MHID   0-07-185054-6
ISSN   2150-6329

ISBN   978-0-07-184448-2 (Cross-Platform edition)
MHID   0-07-184448-1

e-ISBN   978-0-07-185055-1 (e-book alone)
e-MHID   0-07-185055-4

e-ISBN   978-1-259-58790-0 (Cross-Platform edition)
e-MHID   1-259-58790-8

The series editor was Grace Freedson, and the project editor was Del Franz.
Series design by Jane Tenenbaum.

AP Teachers: Order your free online
Teacher's Manual

with teaching strategies, student activity and project ideas, and other ways to incorporate the review materials and practice tests in this *5 Steps to a 5* guide into your classroom curriculum.

Download your free Teacher's Manual from:

http://www.mhprofessional.com/promo/5steps/

or scan this QR code:

CONTENTS

PREFACE

Welcome to AP U.S. Government and Politics. I am, first and foremost, a teacher who has taught Advanced Placement courses to many students who have successfully taken the AP exam. I am also a table leader and reader—one of those crazy teachers who spends a week in the summer reading thousands of student free-response essays. With this guide I hope to share with you what I know, including what I have learned from students and other AP teachers, to help you be successful on the exam.

My philosophy is not to teach *only* for the AP exam. Instead, my goal is to help students develop skills and abilities that lead to advanced levels of aptitude in government and politics. These are the same skills that will enable you to do well on the AP U.S. Government and Politics exam. My aim is to remove your nervousness and to improve your comfort level with the test. I believe that you are already motivated to succeed; otherwise, you would not have come this far. And obviously, you would not have purchased this prep book.

Since you have taken or are already taking a government and politics class, this book is going to supplement your course readings, writing, and analysis. I am going to give you the opportunity to practice the skills and techniques that I know from experience *really work*! I am confident that if you apply the techniques and processes presented in this book, you can succeed.

Let's begin.

Pamela K. Lamb

ACKNOWLEDGMENTS

My love and appreciation to Mark H. Lamb for his constant support, encouragement, and belief in my abilities and in me. Without his collaboration, this book would never have been completed. Special thanks to Frances New for her suggestions and encouragement. To Derek James (DJ) New: May this book someday help you in your studies. To my AP Government and Politics colleagues and friends: Thanks for all the ideas you have shared over the years—I'll see you at the reading. To my students, past, present, and future: Thank you for the inspiration you give to all teachers.

ABOUT THE AUTHORS

Pamela K. Lamb teaches AP U.S. Government and Politics at Del Rio High School in Del Rio, Texas. She is a College Board consultant as well as a longtime reader, table leader, and question leader of AP tests in U.S. Government and Politics.

Stephen Armstrong is a social studies department supervisor in the West Hartford, Connecticut, public schools.

INTRODUCTION: THE FIVE-STEP PROGRAM

The Basics

Not too long ago, you decided to enroll in AP U.S. Government and Politics. Maybe you have always been interested in political affairs, or maybe a respected teacher encouraged you and you accepted the challenge. Either way, you find yourself here, flipping through a book that promises to help you culminate your efforts with the highest of honors, a 5 in AP U.S. Government and Politics. Can it be done without this book? Sure, there are some students out there every year who achieve a 5 on the strength of classwork alone. But I am here to tell you that, for the majority of students in your shoes, using this book is a smart way to make sure you're ready for this difficult exam.

Introducing the Five-Step Preparation Program

This book is organized as a five-step program to prepare you for success on the exam. These steps are designed to provide you with the skills and strategies vital to the exam and the practice that can lead you to that perfect 5. Each of the five steps will provide you with the opportunity to get closer and closer to that prize trophy 5. Here are the five steps.

Step 1: Set Up Your Study Program

In this step you'll read a brief overview of the AP U.S. Government and Politics exam, including an outline of topics and the approximate percentage of the exam that will test knowledge of each topic. You will also follow a process to help determine which of the following preparation programs is right for you:

- Full school year: September through May
- One semester: January through May
- Six weeks: Basic training for the exam

Step 2: Determine Your Test Readiness

In this step you'll take a diagnostic exam in AP U.S. Government and Politics. This pretest should give you an idea of how prepared you are to take the real exam before beginning to study for it.

- Go through the diagnostic exam step by step and question by question to build your confidence level.
- Review the correct answers and explanations so that you see what you do and do not yet fully understand.

Step 3: Develop Strategies for Success

In this step you will learn strategies that will help you do your best on the exam. These strategies cover both the multiple-choice and free-response sections of the exam. Some of these tips are based upon my understanding of how the questions are designed, and others have been gleaned from my years of experience reading (grading) the AP U.S. Government and Politics exam.

- Learn to read multiple-choice questions.
- Learn how to answer multiple-choice questions, including whether or not to guess.
- Learn how to plan and write the free-response questions.

Step 4: Review the Knowledge You Need to Score High

In this step you will learn or review the material you need to know for the test. This review takes up the bulk of this book. It contains:

- A comprehensive review of the themes and concepts of AP U.S. Government and Politics
- Key terms
- Rapid reviews of the main ideas of each chapter

Step 5: Build Your Test-Taking Confidence

In this step you will complete your preparation by testing yourself on practice exams. This book provides you with three complete exams, answers, explanations, and rubrics. Be aware that these practice exams are *not* reproduced questions from actual AP U.S. Government and Politics exams, but they mirror both the material tested by AP and the way in which it is tested.

Finally, at the back of this book you will find additional resources to aid your participation. These include:

- A list of websites related to the AP U.S. Government and Politics exam
- A glossary of terms related to the AP U.S. Government and Politics exam

Introduction to the Graphics Used in This Book

To emphasize particular skills and strategies, we use several icons throughout this book. An icon in the margin will alert you that you should pay particular attention to the accompanying text. We use three icons:

This icon points out a very important concept or fact that you should not pass over.

This icon calls your attention to a strategy that you may want to try.

This icon indicates a tip that you might find useful.

Boldfaced words indicate terms that are included in the glossary at the end of this book.

5 STEPS TO A 5™

AP U.S. Government & Politics

2016

STEP 1

Set Up Your Study Program

CHAPTER 1

What You Need to Know About the AP U.S. Government and Politics Exam

IN THIS CHAPTER

Summary: Learn what topics are tested, how the test is scored, and basic test-taking information.

Key Ideas

✪ A score of 3 or above on the AP exam may allow you to get college credit for your AP course; each college sets its own AP credit policy.

✪ Multiple-choice questions count as one-half of your total score.

✪ Free-response questions count for one-half of your total score.

✪ Your composite score on the two test sections is converted to a score on the 1-to-5 scale.

Background of the Advanced Placement Program

The Advanced Placement program was begun by the College Board in 1955 to construct standard achievement exams that would allow highly motivated high school students the opportunity to be awarded advanced placement as first-year students in colleges and universities in the United States. Today, there are 37 courses and exams with more than two million students from every state in the nation, and from foreign countries, taking the annual exams in May.

The AP programs are designed for high school students who wish to take college-level courses. In our case, the AP U.S. Government and Politics course and exam are designed to involve high school students in college-level studies in political science.

Some Frequently Asked Questions About the AP U.S. Government and Politics Exam

What Is the Format of the AP U.S. Government and Politics Exam?

The following table summarizes the format of the AP U.S. Government and Politics exam.

AP U.S. Government and Politics

SECTION	NUMBER OF QUESTIONS	TIME LIMIT
I. Multiple-Choice Questions	60	Total Time: 45 minutes
II. Free-Response Questions	4	Total Time: 100 minutes

Why Take the AP U.S. Government and Politics Exam?

Most students take the exam because they are seeking college credit. The majority of colleges and universities will consider a 4 or 5 as acceptable credit for their introductory U.S. Government and Politics course. Some schools will accept a 3 on the exam. This means you might be one course closer to graduation before you even attend your first college class or possibly be exempt from an introductory government course. Even if you do not score high enough to earn college credit, the fact that you elected to enroll in AP courses tells admission committees that you are a high achiever and serious about your education.

What Is the Distribution of Grades on the AP U.S. Government and Politics Exam?

Currently nearly 250,000 students take the AP U.S. Government and Politics exam every year. The score breakdown on the test is typically generally as follows:

SCORE	PERCENT OF TEST TAKERS
5	12.0%
4	13.0%
3	25.0%
2	25.0%
1	25.0%

Obviously this is in no way a "pushover" test; you must prepare to do well on it.

Who Writes the AP U.S. Government and Politics Exam?

Development of each AP exam is a multi-year effort that involves many education and testing professionals and students. At the heart of the effort is the AP U.S. Government and

Politics Test Development Committee, a group of college and high school government teachers who are typically asked to serve for three years. The committee creates a large pool of multiple-choice questions. With the help of the testing experts at Educational Testing Service (ETS), these questions are then pretested with college students enrolled in introductory U.S. Government and Politics classes for accuracy, appropriateness, clarity, and assurance that there is only one possible answer. The results of this pretesting allow these questions to be categorized as easy, average, or difficult. After more months of development and refinement, Section I of the exam is ready to be administered.

The free-response essay questions that make up Section II go through a similar process of creation, modification, pretesting, and final refinement so that the questions cover the necessary areas of material and are at an appropriate level of difficulty and clarity. The committee also makes a great effort to construct a free-response exam that will allow for clear and equitable grading by the AP readers.

At the conclusion of each AP reading and scoring of exams, the exam itself and the results are thoroughly evaluated by the committee and by ETS. In this way, the College Board can use the results to make suggestions for course development in high schools and to plan future exams.

What Is Going to Appear on the Exam?

Excellent question! The College Board, after consulting with teachers of U.S. Government and Politics, develops a curriculum that covers material that college professors expect to cover in their first-year classes. Based on this outline of topics, the multiple-choice exams are written such that those topics are covered in proportion to their importance to the expected government and politics understanding of the student. For example, if 10 percent of the curriculum in an AP U.S. Government and Politics class is devoted to the foundations of U.S. government, you can expect roughly 10 percent of the multiple-choice exam to address the foundations of U.S. government. Below is a general outline for the U.S. Government and Politics exam. Remember this is just a guide and each year the exam differs slightly in the percentages.

I. Constitutional Foundations of United States Government	5–15%
II. Beliefs and Behaviors about Government	10–20%
III. Political Parties, Interest Groups, and the Mass Media	10–20%
IV. Institutions of National Government	35–45%
V. Public Policy	5–15%
VI. Civil Rights and Civil Liberties	5–15%

Who Grades My AP U.S. Government and Politics Exam?

Every June a group of government teachers gathers for a week to assign grades to your hard work. Each of these "faculty consultants" spends a day or so getting trained on one question. Because each reader becomes an expert on that question, and because each exam book is anonymous, this process provides a very consistent and unbiased scoring of that question. During a typical day of grading, a random sample of each reader's scores is selected and cross-checked by other experienced "table leaders" to ensure that the consistency is maintained throughout the day and the week. Each reader's scores on a given question are also analyzed statistically to make sure that they are not giving scores that are significantly higher or lower than the mean scores given by other readers of that question. All measures are taken to maintain consistency and fairness for your benefit.

Will My Exam Remain Anonymous?

Absolutely. Even if your high school teacher happens to randomly read your booklet, there is virtually no way he or she will know it is you. To the reader, each student is a number, and to the computer, each student is a bar code.

What About That Permission Box on the Back?

The College Board uses some exams to help train high school teachers so that they can help the next generation of government students to avoid common mistakes. If you check this box, you simply give permission to use your exam in this way. Even if you give permission, your anonymity is still maintained.

How Is My Multiple-Choice Exam Scored?

The multiple-choice section of each U.S. Government and Politics exam is 60 questions and is worth one-half of your final score. Your sheet of little bubbles is run through the computer, which adds up your correct responses. No points are deducted for incorrect answers. Your score is based solely on the number of questions answered correctly. No points are awarded (or deducted) for unanswered questions or for questions answered incorrectly.

How Is My Free-Response Exam Scored?

Your performance on the free-response section is worth one-half of your final score. The free-response section consists of four questions. All four questions are weighed equally in determining your score on this section of the test. Each essay is scored on a scale based on the rubric for that essay. Some free-response questions may be scored from 0 to 6, whereas others may be scored from 0 to 11. Every year, ETS, the U.S. Government and Politics Development Committee, and the chief faculty consultant reevaluate the weighting formulas.

How Is My Final Grade Determined and What Does It Mean?

The composite score for the AP U.S. Government and Politics exam is 120. The composite score is determined by adding the score from the multiple-choice section to the score from the essay section and rounding that sum to the nearest whole number.

Over the years there has been an observable trend indicating the number of points required to achieve a specific grade. Data released from previous AP U.S. Government and Politics exams, which show the approximate ranges for the five scores, are summarized in the following table:

U.S. Government and Politics

COMPOSITE SCORE RANGE	AP GRADE	INTERPRETATION
Mid 80s–120	5	Extremely well qualified for college credit
Mid 70s–mid 80s	4	Well qualified
High 40s–mid 70s	3	Qualified
High 20s–high 40s	2	Possibly qualified
0–high 20s	1	Not qualified

(The ranges change from year to year—use this only as an approximate guideline.)

How Do I Register and How Much Does It Cost?

If you are enrolled in AP U.S. Government and Politics in your high school, your teacher is going to provide all of these details, but a quick summary will not hurt. After all, you do not have to enroll in the AP course to register for and complete the AP exam. When in doubt, the best source of information is the College Board's website: www.collegeboard.com.

Currently the fee for taking the AP U.S. Government and Politics exam is $89. Students who demonstrate a financial need may receive a $22 refund to help offset the cost of testing. There are also several optional fees that must be paid if you want your scores rushed to you or if you wish to receive multiple grade reports.

The coordinator of the AP program at your school will inform you where and when you will take the exam. If you live in a small community, your exam may not be administered at your school, so be sure to get this information.

What Should I Bring to the Exam?

On exam day, you should bring the following items:
- Several pencils and an eraser that does not leave smudges.
- Black or blue colored pens for the free-response section.
- A watch so that you can monitor your time. You never know if the exam room will, or will not, have a clock on the wall. Make sure you turn off the beep that goes off on the hour.
- Your school code.
- Your photo identification and social security number.
- Tissues.
- Your quiet confidence that you are prepared and ready.

What Should I NOT Bring to the Exam?

Leave the following items at home:
- A cell phone, beeper, PDA, walkie-talkie, or calculator.
- Books, a dictionary, study notes, flash cards, highlighting pens, correction fluid, a ruler, or any other office supplies.
- Portable music of any kind. No CD players, MP3 players, or iPods are allowed.
- Panic or fear. It is natural to be nervous, but you can comfort yourself that you have used this book and that there is no room for fear on your exam. Let this test be an opportunity to show what you have learned this year!

CHAPTER 2

How to Plan Your Time

IN THIS CHAPTER

Summary: The right preparation plan for you depends on your study habits and the amount of time you have before the test.

Key Idea

✪ Choose the study plan that's right for you.

Three Approaches to Preparing for the AP U.S. Government and Politics Exam

What kind of preparation program for the AP exam should you follow? Should you carefully follow every step, or are there perhaps some steps you can bypass? That depends not only on how much time you have, but also on what kind of student you are. No one knows your study habits, likes, and dislikes better than you do, so you are the only one who can decide which approach you want or need to adapt. This chapter presents three possible study plans, labeled A, B, and C. Look at the brief profiles below. These may help you determine which of these three plans is right for you.

You're a full-year prep student if:

"*Study groups helped me focus.*"
—DA, AP student

- You are the kind of person who likes to plan for everything very far in advance.
- You buy your best friend a gift two months before his or her birthday because you know exactly what to choose, where you will buy it, and how much you will pay for it.
- You like detailed planning and everything in its place.
- You feel that you must be thoroughly prepared.
- You hate surprises.

If you fit this profile, consider **Plan A**.

You're a one-semester prep student if:

- You buy your best friend a gift one week before his or her birthday because it sort of snuck up on you, yet you have a clear idea of exactly what you will be purchasing.
- You are willing to plan ahead to feel comfortable in stressful situations, but are okay with skipping some details.
- You feel more comfortable when you know what to expect, but a surprise or two is cool.
- You're always on time for appointments.

If you fit this profile, consider **Plan B**.

You're a six-week prep student if:

- You buy your best friend a gift for his or her birthday, but you need to include a belated card because you missed it by a couple of days.
- You work best under pressure and tight deadlines.
- You feel very confident with the skills and background you have learned in your AP U.S. Government and Politics class.
- You decided late in the year to take the exam.
- You like surprises.
- You feel okay if you arrive 10 to 15 minutes late for an appointment.

If you fit this profile, consider **Plan C**.

Calendar for Each Plan

Plan A:
You Have a Full School Year to Prepare

Although its primary purpose is to prepare you for the AP U.S. Government and Politics exam you will take in May, this book can enrich your study of government and politics, your analytical skills, and your essay-writing skills.

SEPTEMBER–OCTOBER (Check off the activities as you complete them.)
— Determine the student mode (A, B, or C) that applies to you.
— Carefully read the Introduction and Chapter 1 of this book.
— Take the Diagnostic Exam in Chapter 3.
— Get on the web and take a look at the AP website(s).
— Skim the Comprehensive Review section. (Reviewing the topics covered in this section will be part of your year-long preparation.)
— Buy a few color highlighters.
— Flip through the entire book. Break the book in. Write in it. Highlight it.
— Get a clear picture of your own school's AP Government and Politics curriculum.
— Begin to use the book as a resource to supplement the classroom learning.
— Read and study Chapters 4 and 5.

NOVEMBER (The first 10 weeks have elapsed.)
— Read and study Chapter 6, Architecture and Development of United States Government.
— Read and study Chapter 7, Federalism.

DECEMBER
— Read and study Chapter 8, Political Culture.
— Read and study Chapter 9, Political Parties.
— Review Chapters 6 and 7.

JANUARY (20 weeks have elapsed.)
— Read and study Chapter 10, Voting and Elections.
— Read and study Chapter 11, Interest Groups and the Mass Media.
— Review Chapters 6 to 9.

FEBRUARY
— Read and study Chapter 12, The Legislative Branch.
— Read and study Chapter 13, The Executive Branch and the Bureaucracy.
— Read and study Chapter 14, The National Judiciary.
— Review Chapters 6 to 11.

MARCH (30 weeks have now elapsed.)
— Take Practice Exam 1 in the first week of March.
— Read and study Chapter 15, Civil Liberties and Civil Rights.
— Read and study Chapter 16, Politics and Public Policymaking.
— Review Chapters 6 to 14.

APRIL
— Take Practice Exam 2 in the first week of April.
— Evaluate your strengths and weaknesses.
— Study appropriate chapters to correct your weaknesses.
— Review Chapters 6 to 16.

MAY (First 2 weeks) (THIS IS IT!)
— Review the Introduction and Chapters 1 to 16—all the material.
— Take Practice Exam 3.
— Score yourself.
— Get a good night's sleep before the exam. Fall asleep knowing that you are well prepared.

GOOD LUCK ON THE TEST!

Plan B:
You Have One Semester to Prepare

Working under the assumption that you've completed or are taking one semester
of government and politics studies, the following calendar will use the skills
you've been practicing to prepare you for the May exam.

JANUARY–FEBRUARY
— Carefully read the Introduction and Chapters 1 to 5 of this book.
— Take the Diagnostic Exam.
— Read Chapters 4 and 5.
— Read and study Chapter 6, Architecture and Development of U.S. Government.
— Read and study Chapter 7, Federalism.
— Read and study Chapter 8, Political Culture.
— Read and study Chapter 9, Political Parties.
— Read and study Chapter 10, Voting and Elections.
— Read and study Chapter 11, Interest Groups and the Mass Media.
— Review Chapters 6 to 11.

MARCH (10 weeks to go.)
— Read and study Chapter 12, The Legislative Branch.
— Review Chapters 6 and 7.
— Read and study Chapter 13, The Executive Branch and the Bureaucracy.
— Review Chapters 8 and 9.

— Read and study Chapter 14, The National Judiciary.
— Review Chapters 10 to 11.
— Read and study Chapter 15, Civil Liberties and Civil Rights.
— Read and study Chapter 16, Politics and Public Policymaking.

APRIL
— Take Practice Exam 1 in the first week of April.
— Evaluate your strengths and weaknesses.
— Study appropriate chapters to correct your weaknesses.
— Take Practice Exam 2 in the third week of April.
— Review Chapters 6 to 11.
— Review Chapters 12 to 16.

MAY (First 2 weeks) (THIS IS IT!)
— Review the Introduction and Chapters 1 to 16—all the material.
— Take Practice Exam 3.
— Score yourself.
— Get a good night's sleep before the exam. Fall asleep knowing that you are well prepared.

GOOD LUCK ON THE TEST!

Plan C:
You Have Six Weeks to Prepare

At this point, we assume that you have been building your government
and politics knowledge base for more than six months. You will, therefore, use this
book primarily as a guide to the AP U.S. Government and Politics exam.
Given the time constraints, now is not the time to try to expand your
AP Government and Politics curriculum. Rather, you should focus on
and refine what you already know.

APRIL 1–15
— Skim the Introduction and Chapters 1 to 5.
— Skim Chapters 6 to 11.
— Carefully go over the Rapid Review sections of Chapters 6 to 11.
— Complete Practice Exam 1.
— Score yourself and analyze your errors.
— Skim and highlight the Glossary at the end of the book.

APRIL 16–MAY 1
— Skim Chapters 12 to 16.
— Carefully go over the Rapid Review sections of Chapters 12 to 16.
— Carefully go over the Rapid Reviews for Chapters 6 to 11.

— Continue to skim and highlight the Glossary.
— Complete Practice Exam 2.
— Score yourself and analyze your errors.

MAY (First 2 weeks) (THIS IS IT!)
— Skim Chapters 6 to 16.
— Carefully go over the Rapid Review sections of Chapters 6 to 16.
— Complete Practice Exam 3.
— Score yourself and analyze your errors.
— Get a good night's sleep.
Fall asleep knowing that you are well prepared.

GOOD LUCK ON THE TEST!

STEP 2

Determine Your Test Readiness

CHAPTER **3**   Take a Diagnostic Exam

CHAPTER 3

Take a Diagnostic Exam

IN THIS CHAPTER

Summary: In the following pages you will find a diagnostic exam that is modeled on the actual AP exam. It is intended to give you an idea of your level of preparation in AP U.S. Government and Politics. After you have completed both the multiple-choice and the free-response questions, check your answers to the multiple-choice questions against the given answers and read over the sample rubrics for the free-response questions.

Key Ideas

✪ Practice the kind of multiple-choice and free-response questions you will be asked on the real exam.

✪ Answer questions that approximate the coverage of topics on the actual exam.

✪ Check your work against the given answers and the free-response rubrics.

✪ Determine your strengths and weaknesses.

✪ Earmark the concepts that you must give special attention.

AP U.S. Government and Politics
Diagnostic Exam 1—Section I

ANSWER SHEET

1 Ⓐ Ⓑ Ⓒ Ⓓ Ⓔ	21 Ⓐ Ⓑ Ⓒ Ⓓ Ⓔ	41 Ⓐ Ⓑ Ⓒ Ⓓ Ⓔ
2 Ⓐ Ⓑ Ⓒ Ⓓ Ⓔ	22 Ⓐ Ⓑ Ⓒ Ⓓ Ⓔ	42 Ⓐ Ⓑ Ⓒ Ⓓ Ⓔ
3 Ⓐ Ⓑ Ⓒ Ⓓ Ⓔ	23 Ⓐ Ⓑ Ⓒ Ⓓ Ⓔ	43 Ⓐ Ⓑ Ⓒ Ⓓ Ⓔ
4 Ⓐ Ⓑ Ⓒ Ⓓ Ⓔ	24 Ⓐ Ⓑ Ⓒ Ⓓ Ⓔ	44 Ⓐ Ⓑ Ⓒ Ⓓ Ⓔ
5 Ⓐ Ⓑ Ⓒ Ⓓ Ⓔ	25 Ⓐ Ⓑ Ⓒ Ⓓ Ⓔ	45 Ⓐ Ⓑ Ⓒ Ⓓ Ⓔ
6 Ⓐ Ⓑ Ⓒ Ⓓ Ⓔ	26 Ⓐ Ⓑ Ⓒ Ⓓ Ⓔ	46 Ⓐ Ⓑ Ⓒ Ⓓ Ⓔ
7 Ⓐ Ⓑ Ⓒ Ⓓ Ⓔ	27 Ⓐ Ⓑ Ⓒ Ⓓ Ⓔ	47 Ⓐ Ⓑ Ⓒ Ⓓ Ⓔ
8 Ⓐ Ⓑ Ⓒ Ⓓ Ⓔ	28 Ⓐ Ⓑ Ⓒ Ⓓ Ⓔ	48 Ⓐ Ⓑ Ⓒ Ⓓ Ⓔ
9 Ⓐ Ⓑ Ⓒ Ⓓ Ⓔ	29 Ⓐ Ⓑ Ⓒ Ⓓ Ⓔ	49 Ⓐ Ⓑ Ⓒ Ⓓ Ⓔ
10 Ⓐ Ⓑ Ⓒ Ⓓ Ⓔ	30 Ⓐ Ⓑ Ⓒ Ⓓ Ⓔ	50 Ⓐ Ⓑ Ⓒ Ⓓ Ⓔ
11 Ⓐ Ⓑ Ⓒ Ⓓ Ⓔ	31 Ⓐ Ⓑ Ⓒ Ⓓ Ⓔ	51 Ⓐ Ⓑ Ⓒ Ⓓ Ⓔ
12 Ⓐ Ⓑ Ⓒ Ⓓ Ⓔ	32 Ⓐ Ⓑ Ⓒ Ⓓ Ⓔ	52 Ⓐ Ⓑ Ⓒ Ⓓ Ⓔ
13 Ⓐ Ⓑ Ⓒ Ⓓ Ⓔ	33 Ⓐ Ⓑ Ⓒ Ⓓ Ⓔ	53 Ⓐ Ⓑ Ⓒ Ⓓ Ⓔ
14 Ⓐ Ⓑ Ⓒ Ⓓ Ⓔ	34 Ⓐ Ⓑ Ⓒ Ⓓ Ⓔ	54 Ⓐ Ⓑ Ⓒ Ⓓ Ⓔ
15 Ⓐ Ⓑ Ⓒ Ⓓ Ⓔ	35 Ⓐ Ⓑ Ⓒ Ⓓ Ⓔ	55 Ⓐ Ⓑ Ⓒ Ⓓ Ⓔ
16 Ⓐ Ⓑ Ⓒ Ⓓ Ⓔ	36 Ⓐ Ⓑ Ⓒ Ⓓ Ⓔ	56 Ⓐ Ⓑ Ⓒ Ⓓ Ⓔ
17 Ⓐ Ⓑ Ⓒ Ⓓ Ⓔ	37 Ⓐ Ⓑ Ⓒ Ⓓ Ⓔ	57 Ⓐ Ⓑ Ⓒ Ⓓ Ⓔ
18 Ⓐ Ⓑ Ⓒ Ⓓ Ⓔ	38 Ⓐ Ⓑ Ⓒ Ⓓ Ⓔ	58 Ⓐ Ⓑ Ⓒ Ⓓ Ⓔ
19 Ⓐ Ⓑ Ⓒ Ⓓ Ⓔ	39 Ⓐ Ⓑ Ⓒ Ⓓ Ⓔ	59 Ⓐ Ⓑ Ⓒ Ⓓ Ⓔ
20 Ⓐ Ⓑ Ⓒ Ⓓ Ⓔ	40 Ⓐ Ⓑ Ⓒ Ⓓ Ⓔ	60 Ⓐ Ⓑ Ⓒ Ⓓ Ⓔ

I _____ did _____ did not finish all the questions in the allotted 45 minutes.

I had _____ correct answers. I had _____ incorrect answers, including questions I left blank.

Scoring Formula:

_____ = _____
   number right   raw score

I have carefully reviewed the explanations of the answers. I need to work on the following types of questions:

AP U.S. Government and Politics
Diagnostic Exam 1

Section I

Total Time—45 minutes

60 Questions

Directions: Each of the questions or incomplete statements below is followed by five suggested answers or completions. Select the one that is best in each case and then fill in the corresponding oval on the answer sheet.

1. American civil liberties were granted by the
   (A) Bill of Rights
   (B) Articles of Confederation
   (C) Declaration of Independence
   (D) Judiciary Article of the United States Constitution
   (E) Supreme Court decision in *Marbury v. Madison*

2. The only president to resign from office was
   (A) Calvin Coolidge
   (B) Spiro Agnew
   (C) Lyndon Johnson
   (D) Richard Nixon
   (E) Zachary Taylor

3. Impeachment cases must be tried in the
   I.   Senate only
   II. House only
   III. Senate and House
   IV. Senate and House with the Supreme Court presiding
      (A) IV
      (B) I
      (C) I and II
      (D) II
      (E) III

4. An example of a government corporation would be
   (A) the U.S. Treasury Department
   (B) the U.S. Postal Service
   (C) the U.S. armed forces
   (D) the Internal Revenue Service
   (E) any independent regulatory agency found within the U.S. government

5. Primary elections are held to
   (A) narrow down the field of candidates within a political party
   (B) expand the field of candidates within a political party
   (C) give the voters more choice in the general election
   (D) allow state legislatures the opportunity to determine political districts
   (E) increase participation of third-party candidates

6. The primary purpose of major U.S. political parties is to control government by
   (A) affecting public policy
   (B) defining party principles
   (C) winning elections through peaceful legal actions
   (D) pushing legislation through Congress
   (E) promoting an individual political cause

7. The independent regulatory commission responsible for the supervision of the nation's banking system and regulation of the money supply is the
   (A) Federal Trade Commission
   (B) Securities and Exchange Commission
   (C) Consumer Product Safety Commission
   (D) Department of the Treasury
   (E) Federal Reserve System

8. Senatorial elections
   (A) occur within single-member districts
   (B) attract less media attention than elections of representatives
   (C) promote frequent personal contact with senatorial constituencies
   (D) provide for a continuous body in the Senate
   (E) result in less diverse constituencies than those of representatives

GO ON TO THE NEXT PAGE

9. The Founding Fathers envisioned a president who would fulfill all of the following roles EXCEPT
    (A) a shaper of public opinion
    (B) a check on bills enacted into law
    (C) the head of state
    (D) the commander of the armed forces
    (E) the executor of bills passed by Congress

10. Before the Supreme Court hears the oral arguments of a case presented for its review, each side must present written documents supporting that side's legal viewpoint. These written documents are known as
    (A) legal documents
    (B) briefs
    (C) viewpoints of the court
    (D) a prospectus
    (E) a writ

11. Which of the following best describes a filibuster?
    (A) A filibuster is an oratorical tactic that can only be used in the Senate.
    (B) A filibuster is an oratorical tactic that can only be used in the House.
    (C) It is used in both houses to stop or slow down action on legislation.
    (D) It can easily be avoided or stopped.
    (E) It is used quite often by the members of Congress and is usually very successful.

12. Interest groups are most often associated with
    (A) matters of economic interest
    (B) matters of political interest
    (C) military issues
    (D) methods of increasing voter participation
    (E) matters of social interest and value

13. In the United States, the average person's political participation is limited to
    (A) voting in local elections
    (B) a basic understanding of government
    (C) voting in presidential elections
    (D) ignoring government altogether
    (E) working for a political party at some level of government

14. The membership of the House of Representatives
    (A) is dependent on the national census
    (B) is a continuous body
    (C) is permanently restricted to 435 members
    (D) is elected in 50 statewide at-large elections
    (E) is apportioned according to the provisions of the New Jersey Plan

15. Which of the following is a major defect of the electoral college?
    (A) The Senate, not the people, decides elections for president.
    (B) Electors are not legally pledged to their candidate.
    (C) Electors are directed by the Constitution as to how to cast their ballot.
    (D) The candidate winning the popular vote always wins.
    (E) Federal law apportions an equal number of electors to each state.

16. In *Lemon v. Kurtzman*, the court established the Lemon Test. According to this test, which of the following would apply?
    (A) Prayer in public schools is unconstitutional.
    (B) Prayer in public schools is constitutional.
    (C) Religious freedom is guaranteed by the constitution.
    (D) Education laws do not apply to religious freedom.
    (E) State aid must be of a secular purpose if it is to be applied to a church school.

17. Which of the following is true about the voting process in America?
    (A) The federal government regulates voter registration in all states.
    (B) State governments regulate voter registration within their respective state.
    (C) All individuals over the age of 18 are required to register to vote.
    (D) Anyone may vote regardless of registration status.
    (E) Local governments are responsible for voter registration laws.

18. In order to ratify the Constitution of the United States
    (A) 9 of the 13 states had to approve the document
    (B) the people had to approve the Constitution by popular vote
    (C) the document had to have unanimous approval by all of the states
    (D) a two-thirds vote by both houses of the new government was necessary
    (E) a three-fourths vote of all state legislatures had to approve the document

GO ON TO THE NEXT PAGE

19. Which of the following is NOT true about the Senate?
    (A) The most influential member is the Senate majority leader.
    (B) Revenue bills cannot be introduced in the Senate.
    (C) The Senate works with the president when treaties are involved.
    (D) The Senate's larger number makes it more powerful.
    (E) The Senate contains 100 members.

20. The purpose of the Twenty-Second Amendment, passed in 1951, was to
    (A) limit presidential terms of office
    (B) allow the president to choose a vice presidential running mate
    (C) provide more checks and balances on the executive office
    (D) allow voters in the District of Columbia to vote
    (E) allow for presidential impeachment

21. Which of the following presidents appointed the first woman to the Supreme Court of the United States?
    (A) Jimmy Carter
    (B) Bill Clinton
    (C) Ronald Reagan
    (D) Franklin Roosevelt
    (E) Gerald Ford

22. Which of the following is a specific power of the House of Representatives?
    I.   impeachment of the president
    II. election of the president when the electoral college fails
    III. initiation of revenue bills
    (A) I only
    (B) II only
    (C) III only
    (D) I, II, and III
    (E) I and II

23. Members of the federal executive bureaucracy tend to represent the interests of
    (A) the president
    (B) the departments in which they work
    (C) the special interests to which they belong
    (D) the political party to which they belong
    (E) themselves

24. In the United States, the powers of government are divided between a national government, state governments, and several regional and local governments. This system is called
    (A) delegated government
    (B) federalism
    (C) democracy
    (D) republican government
    (E) checks and balances

25. A private organization that attempts to get government officials to respond to its philosophy and way of thinking on particular issues is called a(n)
    (A) pressure group
    (B) political pressure group
    (C) interest group
    (D) political power group
    (E) lobbyist

26. The political belief that the president is the steward of the people and should continually act in the best interests of the people is known as the stewardship theory. Which president first promoted this theory?
    (A) Theodore Roosevelt
    (B) Thomas Jefferson
    (C) George Washington
    (D) Franklin Roosevelt
    (E) Woodrow Wilson

27. States, which require the winning candidates of each party to have an absolute majority in a primary election, may also require the holding of a(n)
    (A) open primary
    (B) closed primary
    (C) runoff primary
    (D) nonpartisan primary
    (E) direct primary

28. In the United States, the Congress has created two types of federal courts. These courts are
    (A) special and legislative courts
    (B) district and constitutional courts
    (C) constitutional and appellate courts
    (D) constitutional and legislative courts
    (E) district and appellate courts

29. What right is protected by the Second Amendment of the United States Constitution?
    (A) quarter troops
    (B) bear arms and maintain a militia
    (C) serve in a militia
    (D) petition the federal government
    (E) express and exhibit free speech

GO ON TO THE NEXT PAGE

30. Which of the following is a true statement about political parties in the United States?
    (A) Political parties are addressed in the constitution.
    (B) Membership is voluntary and represents a good cross section of the country's population.
    (C) Membership is voluntary, but only a small portion of the voting public belongs.
    (D) Party membership is strengthening.
    (E) Political parties are becoming less diverse in their membership.

31. An incumbent is a
    (A) first-time office holder
    (B) candidate running for office
    (C) current office holder
    (D) most recently defeated candidate
    (E) candidate with the most votes

32. In developing the United States Constitution, which of the following plans called for a strong national government with three separate branches?
    (A) the Virginia Plan
    (B) the New Jersey Plan
    (C) the Connecticut Plan
    (D) the Philadelphia Plan
    (E) the Hamilton Plan

33. An interest group, a bureaucratic government agency, and a committee of Congress working together would be an example of
    (A) an iron triangle
    (B) a government corporation
    (C) an issue network
    (D) an independent government agency
    (E) an independent regulatory agency

34. The purpose of a poll watcher is to
    (A) direct the voter to the proper polling station
    (B) help the election judge count the votes
    (C) determine exit poll results
    (D) ensure the election process at the poll is fair and honest
    (E) ensure that enough ballots are on hand to meet the needs of voter turnout

35. The president's cabinet is designed to
    (A) issue executive orders
    (B) negotiate executive agreements
    (C) run the executive branch of the government
    (D) set the president's agenda before the Congress
    (E) both advise the president and administer a department of government

36. Which of the following terms best describes the legislative tactic of acquiring funds or projects for a Congressman's home district?
    (A) logrolling
    (B) pork barrel legislation
    (C) gerrymandering
    (D) congressional campaigning
    (E) lobbying

37. What is the total current membership of the electoral college?
    (A) 435
    (B) 535
    (C) 538
    (D) 438
    (E) 270

38. How many courts of appeals are there in the federal court system?
    (A) 1
    (B) 90
    (C) 6
    (D) 3
    (E) 12

39. Adding amendments to the United States Constitution is a two-step process that includes
    (A) proposal by the United States House of Representatives and ratification by the Senate
    (B) proposal by the United States Senate and ratification by the House of Representatives
    (C) proposal and ratification by both houses of Congress
    (D) proposal by the United States Congress and ratification by the states
    (E) proposal by the executive branch and ratification by the legislative branch

40. Each state in the House of Representatives is allowed a certain number of representatives. That number is determined by:
    (A) the population of each state
    (B) constitutional amendment
    (C) presidential mandate
    (D) the number of electors each state has in the electoral college
    (E) a number called for in the Constitution of each state

GO ON TO THE NEXT PAGE

41. In the case of a tie vote in the electoral college during the selection of the president, who is charged with electing the president?
    (A) Senate
    (B) House of Representatives
    (C) Supreme Court
    (D) Senate and Supreme Court
    (E) Supreme Court and House of Representatives

42. Which of the following is an executive power of the Senate?
    (A) reviewing presidential vetoes
    (B) trying impeachment cases
    (C) keeping a check on the House of Representatives
    (D) proposing constitutional amendments
    (E) approving appointments and treaties

43. Which of the following Supreme Court cases established the principle of judicial review in the American court system?
    (A) *McCulloch v. Maryland*
    (B) *Gibbons v. Ogden*
    (C) *Marbury v. Madison*
    (D) *Mapp v. Ohio*
    (E) *Miranda v. Arizona*

44. Which of the following best describes a public interest group?
    (A) A public interest group seeks to benefit its self-interest.
    (B) A public interest group seeks to benefit the nation as a whole rather than its self-interest.
    (C) A public interest group seeks to destroy government bureaucracy.
    (D) A public interest group seeks to provide information to certain groups within the Congress.
    (E) A public interest group seeks to win the support of the president.

45. While the president has the power to make appointments, he or she also has the power to remove some appointed officials from office. Where in the United States Constitution is this power located?
    (A) Article I
    (B) Article II
    (C) Article III
    (D) Article IV
    (E) Article V

46. What is the minimum age requirement for a member of the House of Representatives?
    (A) 25
    (B) 30
    (C) 35
    (D) The same age requirement as for the president
    (E) There is no minimum age requirement

47. Which court was considered to be the most liberal court of the 20th century?
    (A) Warren Court
    (B) Burger Court
    (C) Marshall Court
    (D) Taney Court
    (E) Taft Court

48. The civil service system in the United States was created by
    (A) the Constitution
    (B) executive order
    (C) the Pendleton Act
    (D) the Hatch Act
    (E) the Civil Service Act of 1850

49. A primary election open only to the known voters of a political party would best be described as a(n)
    (A) open primary
    (B) indirect primary
    (C) blanket primary
    (D) wide-open primary
    (E) closed primary

50. How many judges currently serve on the Supreme Court?
    (A) six
    (B) nine
    (C) four
    (D) ten
    (E) five

51. Which of the following is NOT true of the seniority rule?
    (A) The seniority rule ignores ability.
    (B) The seniority rule discourages hard work.
    (C) The seniority rule is not as important today as in the past.
    (D) The seniority rule is significant in the selection of committee chairpersons.
    (E) The seniority rule allows the most qualified individual to be selected for the job.

GO ON TO THE NEXT PAGE

52. Which of the following is NOT an accurate description of the president's ability to deal with the Congress?
    (A) In dealing with Congress, the president works under a system of checks and balances.
    (B) The president must work with political party influences in Congress.
    (C) The president is able to enact legislation that he or she deems necessary.
    (D) The president may veto acts of Congress.
    (E) The president must work with Congress on issues important to both branches of the government.

53. If a special session of Congress is necessary after Congress has adjourned, who has the power to call Congress back into session?
    (A) the speaker of the House and the president *pro tempore*
    (B) the president
    (C) the vice president by virtue of position in the Senate
    (D) the members of Congress
    (E) the members of the House and Senate Special Session Committee

54. When a case is appealed to the Supreme Court of the United States on the request of a lower court that is not sure on the point of law, the lower court must present a(n)
    (A) certificate
    (B) appeal
    (C) writ of assistance
    (D) *writ of certiorari*
    (E) brief solicitation

55. Which U.S. president held the most press conferences?
    (A) Richard Nixon
    (B) George Bush
    (C) Jimmy Carter
    (D) Franklin Roosevelt
    (E) John Kennedy

56. The size of the House of Representatives is determined by
    (A) the president
    (B) Congress
    (C) the Constitution
    (D) the population of the states
    (E) the Supreme Court

57. Bicameralism is
    (A) a legislative body dominated by two major political parties
    (B) a legislative body composed of one house
    (C) a legislative body composed of two houses
    (D) a legislative body that shares power with a judiciary
    (E) a legislative body that shares power with an executive

58. "A President's power originates in his ability to persuade others." This statement can best be attributed to which of the following individuals?
    (A) James David Barber
    (B) Bill Clinton
    (C) Richard Neustadt
    (D) Richard Nixon
    (E) John Locke

59. The political party system in the United States is based on the principle of a(n)
    (A) multi-party system
    (B) single-member district system
    (C) moderate-liberal system
    (D) independent system
    (E) two-party system

60. The Supreme Court of the United States has both original and appellate jurisdiction. The court usually hears cases on appeal and decides only a few cases each year. Who decides which cases the court will hear?
    (A) the chief justice of the Supreme Court
    (B) the members of the Supreme Court as a group
    (C) the attorney general of the United States
    (D) the solicitor general of the United States
    (E) the chief associate judge of the Supreme Court

END OF SECTION I

Section II

Time—100 minutes

Directions: You have 100 minutes to answer all four of the following questions. Unless the directions indicate otherwise, respond to all parts of all four questions. It is suggested that you take a few minutes to plan and outline each answer. *Spend approximately one-fourth of your time (25 minutes) on each question.* Illustrate your essay with substantive examples where appropriate. Make certain to number each of your answers as the question is numbered below. Use a separate sheet of paper if you need more space.

1. Legislative strategies are often used to kill or delay the passage of a bill through Congress.

   (a) Identify three legislative strategies that can kill or delay the passage of a bill through Congress.

   (b) Explain how each of the strategies identified above can kill or delay the passage of a bill through Congress.

GO ON TO THE NEXT PAGE

Participation in Elections for President and Representatives

Percent of Voting-Age Population: 1972 to 1998

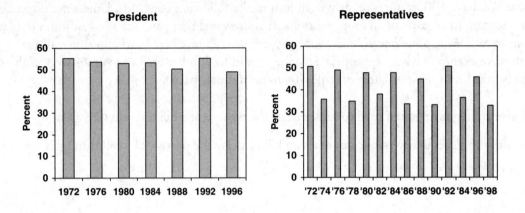

2. The graphs above show participation in elections of the voting-age population for president and members of the House of Representatives. From this information and your knowledge of United States politics, perform the following tasks.

   (a) Identify and discuss two patterns displayed in the graphs.

   (b) Identify two factors that contribute to voter participation in elections. Explain how each affects voter participation.

GO ON TO THE NEXT PAGE

3. Civil rights may be expanded through the passage of new legislation or constitutional amendment.

   (a) Identify and explain two examples of how the expansion of civil rights has been accomplished through the passage of legislation.

   (b) Identify and discuss two examples of how the expansion of civil rights has been accomplished through constitutional amendment.

   (c) Identify and discuss one example of how a restriction has been placed on civil rights through legislation.

   (d) Discuss how the failure to adopt the Equal Rights Amendment (ERA) affected the civil rights of women.

GO ON TO THE NEXT PAGE

4. The Constitution creates a Supreme Court for the United States. By hearing disputes, the Supreme Court influences public policy. Several factors may influence the justices in the judicial decision-making process.

   (a) Identify and discuss two influences on the judicial decision-making process in the Supreme Court.

   (b) Give an example of how the influences you identified have influenced the judicial decision-making process.

END OF SECTION II

› Answers and Explanations

1. **A**. The Bill of Rights established basic rights, including freedom of speech, petition, assembly, religion, and the press; the right to bear arms; freedom from unreasonable search and seizure; the right to a speedy and public jury trial; and freedom from cruel and unusual punishment. The Articles of Confederation (B) did not enumerate civil liberties. Although the Declaration of Independence (C) was a statement of the ideals of the new United States, it did not have the force of law and, therefore, did not establish civil liberties. The Judiciary Article (D) grants only the right of trial by jury in federal cases. *Marbury v. Madison* (E) established the principle of judicial review.

2. **D**. Richard Nixon resigned from office in 1974 as a result of the Watergate scandal. He is the only president to resign thus far. Calvin Coolidge (A) and Lyndon Johnson (C) completed their terms of office. Zachary Taylor (E) died while in office. Spiro Agnew (B) did resign from office, but he was a vice president, not a president.

3. **B**. According to the Constitution, the House of Representatives brings charges of impeachment, whereas the Senate tries, or sits in judgment of, impeachment cases.

4. **B**. The U.S. Postal Service is a government corporation. The U.S. Treasury (A) is a department of the federal government. The armed forces (C) are part of the Defense Department, and the IRS (D) is an independent agency. Independent regulatory agencies (E) are part of the executive branch.

5. **A**. Primary elections are "first elections," held to nominate candidates from within a political party. Primary elections narrow the field of party candidates to one (B), giving voters the choice of only one candidate per party in the general election (C). State legislatures do not use primary results to determine political districts (D). Primary elections are among the factors that limit the influence and participation of third-party candidates.

6. **C**. The primary goal of political parties is to seek to control government through the winning of elections. Choice (D) reflects only one aspect of the role of political parties at the national level. The goals of affecting public policy (A), defining party principles (B), and promoting an individual political cause (E) are secondary goals for major U.S. political parties, which are election oriented.

7. **E**. The Federal Reserve System was created in 1913 to supervise the nation's banking system and to regulate the money supply. The Federal Trade Commission (A) regulates fraudulent trade practices. The Securities and Exchange Commission (B) supervises the exchange of securities to protect investors. The Department of the Treasury (D) is a department, not an independent regulatory commission, of the federal government that collects revenue and administers federal finances. The Consumer Product Safety Commission (C) is an independent regulatory agency that protects the public from faulty consumer products.

8. **D**. Although senators are elected for six-year terms, senatorial elections are staggered so that only one-third of the Senate is elected every two years. Senators are elected in statewide, at-large elections (A), resulting in a larger and, therefore, more diverse, constituency (E). The prestige of the Senate leads to more media interest (B). Because senators are elected from the entire state, their constituencies are generally more diverse than those of representatives.

9. **A**. The world of the late 18th century was so limited, and the nature of the U.S. presidency so newly defined, that the founding fathers could not anticipate the extent to which future presidents would use their power to shape public opinion. The Constitution provides for the presidential role as a check on bills enacted into law through the power of the vote (B) and as administrator, or executor, of bills passed by Congress (E). Article II grants the president the command of the armed forces (D). As both the chief executive and the ceremonial head of the United States, the president is head of state (C).

10. **B.** Briefs are written documents given to the court to present each side's views on the case. Briefs do not present the viewpoint of the court (C). A legal document (A) states a contractual relationship or grants a right. A prospectus (D) is a document that describes major features of a proposed project, whereas a writ (E) is a legal order requiring a person to do or refrain from a specific act.

11. **A.** A filibuster is a stalling tactic used only in the Senate (C, E), where debate is not limited. The House of Representatives limits debate under the authority of the Rules Committee (B). It is difficult to avoid or stop a filibuster because senators are hesitant to place limits on one another (D).

12. **A.** Although interest groups may focus on the subjects mentioned in choices (B) to (E), the largest number of interest groups are based on economic issues.

13. **C.** Voting in presidential elections is the method of participation used by the largest number of Americans. Most Americans do not vote in local elections (A) or work for a political party (E). Choice (B) refers to knowledge rather than participation, while choice (D) involves a lack of political participation.

14. **A.** The number of representatives apportioned to each state depends on the findings of the most recent census. The members of the House of Representatives are elected every two years, preventing a continuous body as in the Senate (B). Congress may vote to alter the "permanent" size of the House (C). Only those states whose population is small enough to allow for only one representative elect representatives in at-large elections; most states elect representatives from single-member districts (D). The Virginia Plan provided for the apportionment of representatives according to population (E).

15. **B.** Electors are not legally pledged to vote for their candidate and may vote for any candidate (C). If no candidate wins a majority of electoral votes, it is the House, not the Senate, that decides the election (A). The candidate winning the popular vote sometimes loses the election, as in the election of 2000 (D). Each state is apportioned electors according to its number of representatives plus senators (E).

16. **E.** The Lemon Test created standards for the establishment clause of the First Amendment, under which state aid given to a church school must be for a secular purpose. Choices (A), (B), (C), and (D) are not included in this court decision.

17. **B.** Voter registration is regulated by state governments (A, E). Registration to vote is not required of anyone in the United States (C); most states, however, require registration in order to vote (D).

18. **A.** According to Article VII of the Constitution, ratification would occur with the approval of 9 of the 13 states.

19. **D.** The Senate (E) has a smaller number of members (100) than the House of Representatives (435). The most influential member is the Senate majority leader, who often also serves as the spokesman for the majority party in the Senate (A). Revenue bills may be introduced only in the House (B). The Senate has the authority to ratify or reject a treaty made by the president (C).

20. **A.** The Twenty-Second Amendment limits the president to two elected terms and not more than ten years in office. The Twenty-Third Amendment allows voters in the District of Columbia to vote in presidential elections (D). No amendments address checks and balances (C), presidential impeachment (E), or the selection of vice-presidential running mates (B).

21. **C.** Sandra Day O'Connor, the first woman appointed to the Supreme Court, was appointed by Ronald Reagan in 1981.

22. **D.** The House of Representatives has the sole power to bring charges of impeachment, elect the president if there is not a majority in the electoral college, and initiate revenue bills.

23. **B.** A bureaucracy is an organization composed of several levels of authority. It often uses specialization to carry out the tasks of its departments and agencies. Members of the federal bureaucracy tend to represent the departments in which they work rather than the president (A), special

interest groups (C), political parties (D), or themselves (E).

24. **B**. U.S. federalism is the division of governmental powers between national, state, and several regional and local governments. Delegated government (A) receives its powers through a constitution. Democracy (C) is rule by the people. A republican government (D) is one in which the people are ruled by elected representatives. Checks and balances (E) are the limits placed by one branch of the federal government over another.

25. **C**. Interest groups are private groups that attempt to pressure government officials to respond to their issue or philosophy. Choices (A), (B), and (D) do not specifically define an interest group. A lobbyist (E) is a representative of a special interest group.

26. **A**. The progressive president Theodore Roosevelt first promoted the stewardship theory, a concept descriptive of the modern presidency. He articulated this philosophy in his 1913 autobiography.

27. **C**. When no candidate receives an absolute majority in a primary, states may require a runoff election between the top candidates. An open primary (A) is one in which any qualified voter may participate. A closed primary (B) is one in which participants must be declared party members. A nonpartisan primary (D) is one in which the candidates do not run on party labels. A direct primary (E) is an election in which voters vote directly for their party's candidates for office.

28. **D**. Constitutional courts are the federal courts created by Congress under Article III of the Constitution. Legislative courts are special courts that hear cases arising from the powers given to Congress under Article I (A). District courts, a type of constitutional court, serve as federal trial courts (B, E). Appellate courts (C), which decide appeals from district courts, are constitutional courts.

29. **B**. The Second Amendment provides the right to bear arms. Quartering troops is addressed in the Third Amendment (A). The First Amendment deals with free speech (E) and petitioning the government (D). No amendment addresses the issue of serving in a militia (C).

30. **B**. Membership in U.S. political parties is voluntary and represents voters from a variety of geographical regions, ethnic and racial groups, income and educational levels, religions, and ideologies. Political parties are not mentioned in the Constitution, and George Washington was elected to the presidency without membership in a party (A). A large portion of the voting public claims party membership (C). More and more U.S. voters are classifying themselves as independents (D), while members of political parties represent more diverse ideologies (E).

31. **C**. Incumbents are current office holders.

32. **A**. The Virginia Plan provided for a strong central government with three branches. The New Jersey Plan (B) called for a weak national government with three separate branches. The Connecticut Compromise (not a proposed plan) created a strong national government with three separate branches (C). There was no Philadelphia Plan (D), and the Hamilton Plan (E) favored a monarch.

33. **A**. An iron triangle is an alliance that develops between bureaucratic agencies, interest groups, and congressional committees or subcommittees in pursuit of a common goal. A government corporation is created by Congress to carry out businesslike activities (B). An issue network (C) is a group of individuals in Washington who regularly discuss and advocate public policies. An independent executive agency (D) is similar to a department but has no cabinet status. An independent regulatory agency (E) is one that is created to regulate or police.

34. **D**. A poll watcher is a representative of a political party or candidate who ensures that the election process is fair and honest. Election judges and other election officials direct voters (A), help count votes (B), and ensure that enough ballots are on hand (E). Political pollsters determine exit poll results (C).

35. **E**. The president's cabinet advises the president; each secretary administers a department of the government. Only the president has the power to issue executive orders (A), negotiate executive agreements (B), run the executive

branch (C), and set his agenda before the Congress (D).

36. **B**. Pork barrel legislation is the term for a member of Congress acquiring funds or projects for his or her home district. Logrolling (A) is an attempt by members of Congress to gain the support of other members for their support of the congressperson's legislation. Gerrymandering (C) involves drawing congressional districts to favor one political party or group over another. Congressional campaigning (D) is the act of running for Congress. Lobbying (E) is the attempt of interest groups to support or reject legislation.

37. **C**. The electoral college is composed of 538 members, with each state having the same number of electors as the sum of its representatives and senators. The Twenty-Third Amendment provides that Washington, D.C., shall have the same number of electors as the smallest state—three.

38. **E**. There are 12 courts of appeals in the federal court system.

39. **D**. Amending the Constitution requires Congress to propose amendments by a two-thirds vote in both houses. The proposed amendment must then be ratified by the state legislatures of three-fourths of the states or by conventions held in three-fourths of the states. Another method of amendment allows Congress to call a national convention when requested by three-fourths of the state legislatures. This convention then initiates the process by proposing the amendment. To date a national convention has not been called to propose an amendment.

40. **A**. The Constitution requires that a state's representation in the House of Representatives be based on the population of the state.

41. **B**. According to the Constitution, if the electoral college fails to choose a president, the House of Representatives is charged with choosing the president.

42. **E**. Approving appointments and treaties are executive powers of the Senate because they are used in conjunction with a power of the president. Reviewing presidential vetoes (A) and proposing constitutional amendments (D) are two of the Senate's legislative powers. Trying impeachment cases (B) is a nonlegislative power of the Senate. The Senate does not check the power of the House of Representatives (C).

43. **C**. *Marbury v. Madison* (1803) established the principle of judicial review. *McCulloch v. Maryland* (1819) upheld the power of the national government by denying the right of a state to tax the Bank of the United States (A). *Gibbons v. Ogden* (1824) upheld the power of the national government over interstate commerce (B). *Mapp v. Ohio* (1961) extended the Fourth Amendment's protection against unreasonable searches and seizures to the states as well as to the national government (D). *Miranda v. Arizona* (1966) held that the Fifth Amendment requires that a person arrested for a crime must be advised of his or her right to remain silent and to have an attorney present (E).

44. **B**. A public interest group, such as Common Cause or Mothers Against Drunk Driving, seeks to benefit the nation as a whole. Public interest groups are concerned with issues such as the environment, consumer protection, crime, and civil rights.

45. **B**. Article II of the Constitution addresses the powers of the president.

46. **A**. The minimum age for a member of the House of Representatives is 25.

47. **A**. Because of its decisions that expanded the rights of criminal defendants, the Supreme Court under Chief Justice Earl Warren is often considered the most liberal court of the 20th century. While the Burger court (B) was responsible for liberal decisions in *Roe v. Wade* and *U.S. v. Nixon*, it is generally considered a more conservative court for its narrowing of the rights of defendants. The Taft Court (E) was a conservative court. The Marshall (C) and Taney (D) courts were 19th-century courts.

48. **C**. The Pendleton Act (1883) created the U.S. civil service system.

49. **E**. A primary election would best be described as a closed primary if only the known members of a political party were able to participate. In an open primary (A), voters may choose candidates of either party, whether they belong to that party or not. In a blanket primary (C), voters may choose the candidates of either party, voting for

a Republican for one office and a Democrat for another. The wide-open primary (D) is another term for the blanket primary. "Indirect" is not a term used to describe primaries (B).

50. **B**. There are currently nine justices on the Supreme Court—a chief justice and eight associate justices.

51. **E**. The seniority rule is the custom that the chair of a congressional committee is awarded to the member of the majority party with the longest participation on the committee. The use of the seniority rule does not require the selection of the most qualified individual to be chosen as a committee chairperson.

52. **C**. The president is only able to suggest legislation. Congress must pass bills enacting legislation.

53. **B**. Only the president may call special sessions of Congress.

54. **A**. Appealing a case to the Supreme Court because a lower court is unsure on a point of law requires the presentation of a certificate. An appeal (B) is a case brought to a higher court from a lower court. A writ of assistance (C) was a document that allowed British officers to search a premise. A *writ of certiorari* (D) is a document from a superior court demanding the record of a case from an inferior court. A brief solicitation (E) is a request for a written argument presented to a court.

55. **D**. Franklin Delano Roosevelt held the most press conferences, partly because of his long tenure in office and the national emergencies of the times.

56. **B**. Congress determines the size of the House of Representatives through the passage of legislation. The Reapportionment Act of 1929 established the current size at 435 members. Although each state's membership in the House is determined by population, changes in population distribution are resolved by reapportionment, thus maintaining the current size of the House at 435 members.

57. **C**. Bicameralism describes a legislative body composed of two houses, such as the United States Congress.

58. **C**. The quotation is attributed to Richard Neustadt.

59. **E**. The United States operates under a two-party system, with only two major parties having a reasonable chance of winning elections. A single-member district (B) is an electoral district from which voters choose one person for each elected office.

60. **B**. The justices of the Supreme Court, using the rule of four, decide which cases they will consider. According to the rule of four, four of the nine justices must agree to hear the case.

› Rubrics for the Free-Response Essay

1. Total Value: 6 points

   Part (a): 1 point for each correctly identified legislative strategy = 3 points
   Part (b): 1 point for each correct explanation of a legislative strategy = 3 points

2. Total Value: 7 points

   Part (a): 1 point for two correctly identified patterns = 1 point
           1 point for each correct discussion of a pattern = 2 points
   Part (b): 1 point for each correctly identified factor = 2 points
           1 point for each correct explanation of a factor = 2 points

3. Total Value: 9 points

   Part (a): 1 point for two correctly identified examples through legislation = 1 point
           1 point for each correct discussion of an example through legislation = 2 points
   Part (b): 1 point for two correctly identified examples through amendment = 1 point
           1 point for each correct discussion of an example through amendment = 2 points
   Part (c): 1 point for correct identification of example of restriction = 1 point
           1 point for correct discussion of restriction due to legislation = 1 point
   Part (d): 1 point for correct discussion of ERA = 1 point

4. Total Value: 6 points

   Part (a): 1 point for each correctly identified influence = 2 points
           1 point for each correct discussion of influence = 2 points
   Part (b): 1 point for each correct example = 2 points

STEP **3**

Develop Strategies for Success

CHAPTER 4

Section I of the Exam: How to Approach the Multiple-Choice Questions

IN THIS CHAPTER

Summary: Use these question-answering strategies to raise your score on the multiple-choice questions.

Key Ideas

✪ Familiarize yourself with the patterns of multiple choice on the AP exam.
✪ Review general guidelines for answering multiple-choice questions.
✪ Learn the skill of eliminating incorrect answer choices.
✪ Learn how to score your answers.
✪ Practice your strategies on the multiple-choice section of a diagnostic exam.

Introduction to the Multiple-Choice Section of the Exam

What Should I Expect in Section I?

For this first section of the U.S. Government and Politics exam, you are allotted 45 minutes to answer 60 objective questions. These are questions that any student in any introductory government and politics class might know. It is not expected that everyone will know the answer to every question; however, you should try to answer as many questions as you can.

The AP U.S. Government and Politics questions always have five answer choices. Points are given for every correct answer. No points are given or deducted for blank answers.

How Should I Begin to Work with Section I?

Take a quick look at the entire multiple-choice section. This brief skimming of the test will put your mind at ease because you will be more aware of the test and what is expected in Section I. Do not spend too much time skimming. Remember, this is a timed exam.

How Should I Proceed Through This Section of the Exam?

Always maintain an awareness of the time. Wear a watch. (Some students like to put it directly in from of them on the desk.) Remember, this will not be your first encounter with the multiple-choice section of the test. You've probably been practicing timed exams in class; in addition, this book provides you with four experiences.

Work at a pace that is comfortable. Every question is worth the same number of points, so don't get bogged down on one or two questions. Don't panic if you do not know the answer to a question. Remember, others taking the exam might not know it either. There has to be a bar that determines the 5s and 4s for this exam. Just do your best.

Reading the questions and answer choices carefully is a must. Read the *entire* question. Don't try to guess what the question is asking; read the question. Read *all* the answer choices. Don't jump at the first answer choice. Pay attention to key terms or negative statements, such as, which of the following is NOT; all of the following EXCEPT.

Types of Multiple-Choice Questions

Multiple-choice questions are not written randomly. There are certain general formats you will encounter.

Is the Structure the Same for All of the Multiple-Choice Questions?

No. There are several basic patterns that the AP test makers employ. Some questions may involve general identification, while others may depend on analysis.

1. The straightforward question may involve defining terms or making a generalization.
2. The negative question might include "all of the following except" and requires extra time because it demands that you consider every possibility.
3. The multiple multiple-choice question uses Roman numerals to list several possible correct answers. You must choose which answer or combinations of answers is correct.
4. The stimulus-based question involves interpreting a chart, graph, table, quote, etc., to determine the answer.

Strategies for Answering the Multiple-Choice Questions

You probably have been answering multiple-choice questions most of your academic life, and you've probably figured out ways to deal with them. However, there may be some points you have not considered that will be helpful for this particular exam.

General Guidelines

- Work in order. This is a good approach for several reasons:
  — It's clear.
  — You will not lose your place on the scan sheet.
  — There may be a logic to working sequentially that will help you answer previous questions. But this is your call. If you are more comfortable moving around the exam, do so.
- Write on the exam booklet. Mark it up. Make it yours. Interact with the test.
- Pace yourself and watch your time. Don't spend too much time on one question so that you run out of time and don't complete questions you might know, but which appear later in the exam. Don't rush. There are no bonus points for finishing early.
- Don't be misled by the length or appearance of a question or of answer choices. There is no correlation between length or appearance and the difficulty of the questions.
- Read the questions and answer choices carefully. Make note of key terms such as NOT or EXCEPT.
- Consider all the choices in a given question. This will keep you from jumping to false conclusions. It helps you slow down and really consider all possibilities. You may find that your first choice is not the BEST or most appropriate choice.
- Remember that all parts of an answer must be correct for the answer to be correct.

> *"The caliber of the multiple-choice questions on an AP exam is extreme—you must know how to deal with them."*
> —HL, AP student

> *"Learn to apply your knowledge by understanding concepts and looking at the whole picture."*
> —MP, AP student

Specific Techniques

- Process of elimination. This is your primary tool, except for direct knowledge of the answer.

  1. Read the five choices.

  2. If no choice immediately strikes you as correct, you can
     — eliminate those that are obviously wrong
     — eliminate those choices that are too narrow or too broad
     — eliminate illogical choices
     — eliminate answers that are synonymous (identical)
     — eliminate answers that cancel each other out

  3. If two answers are close, do one *or* the other of the following:
     — Find the one that is general enough to cover all aspects of the question.
     — Find the one that is limited enough to be the detail the question is looking for.

- Educated guess. You have a wealth of skills and knowledge. A question or choice may trigger your memory. This may form the basis of your educated guess. Have confidence to use the educated guess as a valid technique. Trust your own resources.

Scoring the Multiple-Choice Section

How Does the Scoring of the Multiple-Choice Section Work?

The multiple-choice section of the exam is taken on a scan sheet. The sheet is run through a computer that calculates the number of correct answers. For example, if you correctly answered 47 of the 60 multiple-choice questions, your raw score on Section I of the exam would be 47. This score would then be added to the free-response score for a composite score on the exam. The composite score would be equated to an AP score of 5, 4, 3, 2, or 1.

If I Don't Know the Answer, Should I Guess?

On the multiple-choice section of the test, no points are deducted for incorrect answers. Therefore, it is to your advantage to guess on every question when you are not sure of the correct answer.

The Time Is at Hand

It is now time to try Section I of a second diagnostic exam. Do this entire section in one sitting. Time yourself. Be honest with yourself when scoring your answers.

Note: If the 45 minutes passes before you finish all the questions, stop where you are and score what you have done up to this point. Afterward, answer the remaining questions, but do not count the answers as part of your score. When you have completed all the multiple-choice questions in this diagnostic exam, carefully read the explanations of the answers. Assess which types of questions give you trouble. Use this book to learn from your mistakes.

AP U.S. Government and Politics
Diagnostic Exam 2: Multiple-Choice Questions

ANSWER SHEET

1 Ⓐ Ⓑ Ⓒ Ⓓ Ⓔ	21 Ⓐ Ⓑ Ⓒ Ⓓ Ⓔ	41 Ⓐ Ⓑ Ⓒ Ⓓ Ⓔ
2 Ⓐ Ⓑ Ⓒ Ⓓ Ⓔ	22 Ⓐ Ⓑ Ⓒ Ⓓ Ⓔ	42 Ⓐ Ⓑ Ⓒ Ⓓ Ⓔ
3 Ⓐ Ⓑ Ⓒ Ⓓ Ⓔ	23 Ⓐ Ⓑ Ⓒ Ⓓ Ⓔ	43 Ⓐ Ⓑ Ⓒ Ⓓ Ⓔ
4 Ⓐ Ⓑ Ⓒ Ⓓ Ⓔ	24 Ⓐ Ⓑ Ⓒ Ⓓ Ⓔ	44 Ⓐ Ⓑ Ⓒ Ⓓ Ⓔ
5 Ⓐ Ⓑ Ⓒ Ⓓ Ⓔ	25 Ⓐ Ⓑ Ⓒ Ⓓ Ⓔ	45 Ⓐ Ⓑ Ⓒ Ⓓ Ⓔ
6 Ⓐ Ⓑ Ⓒ Ⓓ Ⓔ	26 Ⓐ Ⓑ Ⓒ Ⓓ Ⓔ	46 Ⓐ Ⓑ Ⓒ Ⓓ Ⓔ
7 Ⓐ Ⓑ Ⓒ Ⓓ Ⓔ	27 Ⓐ Ⓑ Ⓒ Ⓓ Ⓔ	47 Ⓐ Ⓑ Ⓒ Ⓓ Ⓔ
8 Ⓐ Ⓑ Ⓒ Ⓓ Ⓔ	28 Ⓐ Ⓑ Ⓒ Ⓓ Ⓔ	48 Ⓐ Ⓑ Ⓒ Ⓓ Ⓔ
9 Ⓐ Ⓑ Ⓒ Ⓓ Ⓔ	29 Ⓐ Ⓑ Ⓒ Ⓓ Ⓔ	49 Ⓐ Ⓑ Ⓒ Ⓓ Ⓔ
10 Ⓐ Ⓑ Ⓒ Ⓓ Ⓔ	30 Ⓐ Ⓑ Ⓒ Ⓓ Ⓔ	50 Ⓐ Ⓑ Ⓒ Ⓓ Ⓔ
11 Ⓐ Ⓑ Ⓒ Ⓓ Ⓔ	31 Ⓐ Ⓑ Ⓒ Ⓓ Ⓔ	51 Ⓐ Ⓑ Ⓒ Ⓓ Ⓔ
12 Ⓐ Ⓑ Ⓒ Ⓓ Ⓔ	32 Ⓐ Ⓑ Ⓒ Ⓓ Ⓔ	52 Ⓐ Ⓑ Ⓒ Ⓓ Ⓔ
13 Ⓐ Ⓑ Ⓒ Ⓓ Ⓔ	33 Ⓐ Ⓑ Ⓒ Ⓓ Ⓔ	53 Ⓐ Ⓑ Ⓒ Ⓓ Ⓔ
14 Ⓐ Ⓑ Ⓒ Ⓓ Ⓔ	34 Ⓐ Ⓑ Ⓒ Ⓓ Ⓔ	54 Ⓐ Ⓑ Ⓒ Ⓓ Ⓔ
15 Ⓐ Ⓑ Ⓒ Ⓓ Ⓔ	35 Ⓐ Ⓑ Ⓒ Ⓓ Ⓔ	55 Ⓐ Ⓑ Ⓒ Ⓓ Ⓔ
16 Ⓐ Ⓑ Ⓒ Ⓓ Ⓔ	36 Ⓐ Ⓑ Ⓒ Ⓓ Ⓔ	56 Ⓐ Ⓑ Ⓒ Ⓓ Ⓔ
17 Ⓐ Ⓑ Ⓒ Ⓓ Ⓔ	37 Ⓐ Ⓑ Ⓒ Ⓓ Ⓔ	57 Ⓐ Ⓑ Ⓒ Ⓓ Ⓔ
18 Ⓐ Ⓑ Ⓒ Ⓓ Ⓔ	38 Ⓐ Ⓑ Ⓒ Ⓓ Ⓔ	58 Ⓐ Ⓑ Ⓒ Ⓓ Ⓔ
19 Ⓐ Ⓑ Ⓒ Ⓓ Ⓔ	39 Ⓐ Ⓑ Ⓒ Ⓓ Ⓔ	59 Ⓐ Ⓑ Ⓒ Ⓓ Ⓔ
20 Ⓐ Ⓑ Ⓒ Ⓓ Ⓔ	40 Ⓐ Ⓑ Ⓒ Ⓓ Ⓔ	60 Ⓐ Ⓑ Ⓒ Ⓓ Ⓔ

I _____ did _____ did not finish all the questions in the allotted 45 minutes.

I had _____ correct answers. I had _____ incorrect answers, including questions I left blank.

Scoring Formula:

_____ = _____
   number right   raw score

I have carefully reviewed the explanations of the answers. I need to work on the following types of questions:

AP U.S. Government and Politics
Diagnostic Exam 2: Multiple-Choice Questions

Section I

Total Time—45 minutes

60 Questions

Directions: Each of the questions or incomplete statements below is followed by five suggested answers or completions. Select the one that is best in each case and then fill in the corresponding oval on the answer sheet.

1. Which of the following most accurately describes voter behavior in the United States?
   (A) The voting population added by the passage of the Twenty-Sixth Amendment shows the highest percentage of participation in U.S. elections.
   (B) Voters who are not active participants in a religious group are more likely to vote than active members.
   (C) Men are more likely to vote than women.
   (D) Single people are more likely to participate in elections than those who are married.
   (E) Persons with white-collar jobs show a higher percentage of participation in elections than those with blue-collar jobs.

2. Which of the following is true about the president's veto power?
   (A) A bill that has received a pocket veto may be passed over the pocket veto by a two-thirds majority of both houses of Congress.
   (B) Presidents whose party is not the dominant party in the House and Senate frequently have a veto overridden by Congress.
   (C) In the 21st century, the president's veto power was strengthened through the adoption of the line item veto.
   (D) Congress often shows consideration for the president's veto power by revising a vetoed bill and passing it in a form acceptable to the president.
   (E) The veto process demonstrates that the president has little power over the legislative branch.

3. Which of the following statements about voting in 2004 CANNOT be concluded from the information in Table 4-1?
   (A) Asian citizens reported the lowest percentage of those who registered and voted.
   (B) In 2004 the percentage of Hispanic voters of white origin was higher than that of black voters.
   (C) The total number of white voters was greater than those of Asian and black voters combined.
   (D) There was a greater difference in the percentage reported voted between blacks and Asians than between blacks and whites.
   (E) There was less difference in percentage reported voted between the three racial groups when their race was reported in combination with another.

4. Which of the following is true of the relationship between demographics and party preference?
   (A) Voters who own or manage businesses tend to vote Democratic.
   (B) Older Americans tend to vote for Republican candidates.
   (C) Members of minority groups tend to vote Republican.
   (D) Voters with higher incomes tend to prefer the Democratic Party.
   (E) Voters below the age of 21 tend to prefer Republican candidates.

GO ON TO THE NEXT PAGE

Table 4-1 Reported Rates of Voting and Registration by Race: 2004 (Numbers in Thousands)

CHARACTERISTIC	ALONE	IN COMBINATION	ALONE OR IN COMBINATION
White			
Total citizens	162,959	2,284	165,243
Reported registered	119,929	1,598	121,527
Reported voted	106,588	1,342	107,930
Percent reported registered	73.6	70.0	73.5
Percent reported voted	65.4	58.8	65.3
Black			
Total citizens	23,346	562	23,908
Reported registered	16,035	373	16,408
Reported voted	14,016	308	14,324
Percent reported registered	68.7	66.4	68.6
Percent reported voted	60.0	54.8	59.9
Asian			
Total citizens	6,270	416	6,686
Reported registered	3,247	261	3,508
Reported voted	2,768	212	2,980
Percent reported registered	51.8	62.7	52.5
Percent reported voted	44.1	51.0	44.6

Note: This table shows data on reported rates of voting and registration for people who reported they were white, black, or Asian, including people who reported that race alone, people who reported that race in combination with another race, and people who reported that race regardless of whether they also reported another race. For further information, see the Census 2000 brief *Overview of Race and Hispanic Origin; 2000* (C2HBR/01-1), www.census.gov/population/www/cen2000/briefs.html.
Source: U.S. Census Bureau, Current Population Survey, November 2004.

5. The U.S. Supreme Court has used the Fourteenth Amendment to do all of the following EXCEPT
   (A) deny segregation in the public schools
   (B) apply the Bill of Rights to state and local governments
   (C) protect First Amendment freedoms
   (D) defend the institution of slavery
   (E) protect corporations and other private property

6. Social welfare spending
   (A) decreased in the 1930s because of the Great Depression
   (B) increased during Democratic administrations and decreased during Republican administrations
   (C) was restricted during the Reagan administrations
   (D) was extended to more recipients during the Clinton administration
   (E) was restricted to fewer programs during the Johnson administration

GO ON TO THE NEXT PAGE

7. Cases that are appealed to the Supreme Court
   (A) must receive the approval of two-thirds of the justices before they are heard
   (B) cannot be returned to a lower court for reconsideration
   (C) generally result in a reversal of a lower court decision
   (D) are usually accepted because they involve a significant point of law
   (E) are frequently disposed of in brief orders

8. Which is true of a concurring opinion of a case heard by the Supreme Court?
   (A) It is written by a justice who agrees with the majority opinion, but disagrees with the reasoning behind the majority opinion.
   (B) It must be written by the Chief Justice.
   (C) It is an informal poll to determine the opinion of the justices.
   (D) It requires the submission of an *amicus curiae* brief.
   (E) It is filed by a justice or justices who disagree with the majority opinion.

9. Which of the following is true of federalism?
   (A) The Founding Fathers interpreted federalism as dual federalism.
   (B) Interstate highway projects are an example of dual federalism.
   (C) Fiscal federalism involves limited control of the national government over the state.
   (D) Nixon's revenue sharing plan is an example of fiscal federalism.
   (E) Cooperative federalism implies agreement between national and state governments on major social issues.

10. Because of the electoral college system
    (A) candidates focus on states with the largest electoral vote
    (B) the winner of the popular vote for president may not win the election
    (C) the presidential candidate with a plurality in the electoral college wins the election
    (D) the House of Representatives frequently chooses the president
    (E) candidates focus on states with a winner-take-all rule

11. The House committee that controls the conditions for floor consideration of a bill is
    (A) the Judiciary Committee
    (B) the Rules Committee
    (C) the Budget Committee
    (D) the Appropriations Committee
    (E) the Ways and Means Committee

12. What do the Fifth Amendment and the Fourteenth Amendment have in common?
    (A) Both prevent government from depriving a person of life, liberty, and property without due process of law.
    (B) Both speak of powers reserved to the states.
    (C) Both deal with criminal prosecutions.
    (D) Both prevent the government from denying to any person the equal protection of the law.
    (E) Both deal with the privileges of citizens.

13. Which is true of the success of third, or minor, parties?
    I.   Their ideas have often been adopted by major parties.
    II. They have elected members to Congress.
    III. They have split the votes for major party candidates.
    (A) II only
    (B) I and II only
    (C) I and III only
    (D) II and III only
    (E) I, II, and III

14. The Supreme Court has used the free exercise clause of the First Amendment to
    (A) uphold the Religious Freedom Restoration Act of 1993
    (B) rule that school-sanctioned prayer in public schools is unconstitutional
    (C) strike down a federal law prohibiting polygamy
    (D) distinguish between religious belief and religious practice
    (E) require Amish parents to send their children to public school beyond the eighth grade

GO ON TO THE NEXT PAGE

Table 4-2 Reasons for Not Voting by Selected Characteristics: 2004 (Numbers in Thousands)

CHARACTERISTIC	TOTAL	Too busy, conflicting schedule	Illness or disability	Other reason	Not interested	Did not like candidates or issues	Out of town	Don't know or refused	Registration problems	Forgot to vote	Inconvenient polling place	Transportation problems	Bad weather conditions
						PERCENT DISTRIBUTION OF REASONS FOR NOT VOTING							
Total, 18 years and older	16,334	19.9	15.4	10.9	10.7	9.9	9.0	8.5	6.8	3.4	3.0	2.1	0.5
Sex													
Male	7,951	22.5	10.7	10.8	10.6	10.1	11.0	10.0	6.6	3.4	3.1	0.9	0.3
Female	8,383	17.4	19.8	10.9	10.7	9.7	7.1	7.2	7.0	3.5	2.9	3.3	0.6
Race and Hispanic Origin													
White alone	13,341	19.4	15.6	10.9	10.8	10.6	9.4	7.9	6.8	3.4	3.0	1.9	0.4
White alone, non-Hispanic	11,752	18.9	16.2	10.8	10.8	11.1	9.9	7.6	6.2	3.0	3.2	1.9	0.5
Black alone	2,019	20.7	16.5	9.8	10.0	6.4	5.5	13.0	7.2	3.9	2.6	4.2	0.3
Asian alone	479	31.5	6.1	13.7	7.9	4.4	11.6	9.0	6.1	1.4	5.5	1.3	1.5
Hispanic (any race)	1,721	23.5	10.7	11.6	10.5	7.3	6.3	9.8	10.9	6.1	1.5	1.6	0.2
Nativity Status													
Native	15,346	19.5	15.4	10.8	10.9	10.2	8.8	8.5	6.8	3.4	2.9	2.2	0.4
Naturalized	988	26.2	14.1	11.1	6.9	4.8	10.9	10.0	6.9	3.1	3.3	1.6	1.0
Age													
18 to 24 years	2,695	23.2	2.8	10.8	10.0	6.4	12.8	15.2	8.2	6.1	2.5	1.9	0.1
25 to 44 years	6,525	27.6	7.4	11.8	10.3	10.0	8.1	7.6	8.6	3.4	3.3	1.5	0.3
45 to 64 years	4,333	17.2	15.6	10.6	11.0	12.9	10.7	8.6	5.5	3.0	3.0	1.5	0.4
65 years and older	2,781	2.9	45.8	9.0	11.6	8.4	4.5	4.2	3.7	1.7	2.5	4.6	1.2
Marital Status													
Married	7,652	22.0	15.5	11.6	10.3	9.8	9.0	7.0	6.9	3.4	3.1	1.0	0.3
Not married	8,681	18.1	15.2	10.2	11.0	10.0	8.9	9.9	6.8	3.4	2.8	3.1	0.6

PERCENT DISTRIBUTION OF REASONS FOR NOT VOTING

CHARACTERISTIC	TOTAL	Too busy, conflicting schedule	Illness or disability	Other reason	Not interested	Did not like candidates or issues	Out of town	Don't know or refused	Registration problems	Forgot to vote	Inconvenient polling place	Transportation problems	Bad weather conditions
Educational Attainment													
Less than high school graduate	3,437	14.4	25.7	10.3	12.2	8.7	5.5	7.1	4.5	4.1	2.4	4.1	0.9
High school graduate or GED	6,286	20.2	15.1	11.2	12.5	11.3	7.0	8.7	6.2	2.5	3.1	2.0	0.2
Some college or associate's degree	4,512	22.5	9.8	11.1	8.9	9.5	11.1	9.8	7.8	4.3	3.2	1.7	0.3
Bachelor's degree or more	2,099	22.3	11.2	10.3	6.3	8.5	16.0	7.8	10.5	3.1	2.8	0.4	0.9
Duration of Residence													
Less than 1 year	3,388	24.1	6.9	11.9	8.4	8.5	10.2	5.6	15.0	5.3	1.9	2.1	0.2
1 to 2 years	2,480	24.3	10.5	10.2	11.5	9.6	7.4	7.7	8.0	3.5	4.1	3.0	0.2
3 years or longer	10,304	17.5	19.3	10.7	11.1	10.5	9.0	9.4	4.0	2.8	3.1	2.0	0.6
Not reported	162	17.1	14.5	10.5	15.4	6.6	0.9	32	2.3	0.4	–	0.1	–
Region													
Northeast	2,745	19.5	17.5	10.3	10.9	13.4	8.7	8.1	4.8	2.5	2.8	1.5	0.1
Midwest	3,747	17.7	15.1	10.3	12.2	12.3	9.5	10.1	6.2	2.2	2.3	1.8	0.2
South	7,044	20.1	15.5	10.7	10.7	8.4	8.8	8.1	7.0	4.2	3.2	2.6	0.7
West	2,797	22.7	13.3	12.5	8.3	7.1	8.8	8.1	9.4	4.0	3.3	2.0	0.5

– Represents zero or rounds to zero.
Source: U.S. Census Bureau, Current Population Survey, November 2004.

15. When making an appointment to the Supreme Court, presidents
    (A) tend to choose judges from their own political party
    (B) often select a candidate who is neither decidedly liberal nor conservative
    (C) tend to ignore race as a consideration for selecting a judge
    (D) remain impartial by refusing candidate endorsements from members of the Supreme Court
    (E) tend to disregard the religious affiliation of potential candidates

16. According to Table 4-2, which of the following is a correct statement concerning voter apathy?
    (A) The number of voters who reported conflicting schedules as a reason for not voting decreased with an increase in educational level.
    (B) Voters who had immigrated to the United States were more interested in candidates or issues than natural-born citizens.
    (C) Racial groups showed little difference in the percentage of voter indifference.
    (D) A high percentage of voters did not go to the polls because of voter apathy.
    (E) Voters aged 65 or older were more likely to reflect voter apathy than those in other age groups.

17. Which of the following is NOT true concerning the historical development of U.S. political parties?
    (A) Since 1968 the Congress has been controlled by the president's party.
    (B) States' rights was a significant issue in the rise of a two-party system.
    (C) The Republican Party began as a third party.
    (D) The period from 1932 to 1968 was an era of Democratic dominance.
    (E) The period after the Civil War was one of Republican dominance.

18. Today the chief presidential staff is composed of members of the
    (A) Office of Management and Budget
    (B) White House Office
    (C) Council of Economic Advisors
    (D) National Security Council
    (E) Office of Policy Development

19. All of the following are examples of informal amendment to the Constitution EXCEPT
    (A) the creation of lower courts
    (B) judicial review
    (C) the use of executive agreements rather than treaties
    (D) senatorial courtesy
    (E) congressional override of presidential vetoes

20. The technology of the 21st century has changed political parties by
    (A) decreasing the frequency of split-ticket voting
    (B) increasing the importance of the presidential debate
    (C) creating less diversity within major parties
    (D) allowing candidates to become more directly involved with voters
    (E) illuminating the differences between the major parties

21. The size of congressional districts is determined every 10 years by
    (A) gerrymandering
    (B) single-member districts
    (C) the census
    (D) popular sovereignty
    (E) the electoral college

22. Which of the following is a feature that the presidential elections of 1968, 1992, and 2000 share in common?
    (A) Neither candidate in each election won a majority of the electoral vote.
    (B) The elections were decided by the Supreme Court.
    (C) The elections were decided in the Senate.
    (D) The winners received only a plurality of the popular vote.
    (E) The elections were decided in the House of Representatives.

GO ON TO THE NEXT PAGE

23. Senatorial courtesy refers to
    (A) the practice of allowing senators from the majority party in a state where a federal judicial district is located to approve potential judicial nominees
    (B) senatorial immunity from arrest while attending a session in the Senate
    (C) the right of members of Congress to send mail to their constituents at the government's expense
    (D) senatorial immunity from libel or slander suits as a result of their official conduct
    (E) the system in which the chairmanship of a committee is given to the senator with the longest continuous service

24. Which of the following is true of gerrymandering?
    (A) It is intended to draw congressional districts of unequal size.
    (B) It is an attempt to give equal representation for all minority groups.
    (C) It is an effort to draw congressional districts to favor one party or group.
    (D) It violates the principle of the single-member district.
    (E) It is a violation of the Fifteenth Amendment.

25. Which of the following is among the provisions of the First Amendment?
    (A) the right of protection from unreasonable searches and seizures
    (B) the right of peaceful assembly
    (C) the right to a speedy and public trial
    (D) the right to bear arms
    (E) the right to trial by jury

26. The Supreme Court has used the "wall of separation" principle to
    (A) allow prayer in public schools
    (B) prohibit the teaching of evolution in public schools
    (C) require the teaching of creationism in public schools
    (D) allow the use of tax money to purchase textbooks for students in parochial schools
    (E) allow released-time religious instruction outside the public school building

27. Interest groups attempt to influence members of Congress by all of the following EXCEPT
    (A) nominating candidates for public office
    (B) taking an issue to court
    (C) influencing party platforms
    (D) utilizing political action committees (PACs)
    (E) appealing to the public for support

28. Scientific polling includes
    I. controlling how the poll is taken
    II. sampling
    III. formulating public policy
    IV. analyzing and reporting results
    (A) I, III, and IV only
    (B) I, II, and IV only
    (C) II and III only
    (D) II and IV only
    (E) I, II, III, and IV

29. All of the following relate to interstate relations EXCEPT
    (A) interstate compacts
    (B) privileges and immunities
    (C) extradition
    (D) revenue sharing
    (E) full faith and credit

30. Which of the following reflect(s) the principles of the Fifteenth Amendment?
    I. The Twenty-Fourth Amendment
    II. The Civil Rights Act of 1957
    III. *Brown v. Board of Education*
    IV. The Voting Rights Act of 1965
    (A) I only
    (B) III only
    (C) II, III, and IV
    (D) I, II, and IV
    (E) I, II, III, and IV

31. Which of the following is NOT true concerning the vice presidency?
    (A) The vice president may serve no more than two terms.
    (B) The vice president helps determine presidential disability.
    (C) A party's vice presidential nominee is often chosen to balance the ticket.
    (D) Since the 1960s the vice president has often been given a larger role in government.
    (E) The vice president casts tie-breaking votes in the Senate.

GO ON TO THE NEXT PAGE

32. In *Gideon v. Wainwright* (1963), the U.S. Supreme Court declared that
    (A) suspects in police custody must be informed of their rights
    (B) state courts must provide an attorney to poor defendants accused of a felony
    (C) the death penalty is constitutional when it is imposed based on the circumstances of the case
    (D) evidence obtained without a search warrant is excluded from trial in state courts
    (E) searches of criminal subjects are constitutional

33. Which of the following is NOT a constitutional check on the powers of the president?
    (A) power of the purse
    (B) executive agreements
    (C) power of impeachment
    (D) override of presidential vetoes
    (E) judicial review of executive actions

34. Initiative, referendum, and recall
    (A) are examples of issue, or policy, voting
    (B) exist at both the national and state levels
    (C) emerged as a result of the civil rights movement
    (D) allow citizens to nominate candidates
    (E) were eliminated in the Voting Rights Act of 1965

35. Under a single-member district electoral system
    (A) public officials are elected in a winner-take-all arrangement
    (B) minor parties are strengthened
    (C) election results are based on proportional representation
    (D) major parties have less chance of winning than under proportional representation
    (E) the traditional two-party system is weakened

36. Under the system of checks and balances
    (A) the vice president presides over the impeachment trial of the president
    (B) the president may pardon federal offenders
    (C) the judiciary creates lower federal courts
    (D) the House of Representatives confirms judicial appointments
    (E) federal court decisions are absolute

37. All of the following are true of jurisdiction in federal courts EXCEPT
    (A) Concurrent jurisdiction allows certain types of cases to be tried in either federal or state courts.
    (B) The Supreme Court does not have original jurisdiction.
    (C) Appellate jurisdiction applies to courts that hear reviews or appeals of decisions from the lower courts.
    (D) District courts have original jurisdiction.
    (E) The Supreme Court has appellate jurisdiction.

38. Which of the following is true regarding the federal court system?
    (A) Senatorial courtesy plays a key role in the nomination of judges to the Courts of Appeals.
    (B) The size of the Supreme Court is permanently set at eight justices and a Chief Justice.
    (C) Federal judges can serve for unlimited terms of office.
    (D) Supreme Court decisions set precedent.
    (E) Lower courts interpret the law more frequently than appellate courts do.

39. The president can do which of the following without asking the consent of either house of Congress?
    (A) issue an executive order
    (B) appoint Supreme Court justices
    (C) negotiate treaties
    (D) appoint ambassadors
    (E) fill a vacancy in the vice presidency

40. Which is true regarding presidential veto power?
    (A) The president may prevent a bill from becoming law without going through a congressional override attempt.
    (B) Presidential vetoes are frequently overridden.
    (C) Since the Clinton administration, the Congress has given the president the line item veto.
    (D) The Constitution permits the use of the line item veto.
    (E) Veto power has not been a significant source of power for the modern presidency.

GO ON TO THE NEXT PAGE

41. According to traditional democratic theory, government is dependent upon
    (A) bureaucrats
    (B) a system of several strong groups
    (C) interest groups
    (D) the consent of the governed
    (E) a powerful elite

42. Which of the following is true regarding government spending?
    (A) Expenditures to support troop deployment in the Iraqi War are considered non-discretionary spending.
    (B) In recent years, both discretionary and nondiscretionary spending have increased.
    (C) Entitlements are categorized as nondiscretionary spending.
    (D) Student loans are an example of non-discretionary spending.
    (E) Discretionary spending includes interest on the national debt.

43. The media perform all the following functions EXCEPT
    (A) shaping public opinion
    (B) formulating public policy
    (C) providing a link between citizens and the government
    (D) agenda setting by influencing what subjects become significant nationally
    (E) serving as an investigator of personalities

44. Which of the following is required under federal election law?
    (A) A written exam on the Constitution is required in order to register to vote.
    (B) Ballots in the language of the population are required in areas with large linguistic minorities.
    (C) Citizens must register to vote within 30 days after they reach the age of 18.
    (D) Congressional districts must be drawn to include approximately equal numbers of voters from the major parties.
    (E) Prospective voters must pay a fee at the time of registration.

45. Which of the following is NOT an example of domestic policy?
    (A) defense
    (B) crime prevention
    (C) the environment
    (D) energy
    (E) health care

46. Which of the following is a reserved power under the U.S. Constitution?
    (A) regulation of interstate commerce
    (B) making all laws that are "necessary and proper"
    (C) establishment of federal courts below the Supreme Court
    (D) establishment of public school systems
    (E) regulation of immigration

47. Of the following, the strongest influence in a person's political socialization is
    (A) religion
    (B) family
    (C) ethnicity
    (D) education
    (E) income

48. The flag-burning case of *Texas v. Johnson* (1989) was based on the provisions of
    (A) the Second Amendment and due process
    (B) the Fifth Amendment and judicial review
    (C) the Second Amendment and the Establishment Clause
    (D) the Fifth Amendment and the Free Exercise Clause
    (E) the First Amendment and judicial review

49. Compared to the U.S. Constitution, the Articles of Confederation
    (A) based representation in the Congress on population
    (B) created a stronger national judiciary
    (C) reserved more power to the states
    (D) allowed only the national government to coin money
    (E) allowed the Congress stronger authority over interstate and foreign commerce

50. In the debate over the ratification of the U.S. Constitution, the Anti-Federalists
    I. feared a strong national government
    II. wanted the addition of a Bill of Rights
    III. wanted expanded legislative powers
    IV. opposed states' rights
    (A) II only
    (B) I and III only
    (C) I and II only
    (D) III and IV only
    (E) I, II, III, and IV

51. Which of the following is a difference between the House of Representatives and the Senate?
    (A) Revenue bills must originate in the House of Representatives.
    (B) There is limited debate in the Senate but not in the House.
    (C) Impeachment charges are drawn up only by the Senate.
    (D) Filibusters are more common in the House.
    (E) Representation in the Senate is by population, whereas representation in the House is equal for all states.

52. All of the following are checks on the power of the legislative branch EXCEPT
    (A) The courts may rule legislative acts unconstitutional.
    (B) The president may appropriate funds for proposed legislation.
    (C) The president may call special sessions of Congress.
    (D) The president may veto acts of Congress.
    (E) The president may recommend legislation.

53. A vote of cloture ends
    (A) logrolling
    (B) riders
    (C) house debate
    (D) filibusters
    (E) lobbying

54. A proposal to change the child credit allowance in the federal tax code would initially be sent to
    (A) the House Ways and Means Committee
    (B) the Senate Finance Committee
    (C) the House Rules Committee
    (D) the Senate Budget Committee
    (E) the House Appropriations Committee

55. All of the following are true of political action committees (PACs) EXCEPT
    (A) They are political arms of interest groups.
    (B) They arise out of campaign finance reforms.
    (C) They must promote multiple causes.
    (D) They must raise money from multiple contributors.
    (E) They must donate to several candidates.

56. If the president is unable to perform the duties of his office
    (A) only the vice president actually becomes president
    (B) only the Secretary of State informs Congress that the president is disabled
    (C) only the vice president informs Congress of the president's disability
    (D) the president, vice president, and cabinet members inform the Congress of the president's disability
    (E) the president cannot resume the duties of his office without a two-thirds vote of both houses of Congress

57. Which of the following is NOT a value of U.S. democratic political culture?
    (A) compromise
    (B) absolute government
    (C) political equality
    (D) private property
    (E) majority rule/minority rights

58. Which of the following is true of U.S. elections?
    (A) The coattail effect often occurs during off-year elections.
    (B) Single people are more likely to vote than married people.
    (C) Dealigning elections occur with an increase in independents and split-ticket voting.
    (D) "Soft money" refers to unregulated donations to political parties.
    (E) Voter turnout in off-year elections is generally higher than during presidential election years.

GO ON TO THE NEXT PAGE

59. All of the following are true of *Roe v. Wade* EXCEPT
    (A) It is based on the Supreme Court's doctrine of the right to privacy.
    (B) It ruled that states cannot prohibit abortions.
    (C) After the decision, Congress did not propose a constitutional amendment banning abortion.
    (D) After the decision, state legislatures passed laws limiting abortions.
    (E) It prompted right-to-life advocates to pressure presidents and senators to appoint Supreme Court justices who opposed the Court's decision.

60. A constitutional right that persons who have been arrested must be informed of the charges against them is called
    (A) an ex post facto law
    (B) prior restraint
    (C) double jeopardy
    (D) a *writ of habeas corpus*
    (E) a bill of attainder

END OF SECTION I

> Answers and Explanations

1. **E.** Persons with white-collar jobs and higher income levels are more likely to vote than those with blue-collar jobs and lower income levels. The Twenty-Sixth Amendment lowered the voting age from 21 to 18 years. Voters between the ages of 18 and 21 show a low level of participation in elections (A). Active members of religious groups are more likely to vote than those who rarely attend religious services (B). Today women are more likely to vote than men (C). Married people are more likely to vote than those who are single (D).

2. **D.** Congress may alter a bill after it has overridden by a president's veto so that the new form is suitable to the president. A bill that has received a pocket veto dies (A). Very few vetoes have been overridden (B). A form of the line item veto (C) was passed by Congress in 1996, but was declared unconstitutional by the Supreme Court. The fact that few vetoed bills are overridden demonstrates the considerable veto power of the president (E).

3. **B.** The information in the chart does not distinguish Hispanic voters of white origin.

4. **B.** Older Americans tend to be more conservative than younger Americans and, therefore, tend to vote for Republican candidates. Business owners and managers (A), as well as those with higher incomes (D), tend to favor the conservative economic policies of the Republican Party. Members of minority groups tend to favor the domestic policies of the Democratic Party (C). Younger voters tend to prefer the more liberal ideology of the Democrats (E).

5. **D.** The Fourteenth Amendment granted citizenship to blacks, overruling the decision in *Dred Scott v. Sanford*. The Fourteenth Amendment was used in *Brown v. Board of Education* to overturn *Plessy v. Ferguson* and deny segregation in public schools (A). In a series of decisions the Supreme Court has interpreted the Fourteenth Amendment to extend most of the guarantees of the Bill of Rights to state and local governments (B), thus protecting First Amendment freedoms (C). The Court has used the due process clause to protect corporations and other private property (E).

6. **C.** Under Reagan's welfare reform system, benefits were reduced and many recipients removed from welfare rolls. Welfare spending came about as the result of the economic downturn of the Great Depression (A). During the administration of Clinton, a Democrat, welfare spending was reduced by limiting how long a person could receive benefits (B, D). Under the Johnson administration, Great Society programs embraced a wide variety of issues, including health care, school aid, and job training (E).

7. **E.** Many cases appealed to the Supreme Court are disposed of in brief orders and returned to the lower court for reconsideration (B) because they are similar to a case recently decided. Appeals to the Supreme Court must receive the approval of four of the five justices (A). Most appeals are denied because justices agree with the decision of the lower court (C) or believe that they do not deal with a significant point of law (D).

8. **A.** A justice writing a concurrent opinion differs with the majority only because of the reasoning substantiating the majority opinion (E). The concurrent opinion, therefore, does not need to be written by the Chief Justice (B). A poll to determine how each justice is leaning in his or her opinion takes place during the conference phase of the Court's deliberation (C). An *amicus curiae* brief is a statement submitted by an interested party who is not among the attorneys arguing the case (D).

9. **D.** Revenue sharing is an example of fiscal federalism, in which the federal government uses grants to influence the states. The Founding Fathers favored dual federalism, which views the national and state governments each supreme within their own sphere of influence (A). The interstate highway system is an example of cooperative federalism, which involves sharing between the two levels of government (B). Fiscal federalism involves some control over the states by

the national government's granting or withholding money for programs (C). Cooperative federalism may involve differences between the two levels of government. For example, interstate highways were constructed in the South during the civil rights movement, even though the southern states clashed with federal civil rights policies (E).

10. **B**. The winner of the popular vote also needs to win the majority of electoral votes to win the election (C). Candidates focus on swing states, where the majority of voters are apt to vote for either major party (A). Elections rarely go into the House of Representatives (D). All states have a winner-take-all rule in apportioning their electoral votes (E).

11. **B**. The House of Representatives differs from the Senate by having a Rules Committee that sets the conditions for floor debate of a bill. The Rules Committee can facilitate, delay, or prevent House debate.

12. **A**. The Fifth Amendment prevents the federal government from depriving any person of life, liberty, or property without due process of law. The Fourteenth Amendment extends this prohibition to the states. Only the Fifth Amendment deals with criminal prosecutions (C). Only the Fourteenth Amendment deals with the powers reserved to the states (B) and the privileges of citizens (E). The Fourteenth Amendment includes the "equal protection" clause (D).

13. **E**. Minor parties have elected a few members to Congress. Often the ideas of minor parties have been adopted into the platform of major political parties. A minor party may capture a percentage of the vote large enough to sway election results.

14. **D**. The Court has ruled that religious belief is absolute, but that religious beliefs may be restricted, especially if those practices conflict with criminal laws. In 1997 the Supreme Court ruled the Religious Freedom Restoration Act unconstitutional (A). The Court used the establishment clause, not the free exercise clause, to rule in *Engel v. Vitale* that school-sanctioned prayer in public schools is unconstitutional (B). In *Reynolds v. United States* the Court upheld a federal law that prohibited polygamy (C). In *Wisconsin v. Yoder* the Court ruled that Wisconsin could not require Amish parents to send their children to public school beyond the eighth grade (E).

15. **A**. Presidents tend to influence the Court by selecting judges from their own political party. Presidents often want to select a candidate who would tend to vote according to the president's ideological position (B). They often consider race (C) and religious affiliation (E) to provide balance on the court or to satisfy certain segments of society. Presidents may consider endorsements of a particular justice from members of the Supreme Court (D).

16. **B**. Only 4.8% of naturalized citizens reported lack of interest of candidates or issues as opposed to native-born citizens, who reported 10.2% lack of interest. College-educated voters reported busy schedules more frequently than those with less than a high school education (A). Voting patterns among racial groups differed noticeably in most categories (C). Since the chart is restricted to reasons for not voting, it is impossible to determine the percentage of voters who are not casting their ballots (D). Older voters were less likely to list reasons such as too busy, refused, and forgot to vote than younger age groups (E).

17. **A**. Since 1968 U.S. government has been described as divided government, in which one party controls the presidency and the opposing party controls one or both houses of Congress. The earliest Democratic-Republicans, led by Jefferson, favored states' rights (B). The Republican Party began as a third party based largely on opposition to slavery (C). The period from the time of the New Deal to the Nixon presidency was one of Democratic dominance (D). The period after the Civil War was dominated by Republican presidents (E).

18. **B**. The White House Office is made up of personal and political staff members who help with the day-to-day management of the executive branch. The Office of Management and Budget assists the president in the preparation of the annual federal budget (A). The Council of Economic Advisors informs the president about economic developments and problems (C). The National Security Council

(D) advises the president on matters of domestic and foreign national security. The Office of Policy Development gives the president advice about domestic policy (E).

19. **E.** Article I of the Constitution provides for congressional override of presidential vetoes. In the Judiciary Act of 1789, Congress created lower courts in the federal system (A). The concept of judicial review resulted from *Marbury v. Madison* (B). The use of executive agreements rather than treaties allows the president to bypass the Senate (C). Senatorial courtesy is a tradition that has been incorporated into the political system and has lasted over time (D).

20. **D.** New technology has allowed voters to use the Internet to learn of candidate qualifications rather than relying only on party-generated information. Split-ticket voting (splitting the vote among candidates from more than one party) can be accomplished regardless of technology (A). The power of televised presidential debate was already established by the 1960 election (B). Today there is greater diversity within the major parties (C). Today's voters often fail to see a difference between the major parties (E).

21. **C.** After results of the census are compiled, congressional districts are redrawn, if necessary, to maintain populations that are nearly equal in each district. Gerrymandering (A) is the drawing of congressional districts to favor one political party or group over another. Single-member districts (B) are voting districts in which only one representative is chosen from each district. Popular sovereignty (D) is rule by the people. The electoral college (E) is a body of representatives from each state who formally cast ballots for the president and vice president.

22. **D.** In all three elections the winning candidates received only a plurality of the popular vote. Nixon in 1968 and Clinton in 1992 won a majority in the electoral college (A). In 2000, George Bush won a majority of the electoral vote only after the Supreme Court prevented a manual recount of votes in Florida in *Bush v. Gore* (B). Because ultimately all three elections resulted in a majority in the electoral college, they were not decided in the House (E). Presidential elections are not decided in the Senate (C).

23. **A.** Choice (A) is the correct definition. Choices (B) and D are privileges extended to senators in Article I of the Constitution. Choice (C) is a definition of the franking privilege. Choice (E) is a definition of the seniority system.

24. **C.** Gerrymandering involves drawing irregular-shaped districts in order to include populations that favor one party or group over another. All congressional districts must include populations of nearly equal size (A). It is not intended to gain equal representation for all minority groups (B). In fact, gerrymandering is a violation of the Fifteenth Amendment if it is based solely on race (E). Gerrymandered districts remain single-member districts (D).

25. **B.** Choice (B) is a provision of the First Amendment. Protection from unreasonable searches and seizures is guaranteed by the Fourth Amendment (A). The right to a speedy and public trial (C) and trial by jury (E) are provisions of the Sixth Amendment. The Second Amendment grants the right to bear arms (D).

26. **E.** Released-time religious instruction is constitutional if it does not take place within the public school. The Supreme Court has used the "wall of separation" principle to forbid prayer in public schools (A). It has struck down laws that prohibit the teaching of evolution (B) and that require giving equal time to the teaching of creationism (C). The Supreme Court has ruled that the Constitution denies the government the right to spend tax money to support religious institutions (D).

27. **A.** Only political parties nominate candidates for public office. Choices (B), (C), (D), and (E) are all among the strategies typically used by interest groups.

28. **B.** Scientific polling includes sampling, controlling how the poll is taken, and analyzing and reporting results. It is not used to formulate public policy.

29. **D.** Revenue sharing is aid given to state and local governments by the national government. Interstate compacts (A) are agreements between states to work together to solve regional problems. The privileges and immunities clause of the Constitution (B) prohibits states from unreasonably discriminating against residents of

other states. Extradition (C) is the provision that states may return fugitives to a state from which they have fled to avoid criminal prosecution at the request of the governor of the state. The full faith and credit clause of the Constitution (E) requires states to recognize the laws and legal documents of other states.

30. **D.** The Fifteenth Amendment provided that no person could be denied the right to vote based on race or the fact that he was once a slave. The Twenty-Fourth Amendment outlawed poll taxes in federal elections. The use of the poll tax was a strategy designed to keep blacks from voting. *Brown v. Board of Education* dealt with segregation in the public schools, not voting. The Civil Rights Act of 1957 made it a crime to prevent a person from voting in federal elections and created the Civil Rights Division within the Justice Department. The Voting Rights Act of 1965 allowed federal registrars to register voters and outlawed literacy tests in voter registration. Literacy tests had been used by local registrars to keep blacks from voting.

31. **A.** The number of terms a vice president serves is not limited. Under the Twenty-Fifth Amendment, the vice president helps determine presidential disability (B). The vice presidential nominee is often chosen in order to provide geographical or ideological balance to the ticket (C). Since the Kennedy assassination, more attention has been focused on the vice president (D). The vice president presides over the Senate, casting the tie-breaking vote if necessary (E).

32. **B.** In *Gideon v. Wainwright* the Court ruled that, in state trials, those who cannot afford an attorney would have one provided by the state. Choice (A) refers to *Miranda v. Arizona.* Choice (C) refers to *Gregg v. Georgia.* Choice (D) pertains to *Mapp v. Ohio.* Choice (E) refers to *Terry v. Ohio.*

33. **B.** Executive agreements are made by the president with other heads of state and are not subject to Senate ratification. The power of the purse (A) requires that agency budgets be authorized and appropriated by Congress. The power of impeachment (C) is a check of the legislative branch over the executive branch.

Congress may override a presidential veto by a two-thirds majority of both houses (D). The Supreme Court has the power to review and declare unconstitutional the actions of the executive branch (E).

34. **A.** Recall is a special election to allow citizens to remove an official from office before his or her term expires. Initiative allows voters to petition to propose issues to be decided by voters. Referendum allows citizens to vote directly on issues called propositions. They do not exist at the national level (B) and are a result of the Progressive Movement (C). A direct primary allows citizens to nominate candidates (D). They were not eliminated by the Voting Rights Act of 1965 (E).

35. **A.** In a single-member district the individual who receives the most votes is elected from that district or state. Minor parties tend to die out or blend with major parties (B). Election results are not proportional (C). Only major parties have a real chance to win seats in the legislature (D), thus strengthening the existence of the two-party system (E).

36. **B.** The presidential pardon is a check on the judicial branch. The Chief Justice of the Supreme Court presides over the impeachment trial of the president (A). The Congress creates lower federal courts (C). The Senate confirms judicial appointments (D). The Congress may propose constitutional amendments that override Court decisions (E).

37. **B.** The Supreme Court has original jurisdiction in cases affecting ambassadors, other public ministers, and consuls, and in cases in which a state is a party. All other answer choices are true.

38. **D.** Supreme Court decisions often set precedent for future court decisions. Since circuits of the Courts of Appeals cover a wide geographic region, individual senators have less influence and senatorial courtesy does not play a role in nominations (A). Congress has the power to change the number of justices (B). Federal judges are appointed to serve "during good behavior," which generally means for life (C). Appellate courts are more likely than lower courts to interpret the law (E).

39. **A.** An executive order is a directive issued by the president; it has the force of law. The president may negotiate treaties, but treaties must be ratified by a two-thirds vote of the Senate (C). The appointments mentioned in choices (B), (D), and (E) require Senate approval.

40. **A.** If a president chooses to pocket veto a bill, it cannot be overridden by Congress. The Congress seldom overrides a presidential veto (B). In 1996, Congress allowed line item vetoes for appropriations bills. In 1998 the Supreme Court declared this line item veto unconstitutional (C). The Constitution does not mention the line item veto (D). Today even the threat of a veto is sufficient to prompt Congress to pass legislation acceptable to the president (E).

41. **D.** Traditional democratic theory states that government depends on the consent of the governed, given directly or through representatives. Choice (A) describes Max Weber's bureaucratic theory. Choice (B) describes hyperpluralism. Choice (C) defines the pluralist theory, while Choice (E) describes the elite theory of (C). Wright Mills.

42. **C.** Entitlements, including programs such as Medicare, Medicaid, and food stamps, are examples of nondiscretionary spending, or spending required by existing laws for current programs. In recent years the percentage of nondiscretionary spending has increased while the percentage of discretionary spending has increased (B). Student loans are an example of discretionary spending (D). Interest on the national debt is mandatory, or nondiscretionary spending. Defense spending is considered nondiscretionary (A).

43. **B.** Formulating public policy is a function of the government. The other choices are examples of the roles of the media.

44. **B.** In areas where a significant portion of the population uses a language other than English, voting materials must also be printed in that language. Written exams (A) and poll taxes are prohibited by the Voting Rights Act of 1965 and the Twenty-Fourth Amendment (E). Citizens must be registered before the election (C).

Congressional districts must be drawn to contain approximately equal numbers of voters (D).

45. **A.** Domestic policy refers to the social policies of the United States in the areas of crime prevention, education, energy, the environment, health care, and social welfare.

46. **D.** Reserved powers are those powers, such as the establishment of public school systems, that have been reserved to the states. The remaining answer choices are powers of the national government.

47. **B.** Political socialization is the process by which citizens acquire a sense of political identity. Although all answer choices contribute to political socialization, the influence of the family is the strongest.

48. **E.** In *Texas v. Johnson*, the Supreme Court, ruling through the First Amendment guarantee of freedom of speech and through judicial review, declared that flag burning is a form of symbolic speech and, therefore, is protected. The Second Amendment (A, C) guarantees the right to bear arms. The Fifth Amendment guarantees due process (A, B). The Establishment Clause and the Free Exercise Clause are associated with the First Amendment guarantee of freedom of religion (C, D).

49. **C.** While the Constitution created a strong national government, the Articles created a "league of friendship" among the states. Under the Articles, each state had one vote, regardless of population (A). The Articles did not provide for a national judiciary (B). Both the states and the national government could coin money (D). Congress could not regulate interstate trade or foreign commerce (E).

50. **C.** The Anti-Federalists believed that the strong national government provided by the Constitution reserved too few powers to the states. They also believed the Constitution did not explicitly guarantee basic rights and, therefore, favored the addition of a Bill of Rights. The Anti-Federalists were against the expansion of legislative powers provided by the Constitution.

51. **A.** Article I of the Constitution provides that all bills regarding revenue must originate in the House. The Senate's rules provide for unlimited

debate (B). Filibusters, therefore, occur only in the Senate. A filibuster is a lengthy speech designed to delay the vote on a bill (D). Impeachment charges are drawn up only by the House (C). While representation in the House is by population, representation in the Senate is equal for each state (E).

52. **B**. Only the legislative branch may appropriate funds. The other answer choices are all correct.

53. **D**. Cloture is used to end a filibuster; it requires a vote of at least 60 senators. Logrolling (A) is an attempt by members of Congress to gain support of other members in return for their support of the members' legislation. House debate already is limited under the House Rules Committee (C). Lobbying (E) is the attempt to influence members of Congress to support or reject legislation.

54. **A**. The House Ways and Means Committee deals with changes in the tax code. Because all revenue bills must originate in the House, choices (B) and (D) are incorrect. The House Rules Committee decides whether the full House will consider a proposed bill after the proposal has made it out of committee (C). The House Appropriations Committee decides how revenue is appropriated or allowed for each proposal in the various committees (E).

55. **C**. PACs are not required to promote multiple causes. They arose from the campaign finance reforms of the 1970s (B). Choices (A), (D), and (E) are true of political action committees.

56. **D**. The president informs Congress of this disability. The vice president and the majority of the cabinet then inform Congress, in writing, of the president's disability (B, C). The vice president becomes only "acting president" (A). The president may resume his duties upon informing Congress that no disability exists.

If the vice president and a majority of the cabinet disagree, Congress has 21 days to decide the issue by a two-thirds vote of both houses (E).

57. **B**. In the United States, the powers of government are restricted by the will of the people. Compromise (A) allows for the combining of different interests and opinions to form public policy that benefits society. Political equality (C) is the equality of every individual before the law. Private property (D) is protected by law and supported by the capitalist system. Although democracy is based upon majority rule, minority rights must be guaranteed (E).

58. **C**. Dealigning elections occur when party loyalty becomes less important to voters, as may be seen with the increase in independent and split-ticket voting. The coattail effect (A) allows lesser-known or weaker candidates from the presidential candidate's party to win by riding the "coattails" of the nominee. It occurs only during presidential election years. Married people are more likely to vote than single people (B). "Soft money" (D) is restricted by the Bipartisan Campaign Reform Act of 2002. Voter turnout is generally higher in presidential election years (E).

59. **B**. In *Roe v. Wade* the Court ruled that states may prohibit an abortion during the last three months of pregnancy. The other answer choices are true regarding *Roe v. Wade*.

60. **D**. A *writ of habeas corpus* requires a judge to evaluate whether there is sufficient cause to keep a person in jail. An ex post facto law (A) is one applied to acts committed before the law's passage. Prior restraint (B) is the censorship of information before it is published or broadcast. Double jeopardy (C) involves being tried twice for the same offense. A bill of attainder (E) prohibits a person from being found guilty of a crime without a trial.

CHAPTER **5**

Section II of the Exam: How to Approach the Free-Response Essay

IN THIS CHAPTER

Summary: Use these question-answering strategies to raise your score on the free-response essays.

KEY IDEA

Key Ideas

✪ Review the themes that may be covered on the free-response essays.
✪ Learn how the essays are scored.
✪ Review key vocabulary found in essay prompts.
✪ Acquire strategies for responding to the essay prompts.
✪ Become familiar with rubrics.

Introduction to the Free-Response Essay

The free-response section of the U.S. Government and Politics exam contains four mandatory free-response or essay questions. This means no choice between questions; you must answer all four. Don't worry though; often a question will allow choice within the question (such as, "choose one of the three court cases listed"). You will be given 100 minutes for the free-response section; therefore, you should plan on devoting approximately 25 minutes per question. Questions will cover the themes, issues, concepts, and content from all six areas of the course (constitutional underpinnings; political beliefs and behaviors; political parties, interest groups, and the mass media; institutions of national government; public policy; and civil rights and civil liberties).

What Is a Free-Response Essay?

The free-response questions are specific; therefore, your responses must be focused. Responses do not necessarily require a thesis statement, and you must pay close attention to what is being asked. Remember, to gain the highest possible score, answer the question that is asked.

What Is the Purpose of the Free-Response Essay?

The free-response essay assesses your ability to think critically and analyze the topics studied in U.S. Government and Politics. The essays allow students to demonstrate an understanding of the linkages among the various elements of government.

What Are the Pitfalls of the Free-Response Essay?

The free-response question can be a double-edged sword. Students can experience test anxiety (what's "free" in the free-response?) or suffer from overconfidence because of the open nature of this essay. The greatest pitfall is *the failure to plan*. Remember to pace yourself; no one question is more important than another. *Plan your strategy for answering each question, and stick to it.* Don't ramble in vague and unsupported generalities. Rambling may cause you to contradict yourself or make mistakes. Even though your time is limited, creating a general outline may help you in this section.

How Do I Prepare for the Free-Response Essay?

You need to begin preparing for the free-response essay as soon as the course begins. Focus on your writing skills, and practice as if you were writing for the AP exam every time you are assigned an essay in your government and politics class. Determine your strengths and weaknesses, and work to correct areas of weakness. Don't worry, your teacher will probably give you plenty of opportunities to complete these types of essays.

"You must be prepared to read with comprehension and write with consistency."
—JW, AP teacher

- Broaden your knowledge base by reading your textbook and supplemental texts. They will give you basic information to draw from when writing the free-response essay. Do not skim the text—READ—paying attention to details and focusing on people, events, examples, and linkages between different areas of government and politics (for example, interactions between the branches of government or how the media influence lawmakers). Watch the news, and pay attention to current events relating to government and politics.
- Pay attention in class to lectures and discussions. Take notes and study them.
- Take advantage of practice writing whenever possible. Watch and correct grammar, spelling, and punctuation in classroom essays. Check out the previous year's free-response questions, rubrics, and sample scored student essays on the College Board website, www.apcentral.collegeboard.com. You will have to register to access the specific course sites, but it is worth your time.

"Pay close attention to examples: You can use them in your essays."
—DC, AP student

What Criteria Do the AP Readers Use to Score a Free-Response Essay?

The readers look for responses that answer the questions asked. Remember, each free-response is scored by a different AP reader, trained to score that particular question. Care is given to compare each student essay to the standards established in the rubric. The same standards are applied to all essays, and no modifications in the rubrics occur. In general, students should:

- Recognize the subject matter of the question. When you see "Congress," don't just start writing about Congress. Analyze what the question asks about Congress.
- Recognize what task you are being asked to perform in relation to the question; for example, list, explain, describe, identify and explain, or explain and give examples (sometimes you will be asked to perform more than one task).
- NOTE: Remember that there is a general order to the tasks within the question. Organize your essay to answer the question or address the tasks in the order asked.

Types of Free-Response Prompts

Free-response questions are generally straightforward and ask you to perform certain tasks. Understanding what the prompt is asking you to do will help you perform the task correctly.

Prompt Vocabulary

- analyze—examine each part of the whole in a systematic way; evaluate
- define—briefly tell what something is or means
- describe—create a mental picture by using details or examples
- discuss—give details about; illustrate with examples
- explain—make something clear by giving reasons or examples; tell how and why
- argue/defend/justify/support—give evidence to show why an idea or view is right or good
- categorize/classify—sort into groups according to a given set of traits or features
- compare and contrast—point out similarities (compare) and differences (contrast)
- determine cause and effect—decide what leads to an event or circumstance (cause) and what results from an event or circumstance (effect)
- evaluate/judge—determine the worth or wisdom of an opinion, belief, or idea

> *"Pay attention to vocabulary terms."*
> —AL, AP student

Developing the Free-Response Essay

Strategies for Writing the Free-Response Essay

- Read the question carefully, in its entirety, and determine what you are being asked to write about. Analyze the question and identify the topics, issues, and key terms that define your task (define, discuss, explain). Underline key terms to focus your attention.
- Brainstorm ideas.
- Organize ideas and outline your essay before you begin to write. Use the blank space in your test booklet to plan. (Brainstorming and outlining should take about five to eight minutes per question.)
- Write the essay. Include an introduction that restates the question, the factual information, evidence and examples, and a conclusion. Stick to your outline and keep sentences simple. If time is short, forget the introduction and conclusion and jump into the essay, using bulleted lists with explanations or an outline.
- Reread the question and your essay to determine if you answered the question or questions. NOTE: Many of the free-response questions will have several parts; make sure you answer them all.
- Proofread for grammar, spelling, and punctuation errors. Even though these errors will not count against you, they can make your essay harder to read and can make your answer less understandable.

> *"Knowing how to evaluate provided me with confidence in my free-response answers."*
> —DK, AP student

> *"The free-response essays often involve the student choosing between options—look at all options before you begin writing."*
> —LA, AP teacher

Rubrics for the Free-Response Essay

What Is a Rubric?

Rubrics are scoring guidelines used to evaluate your performance on each of the free-response essays. They are based on the sum of points earned by meeting the preestablished criteria.

How Are Rubrics Developed and Applied?

The number of points students may earn for each free-response question is assigned by members of the Test Development Committee. The chief faculty consultant, exam leaders, and question leaders develop preliminary rubrics for each question based on these points. These rubrics are sampled against actual student essays and revised if necessary. Table leaders are then trained using these standards. When the reading begins, table leaders train the AP readers at their table (usually five to seven readers) in the use of the rubric for that particular question. Once the reading begins, the rubrics are not changed.

Common Characteristics of Rubrics

Since each free-response question is different, each scoring rubric will differ. There are, however, several characteristics common to all U.S. Government and Politics rubrics. Each rubric:

- Addresses all aspects and tasks of the question. Points are awarded for each task or response requested—one point for a correct identification and two points for the discussion.
- Contains evaluative criteria. These distinguish what is acceptable from what is not acceptable in the answer; for example, accept AARP as an interest group but do not accept the Democratic Party.
- Has a scoring strategy, a scale of points to be awarded for successfully completing a task. For example, identification of an interest group is worth one point.
- Awards points for correct responses; points are not deducted.
- Can be applied clearly and consistently by different scorers. If more than one reader were to score a particular essay, it would receive the same score, based on the same standards.

Final Comments—Some Helpful Hints

When writing your free response, consider these do's and don'ts.

- **Don't** use words that you are uncomfortable using or not familiar with. Readers are not impressed if you use "big words" but don't understand what they mean or use them incorrectly.
- **Don't** try to "fake out" the reader. They are government professors and teachers. Trying to do this will *always* hurt you more than help you.
- **Don't** preach, moralize, editorialize, or use "cute" comments. Remember, you want the reader to think positively about your essay.
- **Don't** "data dump" or create "laundry lists." Do not provide information (names, court cases, laws) without explanation or relevant link.
- **Do** write neatly and legibly. Write or print in blue or black ink (not pencil; it's harder to read) as clearly as you can.
- **Do** use correct grammar, spelling, and punctuation. They make your essay much easier to score.

> "Be sure your free-response essay is brief and gets directly to the point."
> —JB, AP student

- **Do** answer all questions and all parts of each question. You may answer the questions in any order. Answer the questions you feel you know best, first. That way, if you run out of time and don't finish, no harm is done. Even though the essays are graded on different scales, they are weighted equally and together count for half your total score. (Each essay is 12.5 percent of your total score.)

- **Do** support your essay with specific evidence and examples. If the question asks for examples, supply not only the example but also a discussion of how that example illustrates the concept. Provide however many examples the question asks for; hypothetical examples may sometimes be used, if they are backed up with facts.

- **Do** pay attention to dates and terms like "modern." When time frames are used, keep your evidence and examples within that time frame (modern presidency would not include Jefferson, Jackson, Lincoln).

- **Do** stop when you finish your essay. Proofread! If you ramble on after you have answered the question completely, you might contradict yourself, causing the reader to question your answer.

- **Do** your best!

> "Remember, on free-response questions, AP means answer **all parts** of the question."
> —MN, AP teacher

Test Your Free-Response Skills

It is now time to try the free-response section of the second diagnostic exam. Once again, do this entire section in one sitting. Time yourself. Be honest with yourself when scoring your answers.

If the 100 minutes passes before you finish all the questions, stop where you are and score what you have done up to this point. Afterward, answer the remaining questions, but do not count the answers as part of your score. When you have completed all of the free-response questions on this exam, assess which ones gave you trouble. Use this book to learn from your mistakes.

AP U.S. Government and Politics
Diagnostic Exam 2: Free-Response Essay

Section II

Time—100 minutes

Directions: You have 100 minutes to answer all four of the following questions. Unless the directions indicate otherwise, respond to all parts of all four questions. It is suggested that you take a few minutes to plan and outline each answer. *Spend approximately one-fourth of your time (25 minutes) on each question.* Illustrate your essay with substantive examples where appropriate. Make certain to number each of your answers as the question is numbered below. Use a separate sheet of paper if you need more space.

1. The modern presidency exercises powers far beyond those envisioned by the Founding Fathers.
    (a) Identify one example of the power held by modern presidents in each of the following categories:
        • legislative powers
        • administrative (executive) powers
        • judicial powers
        • national security powers

    (b) Select two examples from Part (a) and analyze how they strengthen the power of the modern presidency.

2. Since the 1930s, entitlements have constituted a significant element in U.S. social programs. Social Security is the most extensive entitlement program in the United States. Using data from the charts in Figure 5-1, perform the following tasks:
    (a) Define entitlement.

GO ON TO THE NEXT PAGE

TABLE 1

Social Security Beneficiaries (thousands)

Year	Retired Workers	Disabled Workers	Wives and Husbands	Children	Others	SSI
1940	112		30	55	26	2,143
1950	1,171		508	700	498	2,952
1960	8,061	455	2,346	2,000	1,981	2,781
1970	13,349	1,493	2,952	4,122	3,778	3,098
1980	19,562	2,859	3,477	4,607	4,988	4,192
1990	24,838	3,011	3,367	3,187	5,421	4,817
2000	28,499	5,042	2,963	3,803	5,107	6,602

SOURCE: Social Security Administration (2001), Table 5.A4; Myers (1985), Table 11.7; and Social Security Administration (2002), Table IV.B9.

TABLE 2

Annual Social Security Payments

Year	Insurance Payments (billions)	Insurance Payments as % of Federal Spending	Insurance Payments as % of GDP	SSI Payments (billions)
1940	$ 0.04	0.4	0.035	$ 0.49
1950	$ 0.96	2.3	0.33	$ 1.5
1960	$ 11.2	12.2	2.13	$ 1.9
1970	$ 31.9	16.3	3.07	$ 2.9
1980	$120.5	20.6	4.31	$ 8.1
1990	$247.8	19.9	4.27	$14.8
2000	$407.6	22.0	4.13	$34.1

SOURCE: Social Security Administration (2001), Table 4.A4; Myers (1985), Table 11.8; and Social Security Administration (2002), Tables IV.C2 and IV.C4.

Figure 5-1 Social Security Beneficiaries.

(b) Identify two trends in the demographic makeup of Social Security beneficiaries.

GO ON TO THE NEXT PAGE

(c) Identify two trends in the percentage of federal spending allotted to Social Security payments.

(d) Give a reason for each trend in Part (b).

(e) Give a reason for each trend in Part (c).

3. The U.S. Constitution was written to resolve the weaknesses of the Articles of Confederation by creating a strong national government.
   (a) Identify three weaknesses of the Articles of Confederation.

   (b) Explain how each of these weaknesses was resolved by the U.S. Constitution.

GO ON TO THE NEXT PAGE

4. Many Supreme Court decisions have defined the nature of race relations in the United States. Use the three decisions listed below to perform the following tasks:
   - *Plessy v. Ferguson* (1896)
   - *Brown v. Board of Education* (1954)
   - *California Board of Regents v. Bakke* (1978)
     (a) Explain the decision of the Court in each case.

     (b) Analyze the effect of each decision on U.S. society.

END OF SECTION II

› Rubrics for the Free-Response Essay

1. Total value: 8 points

    Part (a): 1 point for each identification = 4 points
    Part (b): 2 points for each analysis = 4 points

2. Total value: 9 points

    Part (a): 1 point for each definition = 1 point
    Part (b): 1 point for each trend = 2 points
    Part (c): 1 point for each trend = 2 points
    Part (d): 1 point for each reason = 2 points
    Part (e): 1 point for each reason = 2 points

3. Total value: 6 points

    Part (a): 1 point for each weakness = 3 points
    Part (b): 1 point for each resolution = 3 points

4. Total value: 6 points

    Part (a): 1 point for each explanation = 3 points
    Part (b): 1 point for each analysis = 3 points

STEP 4

Review the Knowledge You Need to Score High

CHAPTER 6

Architecture and Development of U.S. Government

IN THIS CHAPTER

Summary: Government is the institution that creates public policy. The democratic government of the United States traces its roots from the Greco-Roman era to the Enlightenment. The key founding documents of U.S. government, the Declaration of Independence and the Constitution, set forth the principles that define the character of American democracy. The U.S. Constitution is a flexible document that provides for its own changes, or amendments. Among the key principles of U.S. government inherent in the Constitution are federalism, separation of powers, and a system of checks and balances. The power of the Supreme Court broadened with the establishment of judicial review in *Marbury v. Madison* (1803).

Key Terms

government
public policy
democracy
direct democracy
representative democracy
traditional democratic
   theory
pluralist theory
elite theory
bureaucratic theory
hyperpluralism
social contract
natural rights

Declaration of
   Independence
Articles of Confederation
federal system
Connecticut (Great)
   Compromise
Virginia Plan
Three-Fifths Compromise
Commerce and Slave
   Trade Compromise
ratification
Federalists
Federalist Papers

Anti-Federalists
Bill of Rights
constitution
limited government
popular sovereignty
separation of powers
checks and balances
federalism
amendments
judicial review
Marbury v. Madison

Principles of Government

What Is Government?

Political scientist Harold Laswell defined government as "who gets what, when, and how." In any nation a **government** is composed of the formal and informal institutions, people, and processes used to create and conduct public policy. **Public policy** is the exercise of government power in doing those things necessary to maintain legitimate authority and control over society.

Purposes of Government

Every nation must decide for itself what goals will be translated into public policy and the methods by which those goals will be translated. The Preamble of the United States Constitution addresses the goals of public policy for the United States:

- forming a more perfect union: creation of a strong union of the states, while also maintaining state sovereignty
- establishing justice: reasonable, fair and impartial law
- insuring domestic tranquility: preservation of public order
- providing for the common defense: protection and maintenance of national defense
- promoting the general welfare: providing public services and economic health of the nation
- securing the blessings of liberty: promoting individual freedoms

Forms of Government

Greek philosopher Aristotle attempted to classify governments based on the number of individuals who participated in making political decisions: rule by one, rule by the few, or rule by the many. His early classification system is still useful in describing governments today:

- *anarchy*—lack of government
- *autocracy*—rule by one
  — absolute monarchy—ruler gains power through inheritance; there are no restrictions on the ruler's power
  — constitutional monarchy—ruler gains power through inheritance; formal restrictions limit power, often restricting the monarch to ceremonial status
  — dictatorship—ruler seizes power, keeps power by force and restricts opposition to regime; no restrictions on dictator's power
- *oligarchy*—rule by a few
  — aristocracy: rule by the elite, usually determined by social status or wealth
  — theocracy: rule by religious leaders
- *democracy*—rule by the people
  — **direct democracy**—Citizens meet and make decisions about public policy issues.
  — **representative democracy**—Citizens choose officials (representatives) who make decisions about public policy. This is the system in place in most "democratic" nations.

Theories of Democratic Government

KEY IDEA

Theories of democratic government are theories about who has power and influence over public policy and decision making at the local, state, and national levels of government.

- ***traditional democratic theory***—Government depends on the consent of the governed, which may be given directly or through representatives; may include criteria for the measure of "how democratic."

- *pluralist theory*—Interest groups compete in the political arena, with each promoting its policy preferences through organized efforts. Conflict among groups may result, requiring bargaining and compromise (Robert Dahl).
- *elite theory*—A small number of powerful elite (corporate leaders, top military officers, government leaders) form an upper class, which rules in its own self-interest (C. Wright Mills).
- *bureaucratic theory*—The hierarchical structure and standardized procedures of modern governments allow bureaucrats, who carry out the day-to-day workings of government, to hold the real power over public policy (Max Weber).
- *hyperpluralism*—Democracy is a system of many groups having so much strength that government is often "pulled" in numerous directions at the same time, causing gridlock and ineffectiveness.

Origins of American Government

Influences on American Government

In 1607 the British established a permanent colony at Jamestown, Virginia. Early colonists brought ideas and traditions that would form the basis of American government as a part of the British colonial empire, and as an independent United States. Two of the early traditions were limited government and representative government.

- *Ancient Greeks and Romans*—Democratic government began with the ancient Greeks and Romans. Their concepts and ideas of direct and representative democracy greatly influenced the American founding fathers.
- *Magna Carta (1215)*—The first attempt to limit the power of the British monarch was the Magna Carta, forced upon the monarch by British nobility. The "Great Charter" guaranteed the nobility certain rights such as trial by jury, due process of law, and protections against the arbitrary taking of life, liberty, or property.
- *Parliament*—Parliament began as an advisory group to the monarch, but as the power of the monarch became more and more limited, Parliament grew to become the lawmaking body of Britain.
- *Petition of Right (1628)*—The Petition of Right extended the protections of the Magna Carta to include commoners. The monarch's powers were further limited by restricting the monarch from taxing without the consent of Parliament, declaring martial law or military rule during peacetime, or housing the military in private homes without the owners' consent. Guarantees of trial by jury, even for critics of the monarch, were recognized. The Petition of Right was a challenge to the accepted belief in divine-right of the king.
- *English Bill of Rights (1689)*—The English Bill of Rights was an agreement between Parliament and King William and Queen Mary, to prevent future monarchs from abusing their powers. The Bill of Rights guaranteed free parliamentary elections; the rights of citizens to a fair and speedy trial; freedom from excessive bails and cruel and unusual punishment; the right to petition the king; and protections against standing armies during peacetime. Suspension of public laws was prohibited, and taxation without the consent of Parliament was made illegal.
- *Enlightenment philosophers*—During the Enlightenment Era, philosophers such as John Locke supported the concept of a social contract. Locke viewed the **social contract** as a voluntary agreement between the government and the governed. In *Two Treatises on Civil Government* (1689), Locke argued that people are born with **natural rights** to life, liberty, and property (natural law). Locke also believed that governments are created

to support those rights, but that if the government fails to do so, the people may choose to change their government. Thomas Jefferson adopted these ideas in the **Declaration of Independence**. Another Enlightenment thinker, Montesquieu, wrote about the need for branches of government.

Colonial Experiences

From 1607 to 1776, the American colonies were in a continuous state of political self-development. This was due to several factors, such as the long distance from England, indifference of the colonists to the king's authority, and the disputed political authority in England. As the colonies developed, they made the most of their English heritage but made changes to create a new and unique style of government. This new government was founded on the principles of equality, liberty, and limited government.

- *Colonial charters*—Each colony was founded on the basis of a charter from the king. The charter authorized the colony's existence and established its political authority. Royal, proprietary, and charter colonies were founded, each operating with executive, legislative, and judicial roles. The authority of governors, legislatures, and judges depended on the type of colony and its charter.
- *House of Burgesses*—In 1619 Virginia established the first representative legislature in the American colonies. Only adult male property owners could vote for its members.
- *Mayflower Compact*—In 1620 colonists aboard the Mayflower signed an agreement, a social contract, called the Mayflower Compact. This agreement established a government for the colony based on the ideas of consent of the governed and limitations on the authority of government.
- *Difficulties with Britain*—As the colonies grew, so did problems with Britain. Prior to 1750, the British provided defense and manufactured goods for the colonies. The colonies in return provided raw materials and markets for manufactured goods. Britain allowed the colonies to control their own internal affairs. After the French and Indian War (1756–1763), however, the British government expected the colonies to help pay the cost of the war and pay for their own future defense. The British government began enforcing taxes already levied and passed new taxes to replenish the king's treasury. These new taxes included the Sugar Act (1764), the Stamp Act (1765), and the Townshend Acts (1767). As the colonists began protesting, violence and conflict began to break out between the colonies and Britain. After the Boston Massacre (1770) and Boston Tea Party (1772), the British government passed a series of punishing acts collectively known as the Coercive or Intolerable Acts. In response the colonies began to unite in an effort to influence the British government and to express dissatisfaction with British policies.
- *Continental Congresses*—The First Continental Congress included delegates from 12 colonies (all except Georgia) who met in Philadelphia in 1774. This Continental Congress resolved to send a Declaration of Rights to the king in protest of Britain's policies. They also agreed to meet again the following year. The Second Continental Congress began meeting in May 1775, more than one month after the battles of Lexington and Concord. The Second Continental Congress became America's first national government. Delegates from all 13 colonies were present, among them John Hancock, George Washington, Ben Franklin, Thomas Jefferson, John Adams, and Patrick Henry. The Second Continental Congress created the Continental Army and appointed George Washington as its commander-in-chief, borrowed money from France and the Netherlands, created a monetary system, made treaties with foreign governments, and commissioned the writing of the Declaration of Independence and the **Articles of Confederation**.

Declaration of Independence

The Declaration of Independence is mainly the work of Thomas Jefferson. The principles are largely based on the works of Enlightenment philosopher John Locke. The Declaration of Independence can be divided into three parts: a theory of government based on social contract and natural rights, a list of grievances against the king and "others" (Parliament), and a statement of colonial unity and separation from Britain.

Articles of Confederation

The Articles of Confederation (1781–1789), written by the Second Continental Congress in November 1777, became the first national constitution for governing the American states. The Articles created a confederation or "league of friendship" among the states. The Confederation would be composed of a relatively weak national government with a unicameral legislature. Writers of the Articles did not want to replicate the strong national government of Great Britain. Congress would have limited powers such as borrowing money, creating a national army and navy, declaring war, creating post offices, and signing treaties with foreign governments. Congress was not given the power to tax, draft soldiers for military service, or regulate commerce. There was no national executive or judicial branch under the Articles of Confederation. Each state was equal, with one vote, regardless of population or size. The votes of 9 of the 13 states were required for legislation to pass the Confederation Congress; amending the Articles of Confederation required a unanimous vote.

The weaknesses evident in the Articles of Confederation allowed the states to focus on their own powers. With no central government to control them, the states taxed each other, printed their own money, made treaties with foreign governments, and often refused to uphold the laws of the Confederation government. Even with all these problems, the Confederation Congress was able to approve the signing of the Treaty of Paris, which ended the American Revolution in 1783, and pass the Land Ordinance of 1785 and Northwest Ordinance of 1787. The government under the Articles of Confederation, however, could not deal with the nation's problems. Economic chaos and violence broke out, resulting in conferences at Mt. Vernon and Annapolis. These meetings proved to be unsuccessful, and eventually a rebellion of farmers in Massachusetts (Shays Rebellion) led to the calling of a Constitutional Convention.

Constitutional Convention

The Constitutional Convention was convened in Philadelphia in May of 1787, for the purpose of revising the Articles of Confederation. (See Figure 6-1.) Delegates representing all the states except Rhode Island attended.

- Very early in the convention, the delegates decided that they would write a new constitution instead of revising the Articles of Confederation.
- The delegates agreed that the new government would be a republic, a **federal system**, and would be composed of three branches (executive, legislative, judicial).
- Several plans, including the **Virginia Plan** and the New Jersey Plan, were presented to the delegates. (See Figure 6-2.)

Compromises

- Debate over the various plans presented at the Constitutional Convention resulted in the **Connecticut (Great) Compromise**. This compromise settled the disputes between the states over the structure of the legislative branch. Congress would be a bicameral legislature, with representation in the lower house based on the population of the state and equal representation of the states in the upper house.

Weaknesses of the Articles of Confederation and Constitutional Remedies

KEY IDEA

Weaknesses of the Articles of Confederation	How the Constitution Remedied Weaknesses
Articles created a "league of friendship" between the states	The Constitution created a federal system of government between the national and state levels
Congress could not tax; it could only request contributions from the states	National government was given the power to tax
Congress could not regulate interstate trade or foreign commerce	Congress was given the power to regulate commerce between the states and with foreign nations
No separate executive to enforce the acts of Congress	Article II created a separate executive department whose job is to enforce the laws of Congress
No national judiciary to handle state disputes	Article III created a national judiciary with a Supreme Court and lower courts as established by Congress
States and the national government had the authority to coin money	Only the national government has the authority to coin money
Each state had one vote, regardless of size or population	States are represented based on population in the House of Representatives and equality in the Senate
Nine of thirteen states required to pass legislation	Bills need a simple majority in both houses of Congress
Unanimous consent required to amend the Articles of Confederation	Two-thirds of Congress and three-fourths of the states are necessary to amend the Constitution

"Quiz yourself on the material."
—JS, AP student

Figure 6-1

Comparison of the Virginia and New Jersey Plans

Virginia Plan	New Jersey Plan
Bicameral legislature —lower house elected by the people —upper house chosen by lower house from nominees submitted by state legislatures	Unicameral legislature —representatives chosen by state legislatures —each state receives one vote
Representation in each house based on population and/or monetary contributions to the national government by the state	Representation in house would be equal among the states
Single executive chosen by legislative branch, limited to one term only, could veto legislative acts, removed by Congress	Plural executive chosen by legislative branch, no veto powers, removal by the states
Judges chosen by legislative branch	Judges appointed for life by the executive

Figure 6-2

- A second compromise concerned the counting of slaves for the purpose of determining population for representation in Congress and for taxation. Southern states wanted slaves to be counted for representation but not taxation. Northern states wanted slaves counted for taxation but not for representation. The **Three-Fifths Compromise** resolved this issue: each state would count three-fifths of its slave population for purposes of determining both representation and taxation.
- The **Commerce and Slave Trade Compromise** resolved other differences between southern and northern states. Congress was prohibited from taxing exports from the states and from banning the slave trade for a period of 20 years.
- Numerous other compromises were made at the Constitutional Convention concerning the executive and judicial branches as well as the electoral process for choosing a chief executive.

Ratification of the Constitution

Although the delegates at the convention signed the Constitution on September 17, 1787, it still had to be ratified by 9 of the 13 states before it could go into effect. In each state, special ratifying conventions would be held over the next two years. Debate over **ratification** divided citizens into Federalist and Anti-Federalist positions (Figure 6-3).

- The **Federalists** stressed the weaknesses of the Articles of Confederation and the government it created. They supported a stronger central government with expanded legislative powers. The Federalist cause was helped by James Madison, Alexander Hamilton, and John Jay in a collection of 85 essays published in the New York newspapers under the name "Publius." (Hamilton wrote 51, Madison wrote 26, Jay wrote 5, and Hamilton and Madison co-authored 3 of these essays.) These *Federalist Papers* defended the new government created under the Constitution and even today provide insight into the framers' original intent.

Federalists Versus Anti-Federalists

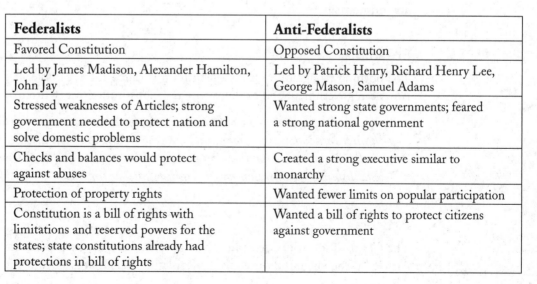

Federalists	Anti-Federalists
Favored Constitution	Opposed Constitution
Led by James Madison, Alexander Hamilton, John Jay	Led by Patrick Henry, Richard Henry Lee, George Mason, Samuel Adams
Stressed weaknesses of Articles; strong government needed to protect nation and solve domestic problems	Wanted strong state governments; feared a strong national government
Checks and balances would protect against abuses	Created a strong executive similar to monarchy
Protection of property rights	Wanted fewer limits on popular participation
Constitution is a bill of rights with limitations and reserved powers for the states; state constitutions already had protections in bill of rights	Wanted a bill of rights to protect citizens against government

Figure 6-3

- The **Anti-Federalists** believed that the new Constitution gave too much power to the national government at the expense of the state governments. Another objection was the lack of a **Bill of Rights,** ensuring fundamental liberties.

The United States Constitution

A **constitution** details the structure of a government. The Constitution of the United States is the oldest national constitution in use today. Although the Constitution is relatively short, it describes the structure and powers of the national government as well as the relationship between the national and state governments.

Basic Principles Within the Constitution

Embodied within the Constitution are the basic principles of:

- *limited government*—belief that government is not all-powerful; government has only those powers given to it
- *popular sovereignty*—the people are the source of government's authority
- *separation of powers*—power is separated among three branches of government; each has its own powers and duties and is independent of and equal to the other branches
- *checks and balances*—each branch is subject to restraints by the other two branches (see Figure 6-4)
- *federalism*—a division of governmental powers between the national government and the states

Checks and Balances

The constitutional system of checks and balances prevents one branch of the federal government from becoming more powerful than the other two.

The Constitution may be divided into three major parts: the Preamble, articles, and **amendments**.

Preamble

The opening paragraph of the Constitution is called the Preamble. It lists the six goals for American government and explains why the Constitution was written.

> *We the People of the United States, in Order to form a more perfect Union, establish Justice, insure domestic Tranquility, provide for the common defense, promote the general Welfare, and secure the Blessings of Liberty to ourselves and our Posterity, do ordain and establish this Constitution for the United States of America.*

Articles

The Constitution is divided into seven articles. Each of the articles covers a specific topic. Article I is the longest, devoted to the legislative branch of government.

- Article I—Legislative Branch
- Article II—Executive Branch
- Article III—Judicial Branch

Separation of Powers and Checks and Balances

Legislative Branch (Passes Laws)

Over Executive:
May override president's veto by two-thirds vote of both houses
May impeach and remove president from office
Senate may refuse to confirm presidential appointments or ratify treaties
Creates executive agencies and programs
Appropriates funds

Over Judiciary:
Creates lower federal courts
Sets salaries of federal judges
May refuse to confirm judicial appointments
May propose constitutional amendments which overrule court decisions
May impeach and remove federal judges

Executive Branch (Enforces Laws)

Over Legislature:
President may veto acts of Congress
President may call special sessions of Congress
President may recommend legislation

Over Judiciary:
President appoints federal judges
President may grant reprieves and pardons to federal offenders
May refuse to enforce court decisions

Judicial Branch (Interprets Laws)

Over Legislature:
May rule legislative acts unconstitutional
Chief justice presides over impeachment of president

Over Executive:
May rule executive actions unconstitutional

Figure 6-4

- Article IV—Intergovernmental Relationships
- Article V—Amendment Process
- Article VI—Supremacy of the Constitution
- Article VII—Ratification Process

Formal Amendment Process

One major weakness of the Articles of Confederation was the amendment process, which required unanimous approval for amendments to become effective. The framers of the Constitution anticipated the need to change the Constitution and provided a process to amend the Constitution (Article V) that required both state and national action. Amending the Constitution requires proposal, a national function, and ratification, a state function. Amendments may be proposed in Congress by two methods and ratified by two methods, creating four possible methods for formally amending the Constitution:

- proposed by two-thirds vote of each house of Congress and ratified by three-quarters of the state legislatures (used 26 times)
- proposed by two-thirds vote of each house of Congress and ratified by special conventions in at least three-quarters of the states (used once, to ratify the Twenty-First Amendment)
- proposed by a national convention called by Congress at the request of two-thirds of the state legislatures and ratified by three-quarters of the state legislatures (never used)
- proposed by a national convention called by Congress at the request of two-thirds of the state legislatures and ratified by special conventions in at least three-quarters of the states (never used)

Formal Amendments

Formal amendments are written changes to the Constitution. They add to, change the wording of, or delete language from the Constitution. Only 27 formal amendments have been added to the Constitution since its adoption. (See Figure 6-5.) The first 10 amendments, the Bill of Rights, were added in 1791.

Informal Amendment Process

Although the United States Constitution has been formally changed only 27 times, there have been many changes in the way in which the American government operates. Most of those changes have come about through the informal amendment process and do not involve actually changing the wording of the Constitution. Informal changes in the Constitution may occur in the following ways:

- *legislative actions*—Congress has passed various acts that have altered or made clear the meaning of the Constitution. For example, under Article III Congress is given the authority to create lower courts, which they did through the Judiciary Act of 1789.
- *executive actions*—The manner in which presidents use their powers can create informal amendments and expand presidential authority. The use of executive agreements rather than treaties allows the president to bypass the Senate.
- *judicial interpretation/judicial review*—The people who serve as judges and the times in which they serve affect how courts interpret laws. The concept of judicial review resulted from **Marbury v. Madison** (1803); it is not mentioned in the Constitution.
- *custom and usage*—Traditions that have been incorporated into the political system and which have lasted over time have changed the meaning of the Constitution. Senatorial courtesy in the Senate and the "no-third-term" tradition in the Presidency (until the Twenty-Second Amendment made it part of the Constitution) are examples.

Marbury v. Madison (1803)

In the election of 1800 political parties played an active role. Federalists supported John Adams, and Democratic-Republicans supported Thomas Jefferson. At the conclusion of the election, Adams and the Federalists had lost control of the presidency and Congress. In an effort to retain some control in the government, the "lame duck" Federalist Congress created numerous new judicial positions, which outgoing President Adams attempted to fill. Late

Constitutional Amendments

- Amendment 1—guarantees freedom of religion, speech, press, assembly, and petition
- Amendment 2—ensures the right to keep and bear arms
- Amendment 3—sets conditions for quartering of troops in private homes
- Amendment 4—regulates search, seizure, and warrants
- Amendment 5—addresses protections against self-incrimination, guarantees of due process, eminent domain, and grand jury indictment for capital crimes
- Amendment 6—guarantees rights to a speedy, public trial and an impartial jury; to confront witnesses; and to have an attorney
- Amendment 7—preserves right to a jury trial in civil cases
- Amendment 8—ensures no excessive bails or fines, nor cruel and unusual punishment
- Amendment 9—unenumerates rights of the people
- Amendment 10—reserves powers of the states and the people
- Amendment 11—restricts lawsuits against states
- Amendment 12—provides for election of president and vice-president by separate ballot in electoral college
- Amendment 13—abolishes slavery
- Amendment 14—guarantees rights of citizenship, due process, and equal protection
- Amendment 15—guarantees citizens' right to vote regardless of race, color, or previous condition of servitude
- Amendment 16—authorizes income tax
- Amendment 17—establishes direct election of senators by popular vote
- Amendment 18—prohibits intoxicating liquors
- Amendment 19—establishes women's suffrage
- Amendment 20—sets terms and sessions of executive and legislative branches; "lame duck"
- Amendment 21—repeals prohibition (18th amendment)
- Amendment 22—limits presidential terms of office
- Amendment 23—allows for voting rights in District of Columbia in presidential elections
- Amendment 24—abolishes poll taxes
- Amendment 25—addresses presidential succession, disability, and vice-presidential vacancies
- Amendment 26—gives 18-year-olds the right to vote
- Amendment 27—addresses congressional pay

Figure 6-5

into the night prior to Jefferson's inauguration, Adams was still signing the commissions of the "midnight appointments" which the secretary of state was to deliver. Not all the commissions were delivered, and when Jefferson took office, he ordered the commissions withheld, intending to make his own appointments. William Marbury expected to receive a commission as a justice of the peace for the District of Columbia. He petitioned the Supreme Court to issue a writ of mandamus (allowed under the Judiciary Act of 1791) ordering Secretary of State James Madison to deliver the commission to Marbury and several others. The Supreme Court under Chief Justice John Marshall ruled that although Marbury was entitled to the commission, the Supreme Court would not order Madison to give it to him because the court did not have authority under the Constitution to decide this type of case, and that the portion of the Judiciary Act of 1791 that allowed the Court to hear these cases was unconstitutional. This case established the principle of judicial review and was the first time the court declared an act of Congress unconstitutional.

› Review Questions

1. All of the following are examples of checks and balances EXCEPT
   (A) presidential veto
   (B) impeachment of the president
   (C) appointment of Supreme Court justices
   (D) ratification of treaties
   (E) declaration of war by Congress

2. Which of the following documents best describes a government based on unity, natural rights, and the social contract theory?
   (A) Articles of Confederation
   (B) Declaration of Independence
   (C) Mayflower Compact
   (D) U.S. Constitution
   (E) Petition of Rights

3. The original purpose of the Constitutional Convention was to
   (A) write a new constitution
   (B) review the problems of the state governments
   (C) revise the Articles of Confederation
   (D) deal with the issue of slavery
   (E) deal with the unsuccessful economic chaos and violence that resulted from the conferences at Mt. Vernon and Annapolis

4. Compared to government under the Articles of Confederation, the Constitution
   I. can more easily be amended
   II. created a federal republic
   III. called for separation of powers among three branches of government
   IV. created a league of friendship among the states
   (A) I only
   (B) I and III only
   (C) II and IV only
   (D) I, II, and III only
   (E) I, II, III, and IV

5. Which of the following was not a weakness of government under the Articles of Confederation?
   (A) The national judiciary resolved arguments between the states.
   (B) Congress lacked the power to tax.
   (C) It lacked a national judiciary.
   (D) It was unable to control commercial interests.
   (E) Unanimous decisions were necessary to amend articles.

6. Slavery and the taxation of exports were important topics to the Founding Fathers. Which compromise describes how the Founding Fathers resolved both of these issues?
   (A) Great Compromise
   (B) Commerce and Slave Trade Compromise
   (C) Connecticut Compromise
   (D) Three-Fifths Compromise
   (E) Electoral Compromise

7. Those who support the pluralist theory of democracy believe that
   (A) government depends on the "consent of the governed"
   (B) democracy is a hierarchical structure with bureaucrats holding the real power
   (C) democracy is based on choosing officials to run the government
   (D) a small number of powerful corporate and military leaders rule in their own self-interest
   (E) interest groups compete to promote their preferences

8. The Supreme Court's decision in **Marbury v. Madison** (1803)
   (A) expanded the powers of Congress
   (B) established the principle of judicial review
   (C) allowed Congress to amend the Constitution
   (D) strengthened the powers of the states
   (E) supported the concept of national supremacy

9. The Bill of Rights includes
   (A) the Preamble
   (B) the Articles of Confederation
   (C) the articles of the Constitution
   (D) all the formal amendments
   (E) the first 10 amendments

10. Amending the Constitution is a multi-step process. Which of the following steps are required to amend the Constitution?
    I. proposal at the national level
    II. proposal at the state level
    III. presidential signature
    IV. ratification at the state level
    (A) II and III only
    (B) I and IV only
    (C) III and IV only
    (D) I, II, and III only
    (E) I, II, III, and IV

› Answers and Explanations

1. **E.** A declaration of war by Congress is an expressed power of Congress under Article I of the Constitution. The presidential veto (A) is a check on the power of the legislative branch. Impeachment is a check by the legislative and judicial branches on the power of the executive branch (B). The appointment of Supreme Court justices (C) is checked by the executive and legislative branches. The Senate must ratify treaties negotiated by the executive branch (D).

2. **B.** The Declaration of Independence was based on the writings of John Locke and his theory of a social contract between government and the governed. The document unified the colonies to fight for independence by advancing the ideas of natural law, which states that there are certain rights that government cannot take away from the people. The Petition of Rights (E) was an English document that challenged the divine right concept. The Mayflower Compact (C) was based on the consent of the governed, but it did not enumerate natural rights. The U.S. Constitution (D) reflects the ideals of unity and the consent of the governed, but does not specifically define the concepts of natural rights and the social contract theory as the Declaration does. The Articles of Confederation (A) did not specifically address the concepts of natural rights and the social contract.

3. **C.** Because of the problems among the states under the Articles of Confederation, the Constitutional Convention was convened to revise the Articles and to strengthen the power of the government. This convention dealt with the problems of the national government and not those of the states (B). Neither was the convention called to deal with the slavery issue (D) nor to write an entirely new plan of government (A). Economic chaos and violence were the causes, not the results, of the conferences at Mt. Vernon and Annapolis (E).

4. **D.** The Constitution created a federal system of government, allowed for an easier amendment process, and created three separate branches of government—legislative, executive, and judicial.

5. **A.** Under the Articles of Confederation, there was no national judiciary. State courts resolved differences among the states. The remaining answer choices are correct.

6. **B.** Differences between northern and southern interests at the Constitutional Convention led to a compromise concerning the slave trade and the taxation of exports from the states. The Commerce and Slave Trade Compromise prohibited Congress from ending the slave trade for a period of 20 years and prohibited the taxation of exports from the states. The Connecticut (Great) Compromise (C, A) resolved the question of representation in Congress. The Three-Fifths Compromise (D) counted slaves as three-fifths of a person for purposes of taxation and representation in Congress. Another compromise created the electoral college (E).

7. **E.** Robert Dahl's pluralist theory is based upon the idea of competing interest groups vying for power. Choices (A) and (C) describe traditional democratic theory. Answer (B) pertains to the bureaucratic theory, and choice (D) represents the elite theory.

8. **B. Marbury v. Madison** established the principle of judicial review, allowing the courts to determine the constitutionality of acts of Congress.

9. **E.** The Bill of Rights, adopted in 1791, includes only the first 10 amendments to the Constitution (D). The Preamble sets forth the purposes of the Constitution (A). The articles are the sections of the Constitution (C). The Articles of Confederation (B) predated the Constitution.

10. **B.** Article V of the Constitution outlines the formal amendment process, which includes congressional proposal of amendments at the national level and state ratification of amendments.

> Rapid Review

- Political scientist Harold Laswell defined government as "who gets what, when, and how."
- Every nation has defined public policy goals. The United States defines its goals in the Preamble of the Constitution.
- Aristotle's methods of classifying governments can still be used today.
- Modern theories about democratic government include traditional democratic theory, pluralist theory, elitist theory, bureaucratic theory, and hyperpluralism.
- The ancient Greeks and Romans, Enlightenment philosophers such as John Locke, British documents, and colonial experiences influenced the establishment of American government.
- The Declaration of Independence was a statement of colonial unity and a justification for separation from Britain.
- The Articles of Confederation, the first national constitution, created a "league of friendship" among the states. This weak national government failed to solve the postwar problems of the United States, and its weaknesses led to the writing of the U.S. Constitution.
- The Constitutional Convention, called to revise the Articles of Confederation, realized the need to create a new form of government with broader powers. The resulting Constitution created a federal system of three branches of government, with checks and balances.
- Various plans for the new government resulted in a series of compromises, including the Connecticut (Great) Compromise, Three-Fifths Compromise, and Commerce and Slave Trade Compromise.
- Debates over ratification of the Constitution led to the creation of the Federalists and Anti-Federalists.
- The Constitution is composed of the Preamble, seven articles, and the 27 formal amendments.
- The Constitution is a plan of government based on several basic principles: limited government, popular sovereignty, separation of powers, checks and balances, and federalism.
- Formal amendments are added to the Constitution through the process outlined in Article V. The proposal stage is accomplished at the national level, while ratification takes place within the states.
- The Constitution may be informally amended through legislative actions, executive actions, judicial interpretations, and custom and usage.
- *Marbury v. Madison* established the principle of judicial review.

CHAPTER 7

Federalism

IN THIS CHAPTER

Summary: One of the basic principles embodied in the United States Constitution is federalism. Federalism arose from the framers' desire to create a stronger national government than under the Articles of Confederation but preserve the existing states and state governments. **Federalism** is a political system where the powers of government are divided between a national government and regional (state and local) governments. Each level of government has certain authority over the same territory and people. A constitution outlines each level of government's authority, powers, and prohibitions.

Key Terms

federalism
delegated powers
implied powers
Necessary and
   Proper (Elastic)
   Clause
inherent powers
concurrent powers
reserved powers
Full Faith and Credit
   Clause

Privileges and Immunities
   Clause
extradition
interstate compacts
Supremacy Clause
McCulloch v. Maryland
dual federalism
cooperative federalism
devolution
fiscal federalism
fiscal policy

grants-in-aid
categorical grants
block grants
revenue sharing
mandates
unfunded mandates

The Constitutional Basis of Federalism

Although the term federalism is not found in the United States Constitution, it is clearly defined in the delegated, concurrent, and reserved powers of the national and state governments (see Figure 7-1):

- *delegated powers*—Expressed, or enumerated, powers given specifically to the national government (Articles I–V).
- *implied powers*—Although not expressed, powers that may be reasonably inferred from the Constitution (Article I, Section 8, Clause 18—the **Necessary and Proper Clause**, or **Elastic Clause**).
- *inherent powers*—Powers that exist for the national government because the government is sovereign.
- *concurrent powers*—Powers that belong to both the national and state governments.
- *reserved powers*—Powers belonging specifically to the state because they were neither delegated to the national government nor denied to the states (Article IV; Amendment 10).
- *prohibited powers*—Powers that are denied to the national government, state governments, or both (Article I, Sections 9 and 10; Amendments); for example, neither the national government nor state governments may pass an ex post facto law or a bill of attainder.

Powers of Government Under Federalism

National Powers (Expressed, Implied, Inherent)	National and State Powers (Concurrent)	State Powers (Reserved)
Regulate foreign and interstate commerce	Levy taxes	Regulate intrastate commerce
Coin and print money	Borrow money	Establish local governments
Provide an army and navy	Spend for general welfare	Establish public school systems
Declare war	Establish courts	Administer elections
Establish federal courts below the Supreme Court	Enact and enforce laws	Protect the public's health, welfare, and morals
Conduct foreign relations	Charter banks	Regulate corporations
Make all laws "necessary and proper"		Establish licensing requirements for certain regulated professions
Acquire and govern U.S. territories and admit new states		
Regulate immigration and naturalization		

Figure 7-1

Federalism in Practice

Interstate Relations

Article IV of the Constitution addresses the issue of relationships between the states. It offers several provisions:

- *Full Faith and Credit Clause*—States are required to recognize the laws and legal documents of other states, such as birth certificates, marriage licenses, driver's licenses, wills.
- *Privileges and Immunities Clause*—States are prohibited from unreasonably discriminating against residents of other states. Nonresidents may travel through other states; buy, sell, and hold property; and enter into contracts (does not extend to political rights such as the right to vote or run for political office, or to the right to practice certain regulated professions such as teaching).
- *extradition*—States may return fugitives to a state from which they have fled to avoid criminal prosecution at the request of the governor of the state.
- *interstate compacts*—States may make agreements, sometimes requiring congressional approval, to work together to solve regional problems. Some examples are "hot-pursuit agreements," parole and probation agreements, the Port Authority of New York and New Jersey, and regulating the common use of shared natural resources.

Guarantees to the States

Article IV of the Constitution provides national guarantees to the states:

- republican form of government
- protections against foreign invasion
- protections against domestic violence
- respect for the geographic integrity of states

Some of the advantages and disadvantages of federalism are shown in Figure 7-2.

Advantages and Disadvantages of Federalism

Advantages of Federalism	Disadvantages of Federalism
Ideally suited to large geographic area because it encourages diversity in local government	Inflexibility inherent in a written constitution
Avoids concentration of political power	Complex, with many governments to deal with
Accommodated already existing state governments	Duplication of offices and functions
States serve as training grounds for national leaders	Conflicts of authority may arise
Keeps government close to the people	

Figure 7-2

Establishing National Supremacy

Article VI of the United States Constitution contains the **Supremacy Clause**, which helps to resolve conflicts between national and state laws. Because two levels of government are operating within the same territory and over the same people, conflicts are bound to arise. The Supremacy Clause states that the Constitution, its laws and treaties shall be the "supreme law of the land." The Supreme Court upheld this supremacy in *McCulloch v. Maryland* (1819). The Supreme Court continued to expand the powers of Congress over interstate commerce in *Gibbons v. Ogden* (1824).

McCulloch v. Maryland (1819)

The Supreme Court dealt with the issues of the Necessary and Proper Clause and the Supremacy Clause when Maryland imposed a tax on the Baltimore branch of the Second National Bank of the United States. Chief cashier James McCulloch refused to pay the tax, Maryland state courts ruled in the state's favor, and the United States government appealed to the Supreme Court. The Marshall court ruled that although no provision of the Constitution grants the national government the expressed power to create a national bank, the authority to do so can be implied by the Necessary and Proper Clause (Article I, Section 8, Clause 18). This ruling established the implied powers of the national government and national supremacy, the basis used to strengthen the power of the national government.

Gibbons v. Ogden (1824)

At issue was the definition of commerce and whether the national government had exclusive power to regulate interstate commerce. The New York legislature gave Robert Livingston and Robert Fulton exclusive rights to operate steamboats in New York waters and Aaron Ogden the right to operate a ferry between New York and New Jersey. Thomas Gibbons had received a national government license to operate boats in interstate waters. Ogden sued Gibbons and won in the New York courts; Gibbons appealed to the Supreme Court. The Marshall court defined commerce as including all business dealings, and the power to regulate interstate commerce belongs exclusively to the national government. Today, the national government uses the commerce clause to justify the regulation of numerous areas of economic activity.

Federalism Today

Since the founding of the United States, society has changed, and federalism has evolved to meet the changes and challenges.

Dual Federalism

The earliest (1789–1932) interpretation of federalism is the concept of **dual federalism**, which views the national and state governments each remaining supreme within their own sphere of influence. This form of federalism is often referred to as "layer cake federalism," because each level of government is seen as separate from the other, with the national government having authority over national matters and state governments having authority over state matters. The early beliefs that states had the sole responsibility for educating their citizens and the national government had the sole responsibility for foreign policy issues are examples of dual federalism.

Cooperative Federalism

In the 1930s the interpretation of federalism shifted to that of the national and state governments sharing policymaking and cooperating in solving problems. **Cooperative federalism** or "marble cake federalism" as it came to be known, grew from the policies of the New Deal era and the need for the national government to increase government spending and public assistance programs during the Great Depression. The cooperation of the national and state governments to build the national interstate highway system beginning in the 1950s is an example of cooperative federalism. The expansion of cooperative federalism during (President Lyndon B. Johnson's) Great Society required even greater cooperation from the states in return for federal grants.

New Federalism

During the administrations of Richard Nixon, Ronald Reagan, and George H. W. Bush the national government attempted to implement a reversal of cooperative federalism and place more responsibility on the states about how grant money would be spent. The term **devolution**—a transfer of power to political subunits—has been used to describe the goals of new federalism. An example of new federalism is welfare reform legislation, which has returned more authority over welfare programs to the states. The national government directed where much of the money should be spent in the stimulus-spending bills during the first year of the Obama administration.

Fiscal Federalism

The national government's patterns of spending, taxation, and providing grants to influence state and local governments is known today as **fiscal federalism**. The national government uses **fiscal policy** to influence the states through granting or withholding money to pay for programs:

- *grants-in-aid* programs—Money and resources provided by the federal government to the state and local governments to be used for specific projects or programs. The earliest grants often covered public works projects such as building canals, roads, and railroads, and land grants for state colleges.
- *categorical grants*—Grants that have a specific purpose defined by law, such as sewage treatment facilities or school lunch programs; may even require "matching funds" from the state or local governments; categorical grants may be in the form of project grants (awarded on the basis of a competitive application, such as university research grants) or formula grants (awarded on the basis of an established formula, such as Medicaid).
- *block grants*—General grants that can be used for a variety of purposes within a broad category, such as education, health care, or public services; fewer strings attached so state and local governments have greater freedom in how the money is spent; preferred by states over categorical grants.
- *revenue sharing*—Proposed under the Johnson administration and popular under the Nixon administration, a "no strings attached" form of aid to state and local governments; could be used for virtually any project but never exceeded more than 2 percent of revenues; eliminated during the Reagan administration.
- *mandates*—Requirements that are imposed by the national government on the state and local governments; for example, the Americans with Disabilities Act (1990) mandates that all public buildings be accessible to persons with disabilities. Mandates often require state or local governments to meet the requirement at their own expense (**unfunded mandates**). After the mid-term elections of 1994, the Republican-controlled Congress passed the Unfunded Mandate Reform Act, which imposed limitations on Congress's ability to pass unfunded mandate legislation.

❯ Review Questions

1. A major strength of federalism lies in the fact that it promotes both national and state activities in which of the following manners?
   (A) provides for complex government activities
   (B) avoids concentration of political power
   (C) guarantees the inherent inflexibility of a written constitution
   (D) allows for the duplication of government offices and functions
   (E) provides equal funding for mandates

2. *McCulloch v. Maryland* (1819) was an important Supreme Court case involving federalism because
   (A) it called for a republican form of government
   (B) it provided for a national law protecting against domestic violence
   (C) following this case, the Supreme Court became the third powerful branch of the national government
   (D) the Supremacy Clause of the Constitution was upheld
   (E) the Supremacy Clause of the Constitution was established

3. Article IV of the United States Constitution addresses which of the following relationships between the states?
   I. full faith and credit
   II. interstate compacts
   III. respect for geographic integrity
      (A) I only
      (B) II only
      (C) III only
      (D) I and II only
      (E) II and III only

4. Which of the following is not a concurrent power of national and state governments?
   (A) protecting the public's health, welfare, and morals
   (B) borrowing money
   (C) chartering banks
   (D) establishing courts
   (E) levying taxes

5. Cooperative federalism can best be described as
   (A) the national government's ability to help the states through the spending of tax dollars and the providing of project grants
   (B) placing more responsibility on the states as to how grant money is to be spent
   (C) "layer cake federalism"
   (D) an extension of new federalism
   (E) "marble cake federalism"

6. The president most responsible for the implementation of new federalism was:
   (A) George H. W. Bush
   (B) Richard Nixon
   (C) Ronald Reagan
   (D) Bill Clinton
   (E) Gerald Ford

7. Which of the following is an example of fiscal federalism?
   I. mandates
   II. revenue sharing
   III. grants-in-aid
   IV. project
      (A) I and II only
      (B) II and III only
      (C) I, II, and III only
      (D) I, II, and IV only
      (E) I, II, III, and IV

8. Which of the following has the fewest "strings" attached when it comes to spending government monies?
   (A) mandates
   (B) categorical grants
   (C) block grants
   (D) revenue sharing
   (E) grants-in-aid

9. Federalism as a form of government has many disadvantages. A major disadvantage of federalism is
   (A) conflicts may arise over authority of government
   (B) there is concentration of political power
   (C) government is not close to the people
   (D) existing state governments are not accommodated
   (E) geography is not considered

10. Prohibited powers are powers that are denied to both the national and state governments. These denied powers may be found in
   (A) Article I, Section 8
   (B) Article I, Sections 9 and 10
   (C) Article IV, Section 4
   (D) Article I, Section 8, Clause 18
   (E) Article IV, Section 1

›Answers and Explanations

1. **B**. Governmental power is divided between the national and state governments, each operating within the same geographic territory with power over a single population. Providing for complex governmental activities (A) and allowing for the duplication of government offices and functions (D) are not usually considered major strengths of federalism. The Constitution is a very flexible document (C). One type of mandate, the unfunded mandate, requires state or local governments to meet the mandate's requirement at their own expense (E).

2. **D**. *McCulloch v. Maryland* upheld Article VI of the Constitution, which declares the Constitution the "supreme law of the land" (E). The Supreme Court (C) was established by Article III of the Constitution as the highest court of the judicial branch. Answer choices (A) and (B) were not provisions of the decision in *McCulloch v. Maryland*.

3. **D**. Geographic integrity of the states is a guarantee of the national government to the states, not of the states to each other.

4. **A**. Protecting the public health, welfare, and morals is a reserved power of the states. The other answer choices represent concurrent powers, or those shared by both the national and state governments.

5. **E**. Cooperative federalism involves the national government and state governments working together to solve problems, often with a blending (similar to that of a marble cake) of responsibilities. Choices (A) and (B) are not the best descriptions of cooperative federalism because neither reflects mutual sharing and planning between the national and state governments. "Layer cake federalism" (C) describes dual federalism.

New federalism (D) places more responsibility on the states about how grant money is spent.

6. **B**. Richard Nixon began the program of new federalism to place responsibility on the states for the spending of grant money. New federalism continued under succeeding presidents, particularly Ronald Reagan (C) and George H. W. Bush (A).

7. **E**. Mandates, revenue sharing, grants-in-aid, and project grants (a type of categorical grant) are forms of fiscal federalism.

8. **D**. Revenue sharing has a "no strings attached" policy for the states receiving money. Some mandates require the use of state or local funds (A). Categorical grants (B) may require matching funds from state or local governments. Block grants (C) have fewer strings attached than categorical grants. The federal government requires grants-in-aid (E) to be used for specific projects or programs.

9. **A**. Conflicts between national and state authority may arise under the system of federalism. While federalism provides for a strong national government, power is not concentrated in the national government (B). State governments remain close to the people (C), and the needs of state governments are accommodated under federalism (D). The national government respects the geographic integrity of each state (E).

10. **B**. Article I, Section 9 denies certain powers to the national government; Article I, Section 10 denies powers to the state governments. Article I, Section 8 (A) details the powers of Congress. Article IV, Section 4 (C) guarantees each state a republican form of government. Article I, Section 8, Clause 18 (D) is the "necessary and proper clause." Article IV, Section 1 (E) contains the "full faith and credit clause."

› Rapid Review

- Federalism is a system of government in which the powers of government are divided between a national government and regional (state and local) governments.
- There are both advantages and disadvantages to federalism as a form of government.
- Federalism can be found in the delegated, reserved, and concurrent powers of the Constitution.
- Article IV of the Constitution provides for interstate relations, including full faith and credit, privileges and immunities, extradition, interstate compacts.
- Article IV of the Constitution provides national guarantees to the states.
- *McCulloch v. Maryland* and *Gibbons v. Ogden* upheld national supremacy and expanded the powers of Congress under the commerce clause, respectively.
- As practiced in the United States, federalism has evolved through many phases, including dual federalism, cooperative federalism, new federalism, and fiscal federalism.

Political Culture

IN THIS CHAPTER

Summary: A **political culture** is a set of basic values and beliefs about a country or government that is shared by most citizens (freedom is precious, for example) and that influences political opinions and behaviors. The U.S. political culture gives citizens a sense of community, creates support for the democratic processes (majority rule, free elections), helps shape attitudes toward public officials, and teaches civic responsibility. The political culture provides a setting for a political system to function.

Key Terms

political culture	sampling	liberal
political socialization	sampling errors	moderate
opinion leaders	ideology	conservative
public opinion	political ideology	reactionary
straw polls	radical	

American Democratic Values

Although the United States is a diverse society, it is united under a common political culture, or common set of beliefs and attitudes about government and politics. This political culture translates into a consensus of basic concepts that support democracy. Democracy is not guaranteed; therefore the American people must continue to practice these concepts:

- *majority rule/minority rights*—Although democracy is based upon majority rule, minority rights must be guaranteed.
- *equality*—Equality of every individual before the law and in the political process.
- *private property*—Ownership of property is protected by law and supported by the capitalist system.
- *individual freedoms*—Guarantees of civil liberties and protections of infringements upon them.

- *compromise*—Allows for the combining of different interests and opinions to form public policy to best benefit society.
- *limited government*—Powers of government are restricted in a democracy by the will of the people and the law.

It is vital to note that the importance of each of the above changes over time. During the presidency of George W. Bush (2001–2009), some believed that, because of the "War on Terror," the power of the government should be greatly expanded. During the first two years of the Obama presidency, members of the "Tea Party" and others claimed that the powers of the federal government had gotten too big.

Political Socialization

Political socialization is the process by which citizens acquire a sense of political identity. Socialization is a complex process that begins early in childhood and continues throughout a person's life. It allows citizens to become aware of politics, learn political facts, and form political values and opinions. Although the paths to political awareness, knowledge, and values differ, people are exposed to a combination of influences that shape their political identities and opinions:

- Family and home influences often help shape political party identification. It is strongest when both parents identify with the same political party.
- Schools teach patriotism, basic governmental functions and structure, and encourage political participation.
- Group affiliations (interest groups, labor unions, professional organizations) provide common bonds between people which may be expressed through the group or its activities.
- Demographic factors (occupation, race, gender, age, religion, region of country, income, education, ethnicity).
- Mass media inform the public about issues and help set the political and public agendas.
- **Opinion leaders**, those individuals held in great respect because of their position, expertise, or personality, may informally and unintentionally exercise influence.
- Events may instill positive or negative attitudes. For example, the Watergate scandal created a mistrust of government. In the immediate aftermath of the attacks on the World Trade Center on September 11, 2001, patriotic spirit increased in many parts of the United States.

Public Opinion

Public opinion is a collection of shared attitudes of many different people in matters relating to politics, public issues, or the making of public policy. It is shaped by people's political culture and political socialization. Public opinion can be analyzed according to distribution (physical shape of responses when graphed), intensity (how strongly the opinions are held), and stability (how much the opinion changes over time). A consensus occurs when there is general agreement on an issue. Public opinion that is strongly divided between two very different views is a divisive opinion.

Measuring Public Opinion

The measurement of public opinion is a complex process often conveying unreliable results. Elections, interest groups, the media, and personal contacts may signal public opinion on certain issues; however, the most reliable measure of public opinion is the public opinion poll. Businesses, governments, political candidates, and interest groups use polls.

Early polling in the United States involved the use of **straw polls**, asking the same question of a large number of people. They were unreliable because they did not necessarily include a cross-section of the general population of the United States. The most famous mishap occurred in 1936 when the *Literary Digest* mailed postcards to more than 10 million people concerning the outcome of the 1936 presidential election. With over 2 million responses, the magazine incorrectly predicted the defeat of Franklin Roosevelt and victory of challenger Alf Landon. The magazine had used automobile registrations and telephone directories to develop its sample, not realizing that during the Depression many people did not have cars or telephones. Many voters who supported Roosevelt had not been polled. The mailings had also been done early, and some voters changed their minds between answering the poll and actually voting.

Modern polling began in the 1930s when George Gallup helped develop the use of a scientific polling process that includes:

- *sampling*—Those chosen to participate in the poll must be representative of the general population and chosen at random.
- *preparing valid questions*—Directions should be clear and questions should be phrased and ordered in a way that does not lead the respondent to a particular answer (clear, fair, and unbiased).
- *controlling how the poll is taken*—Make sure the respondent has some knowledge of the issues addressed in the poll and that the pollster's appearance and tone do not influence the responses. Survey methods may include telephone, mail, and in-person interviews.
- *analyzing and reporting results*—Reporting the results of polls without providing information about how the poll was conducted, **sampling errors**, or when the poll that was taken can lead to misinformation and error.

Today, the use of statistical analysis through computers has made polling an even more accurate research tool.

Ideology

An **ideology** is a consistent set of beliefs. A **political ideology** is a set of beliefs about politics and public policy that creates the structure for looking at government and public policy. Political ideologies can change over time. Differences in ideology generally occur in the arena of political, economic, and social issues.

Ideology: A Political Spectrum

- *radical*—favors rapid, fundamental change in existing social, economic, or political order; may be willing to resort to extreme means, even violence or revolution to accomplish such change (extreme change to create an entirely new social system)
- *liberal*—supports active government in promoting individual welfare and supporting civil rights, and accepts peaceful political and social change within the existing political system
- *moderate*—political ideology that falls between liberal and conservative and which may include some of both; usually thought of as tolerant of others' political opinions and not likely to hold extreme views on issues
- *conservative*—promotes a limited governmental role in helping individuals economically, supports traditional values and lifestyles, favors a more active role for government in promoting national security, and approaches change cautiously
- *reactionary*—advocates a return to a previous state of affairs, often a social order or government that existed earlier in history (may be willing to go to extremes to achieve their goals)

› Review Questions

1. Which of the following is not a concept found in the political culture of the American democratic society?
   (A) private property
   (B) equality
   (C) majority rule
   (D) minority rule
   (E) compromise

2. The process by which citizens acquire a sense of their own political identity would best be defined as
   (A) public opinion
   (B) political socialization
   (C) demographics
   (D) political culture
   (E) patriotism

3. Which of the following would be a true statement regarding public opinion?
   (A) Public opinion teaches patriotism.
   (B) Public opinion allows citizens to become aware of politics, learn facts, and form political values.
   (C) Public opinion is shaped by an individual's political culture and political socialization.
   (D) A change in public opinion is always a slow process.
   (E) Public opinion is usually based on the ideas of small select groups within a given political socialization area.

4. Attempting to measure public opinion by asking the same question of a large number of people is
   (A) a straw poll
   (B) a sampling poll
   (C) a controlling poll
   (D) a scientific poll
   (E) a literary poll

5. There are many different ideologies within the political spectrum. An ideology that promotes a limited governmental role in helping individuals and supports traditional values and lifestyles would best be defined as a
   (A) liberal ideology
   (B) reactionary ideology
   (C) radical ideology
   (D) moderate ideology
   (E) conservative ideology

› Answers and Explanations

1. **D**. Majority rule/minority rights is a concept found in U.S. political culture. The other answer choices reflect ideals of U.S. democratic society.

2. **B**. Political socialization is the process of acquiring a political identity. Public opinion (A) is a collection of shared attitudes of many different people. Demographics (C) and patriotism (E) are factors that shape political socialization. Political culture (D) is a set of basic values and beliefs about a country or government that is shared by most citizens.

3. **C**. Public opinion is shaped by an individual's political culture and political socialization. Institutions such as the family and schools teach patriotism (A). Public opinion is shaped by facts and political values (B). Change may be slow or sudden and may be analyzed (D). Public opinion is based on attitudes shared by many different people (E).

4. **A**. A straw poll is an attempt to measure public opinion by asking the same question of a large number of people. Sampling (B) and controlling (C) are features of scientific polling (D). A literary poll (E) refers to an inaccurate poll taken in the election campaign of 1936.

5. **E**. A conservative ideology promotes a limited governmental role in helping individuals and supports traditional values and lifestyles. Liberal ideology (A) supports active government involvement. Reactionary ideology (B) desires a return to an earlier social order or government. Radical ideology (C) favors rapid, fundamental change. Moderate ideology (D) falls between liberal and conservative on the political spectrum.

> Rapid Review

- A political culture is a set of basic values and beliefs about a country or government that is shared by most citizens.
- America is a heterogeneous (diverse) society with many political cultures.
- Democracy is not guaranteed. In order to ensure democracy, political concepts must be practiced.
- Political socialization is the process of citizens acquiring a political identity. Several factors influence the process of political socialization.
- Public opinion is a collection of ideas and attitudes about government that are shared by the general public.
- Public opinion is shaped by an individual's political culture and political socialization.
- Public opinion polls are the most reliable measure of public opinion.
- Modern polling began in the 1930s with George Gallup. Today, polling is more scientific and based on statistical analysis.
- An ideology is a consistent set of beliefs. A political ideology is beliefs based on politics and public policy.
- Ideological placement on a political spectrum may include classification as radical, liberal, moderate, conservative, or reactionary.

CHAPTER 9

Political Parties

IN THIS CHAPTER

Summary: Political parties are voluntary associations of people who seek to control the government through common principles based upon peaceful and legal actions, such as the winning of elections. Political parties, along with interest groups, the media, and elections serve as a linkage mechanism that brings together the people and the government while holding the government responsible for its actions. Political parties differ from interest groups in that interest groups do not nominate candidates for office.

Key Terms

political parties	New Deal coalition	realignment
two-party system	divided government	national chairperson
single-member	gridlock	soft money
districts	dealignment	straight ticket

Roles of Political Parties

- *party in the electorate*—all of the people who associate themselves with one of the political parties
- *party in government*—all of the appointed and elected officials at the national, state, and local levels who represent the party as members; office holders
- *party in organization*—all of the people at the various levels of the party organization who work to maintain the strength of the party between elections, help raise money, and organize the conventions and party functions

Party Systems

One-Party System

In a one-party system only one party exists or has a chance of winning election. Generally, membership is not voluntary and those who do belong to the party represent a small portion of the population. Party leaders must approve candidates for political office, and voters have no real choice. The result is dictatorial government.

Two-Party System

In a **two-party system** there may be several political parties but only two major political parties compete for power and dominate elections. Minor parties generally have little effect on most elections, especially at the national level. The Electoral College system makes it difficult for third-party candidates to affect presidential elections. It would be difficult for a third-party presidential candidate to actually win a state, which is necessary to capture electoral votes. Systems that operate under the two-party system usually have a general consensus, or agreement, among citizens about the basic principles of government, even though the parties often differ on the means of carrying them out. The use of **single-member districts** promotes the two-party system. Voters are given an "either-or" choice, simplifying decisions and the political process. The two-party system tends to enhance governmental stability; because both parties want to appeal to the largest number of voters, they tend to avoid extremes in ideology.

Multi-Party System

Multi-party systems exist when several major parties and a number of minor parties compete in elections, and any of the parties stands a good chance of winning. This type of system can be composed of from 4 to 20 different parties, based on a particular region, ideology, or class position, and is often found in European nations, as well as in other democratic societies. The multi-party system is usually the result of a proportional representation voting system rather than one with single-member districts. The idea behind multi-party systems is to give voters meaningful choices. This does not always occur because of two major problems: in many elections, no party has a clear majority of the vote, and not receiving a majority forces the sharing of power by several parties (coalitions). The multi-party system tends to promote instability in government, especially when coalition governments are formed.

What Do Political Parties Do?

- *Recruit candidates*—Find candidates interested in running for public office, especially if no incumbent is running.
- *Nominate and support candidates for office*—Help raise money and run candidate campaigns through the party organization.
- *Educate the electorate*—Inform the voters about the candidates and encourage voters to participate in the election.
- *Organize the government*—The organization of Congress and state legislatures is based on political party controls (majority vs. minority party); political appointments are often made based on political party affiliation.

Party Identification and Membership

Membership in American political parties is voluntary. There are no dues to pay; membership is based on party identification. If you believe you are a member of a particular political party, then you are. Most states require citizens to identify their political party when registering to vote. Most people choose to belong to a political party that shares their views on issues or the role of government. Several factors may influence party identification:

- ideology
- education
- income
- occupation
- race or ethnicity
- gender
- religion
- family tradition
- region of the country
- marital status

However, a large number of Americans choose not to join any political party, instead registering as independents.

The Two-Party Tradition in America

The Constitution did not call for political parties, and the Founding Fathers at first did not intend to create them. James Madison, in *Federalist #10*, warned of the divisiveness of "factions." George Washington was elected president without party labels and in his farewell address warned against the "baneful effects of the spirit of the party." During the process for ratification of the Constitution, Federalists and Anti-Federalists conflicted over ideals concerning the proper role of government. This conflict resulted in the development of the first political parties: the Federalists and Jeffersonian Republicans, or Democratic-Republicans as they were later called.

Why a Two-Party Tradition?

Although there have been numerous minor parties throughout its history, why has the United States maintained the two-party tradition?

- *historical roots*—British heritage, Federalist and Anti-Federalist divisions
- *electoral system*—single-member districts mean that only one representative is chosen from each district (one winner per office)
- *election laws*—vary from state to state, which makes it difficult for minor parties to get on the ballot in many states

Rise of Political Parties: Party Development (1789–1800)

The earliest political parties began to develop under the administration of George Washington. Alexander Hamilton, secretary of the treasury, supported a strong national government; his followers became known as Federalists. Secretary of State Thomas Jefferson supported states' rights and a less powerful national government. The clash between these two individuals and their supporters led to the development of political parties. In the election of 1796, Jefferson challenged John Adams, the Federalist candidate, for the presidency but lost. By 1800 Jefferson was able to rally his supporters and win the presidency.

Democratic Domination (1800–1860)

The Democratic-Republicans dominated the government from 1800 to 1824, when they split into factions. The faction led by Andrew Jackson, the Jacksonian Democrats or Democrats, won the presidency in 1828. The major opposition to the Democrats during this time was the Whig Party. Although the Whigs were a powerful opposition party in the U.S. Congress, they were able to win the presidency only twice, in 1840 with the victory of William Henry Harrison and in 1848 with that of Zachary Taylor. From that election until the election of 1860, Democrats dominated American politics. The Democratic Party became known as the party of the "common man," encouraging popular participation, and helping to bring about an expansion of suffrage to all adult white males.

Republican Domination (1860–1932)

The Republican Party began as a third party, developed from a split in the Whig Party. The Whigs had been the major opposition to the Democrats. By 1860 the Whig Party had disappeared and the Republican Party had emerged as the second major party. The Republican Party was composed mostly of former members of other political parties, appealing to commercial and antislavery groups. The Republican Party was successful in electing Abraham Lincoln president in 1860, and by the end of the Civil War had become a dominant party. Sometimes called the Grand Old Party or GOP, the Republican Party often controlled both the presidency and Congress.

Return of Democrats (1932–1968)

With the onset of the Depression, new electoral coalitions were formed and the Republicans lost their domination of government. Franklin Delano Roosevelt was able to unite blacks, city dwellers, blue-collar (labor union) workers, Catholics, Jews, and women to create a voting bloc known as the **New Deal coalition**. The election of 1932 brought the Democrats back to power as the dominant party in American politics. Roosevelt was elected to the presidency an unprecedented four times. From 1932 to 1968 only two Republican presidents (Eisenhower and Nixon) were elected. Not until 1994 did the Republicans gain control of both houses of Congress.

Divided Government (1968–Present)

Since 1968 **divided government** has characterized American institutions, a condition in which one political party controls the presidency and the opposing party controls one or both houses of Congress. This division creates a potential **gridlock** when opposing parties and interests often block each other's proposals, creating a political stalemate. In the election of 2000, George W. Bush won the presidency and the Republican Party won control of the House of Representatives and Senate (until Jim Jeffords changed affiliation to Independent). In the mid-term election of 2002, the Republicans again gained control of the executive and legislative branches, creating a unified government. In the 2006 off-year election, the Democrats won control of both houses of Congress, returning divided government to U.S. politics. In the 2008 elections, the Democrats won control of the presidency and both houses of Congress, although few predicted that this would permanently end the era of divided government.

Electoral Dealignment

When significant numbers of voters no longer support a particular political party, **dealignment** has occurred. Often, those voters identify as independents and believe they owe no loyalty to any particular political party.

Electoral Realignment

Historically, as voting patterns have shifted and new coalitions of party supporters have formed, electoral **realignment** has occurred. Several elections can be considered realigning elections, where the dominant party loses power and a new dominant party takes its place. The elections of 1860 and 1932 are examples. Many consider the 1980 election in this light; the long-term impact of the 2008 and 2010 elections will be studied in the future.

Third or Minor Parties

Although the Republican and Democratic parties have dominated the political scene, there have been minor, or third, parties throughout U.S. history. Minor parties usually have great difficulty in getting candidates elected to office, although they have been more successful at the state and local levels. A few minor party candidates have been elected to Congress, but no minor party candidate has ever been elected president. Minor parties have been instrumental in providing important reforms that have been adopted by the major parties. Success rather than failure often brings an end to minor parties, as the major parties often adopt popular reforms or ideas, especially if they appeal to the voters.

Types of Third Parties

Some third parties have been permanent, running candidates in every election; however, many third parties disappear after only a few elections. Several types of minor parties have emerged:

- *ideological*—Those based on a particular set of social, political, or economic beliefs (communist, socialist, libertarian).
- *splinter/personality/factional*—Those that have split away from one of the major parties; usually formed around a strong personality who does not win the party nomination; may disappear when that leader steps aside (Theodore Roosevelt's "Bull Moose" Progressive, Strom Thurmond's States' Rights, George Wallace's American Independent).
- *single issue*—Parties that concentrate on a single public policy matter (Free Soil, Right to Life, Prohibition).
- *protest*—Usually rooted in periods of economic discontent; may be sectional in nature (Greenback, Populist); some observers place the "Tea Party," which supported many candidates in the 2010 congressional elections, in this category.

Structure and Organization of Political Parties

A political party must have an effective organization to accomplish its goals. Both of the major parties are organized in much the same manner. Both parties are highly decentralized, or fragmented. The party of the president is normally more solidly united than the opposition. The president is automatically considered the party leader, while the opposition is often without a single strong leader. Usually one or more members of Congress are seen as the opposition leaders.

National Convention

The national convention serves as the party's national voice. Party delegates meet in the summer of every fourth year to select the party's candidates for president and vice president. They are also responsible for writing and adopting the party's platform, which describes the policy beliefs of the party.

National Committee

The national committee manages the political party's business between conventions. They are responsible for selecting the convention site, establishing the rules of the convention, publishing and distributing party literature, and helping the party raise campaign contributions.

National Chairperson

The party's national committee, with the consent of the party's presidential nominee, elects the **national chairperson**. The chairperson is responsible for directing the work of the national committee from their national headquarters in Washington, D.C. The chairperson is involved in fundraising, recruiting new party members, encouraging unity within the party, and helping the party's presidential nominee win election.

Congressional Campaign Committee

Each party has a committee in the House of Representatives and Senate that works to ensure the election or reelection of the party's candidates by raising funds and determining how much money and support each candidate will receive. The committee often works to defeat an opposition party member who appears weak and might be open to defeat.

State and Local Organization

State law largely determines state and local party organization. Differences exist from state to state; however, state and local parties are structured in much the same way as the national party organization. Generally, state parties today are more organized and better funded than in previous years. As a result of **soft money**, money that is distributed from the national political party organization and that does not have to be reported under the Federal Election Campaign Act (1971) or its amendments, state parties have become more dependent on the national party organization and are subject to their influence. In 2002, however, the use of soft money was significantly restricted by the Bipartisan Campaign Reform Act, also known as the McCain-Feingold Act. The Supreme Court, in *Citizens United v. FEC* (2010), ruled that limiting the ability of businesses, unions, and other groups to fund their own efforts to elect or defeat candidates for office is unconstitutional.

Future of Political Parties

The future of political parties in the United States is uncertain. In recent decades, political parties have been in decline. This decline may be attributed to several factors:

- *third-party challenges*—In recent elections third-party challengers have taken votes from the major candidates, lessening their ability to win a majority of the vote.
- *loss of support by party loyalists*—The number of independent voters has increased.

- *increase in split-ticket voting*—Many voters no longer vote a **straight ticket** (only for candidates of one political party) but rather split their vote among candidates from more than one party.
- *lack of perceived differences between the parties*—Voters often believe there are no major differences in the parties or their candidates.
- *party reforms*—Changes within the parties themselves to create greater diversity and openness have allowed for greater conflict within some parties.
- *methods of campaigning*—New technologies have allowed candidates to become more independent of parties and more directly involved with the voters.

> Review Questions

1. Which of the following best describes a multi-party system?
   (A) Membership in the party of choice is not generally voluntary.
   (B) There is usually a general consensus of agreement as to basic principles of government.
   (C) Multi-party systems usually give the voters meaningful choices.
   (D) Parties tend to avoid extreme ideologies.
   (E) Minor parties have little effect on most elections.

2. Which of the following is NOT a responsibility of a political party?
   (A) organize the government
   (B) represent special interests
   (C) recruit candidates
   (D) educate voters
   (E) raise campaign money

3. The Republican and Democratic parties have dominated the political scene throughout American history. Minor parties have often surfaced to fill the void left by the major parties. A splinter minor party can best be characterized by
   (A) the single issues supported by the party
   (B) the fact that it is usually built around the working-class American
   (C) the permanence of its presence on the political scene
   (D) its presence during times of economic discontent
   (E) the fact that it is the result of a revolt within a major party

4. The Republicans dominated party politics during which span of years?
   (A) 1860–1932
   (B) 1932–1968
   (C) 1968–present
   (D) 1800–1860
   (E) 1789–1800

5. The national convention serves what major purpose for a political party?
   (A) to allow the people to direct the work of the national committee through a system of national participation
   (B) to establish the rules of party campaigning
   (C) to serve as the party's national voice in the selection of the party's candidate
   (D) to manage the political party's business by the vote of party constituents
   (E) to allow the political party to meet as a whole in order to raise funds, recruit new members, and encourage unity within the party

6. Which of the following best describes state party organizations?
   (A) They are independent of the national party.
   (B) They are subject to their own jurisdiction according to party doctrines.
   (C) They are determined and organized by the national party in accordance with national law.
   (D) Their funding has been affected by campaign reform law.
   (E) They have the same organizational structures in all states because they are regulated by state law.

7. Membership in an American political party is voluntary and based on party identification. Which factors influence party identification?
   I. education
   II. gender
   III. public opinion
   (A) I only
   (B) II only
   (C) III only
   (D) I and II only
   (E) I and III only

8. Which of the following best describes the structure and organization of a political party?
   (A) They are close-knit and very organized.
   (B) They are highly decentralized or fragmented.
   (C) After election day they are usually less responsible to the people.
   (D) The president plays no role in party leadership after his election.
   (E) During the founding of our country, both parties organized in the same manner, along the same lines, and with the same political ideas in mind.

9. The shifting of voting patterns and formation of new coalitions of party supporters is known as
   (A) alignment
   (B) realignment
   (C) divided government
   (D) dealignment
   (E) party positioning

10. The future of political parties in the United States is uncertain due to
    I. decline of third-party challenges
    II. perceived differences between the parties
    III. increase in split-ticket voting
    IV. lack of party reform
    (A) I only
    (B) III only
    (C) II and III only
    (D) I and III only
    (E) I, II, and IV only

› Answers and Explanations

1. **C.** Multi-party systems tend to give voters a greater variety of major and minor party candidate choices. As a result, minor parties may affect elections (E). Party membership is voluntary (A). Parties represent a wide variety of ideologies (D). Multi-party systems often result in government by coalition, indicating a general lack of consensus (B).

2. **B.** Interest groups, not political parties, represent special interests. The other answer choices represent roles of political parties.

3. **E.** Splinter parties usually develop around a personality (A) within a major party. They split from that party when their candidate fails to receive the party nomination. A splinter party may disappear when their leader steps aside (C). Splinter parties are not often associated with the working class or with times of economic distress. An example is Theodore Roosevelt's Progressive Party (B, D).

4. **A.** Republicans often controlled Congress and the executive branch between 1860 and 1932. The years from 1800 to 1860 (D) and 1932 to 1968 (B) were eras of Democratic dominance. The period of 1968 to the present has been characterized by divided government (C). The period from 1789 to 1800 was one of party development (E).

5. **C.** Two major functions of the national convention are to write the party platform and to nominate the party's candidates for president and vice president. The national committee directs the party (A) and its campaign (B), manages the party's business (D), and promotes party unity and fundraising (E).

6. **D.** State parties have often received soft money from the national organization. In 2002 the use of soft money was restricted by the Bipartisan Campaign Reform Act.

7. **D.** Education and gender are two of the several factors that influence party identification. Public opinion develops in part from party identification.

8. **B.** Political parties tend to be highly decentralized and fragmented (A), especially at the national level and when no election is immediate. The president is the party leader after his election (D). Early political parties reflected different political ideas (E). After election day, political parties continue to communicate with their registered members through party mailings (C).

9. **B.** Realignment creates new voting coalitions, such as the New Deal coalition that elected Franklin Roosevelt in 1932.

10. **B.** The future of political parties is uncertain because of the increase in split-ticket voting, an increase in third-party challenges, a lack of perceived differences between the parties, and an increase in party reforms.

› Rapid Review

- Political parties are voluntary associations of voters.
- Political parties are different from interest groups.
- Political parties serve the party in the electorate, in government, and in organization.
- One-party, two-party, and multi-party systems exist throughout the world.
- Political parties recruit candidates, nominate and support candidates for office, educate the electorate, and organize the government.
- Party identification may be based on several factors.
- The Constitution does not call for political parties. Two parties developed from factions during the ratification process.
- Historically, there have been periods of one-party domination of the government. More recently, divided control of the branches of government has led to potential gridlock.
- Minor parties have existed throughout American history. There are four major types of minor parties: ideological, splinter/personality, single-issue, and protest parties.
- Political parties must have organization to accomplish their goals. American political parties tend to be decentralized and fragmented.
- The future of political parties in America is uncertain; some maintain that the two-party system is in jeopardy.

CHAPTER 10

Voting and Elections

IN THIS CHAPTER

Summary: Most people think of political participation in terms of voting; however, there are other forms of political participation, and sometimes they are more effective than voting. Political participation includes all the actions people use in seeking to influence or support government and politics.

Key Terms

suffrage	open primary	maintaining elections
electorate	blanket primary	deviating elections
direct primary	runoff primary	critical elections
recall	general elections	realigning elections
referendum	off-year elections	dealigning elections
initiative	coattail effect	split-ticket voting
political efficacy	caucus	Watergate
Motor Voter Law	presidential preference	freedom of
primary elections	primary	expression
closed primary	electoral college	soft money

Participation and Voting

KEY IDEA

Forms of Political Participation

- voting in elections
- discussing politics and attending political meetings
- forming interest groups and PACs
- contacting public officials
- campaigning for a candidate or political party

- contributing money to a candidate or political party
- running for office
- protesting government decisions

Most of these behaviors would be considered conventional or routine, within the acceptable channels of representative government. Less conventional behaviors have been used when groups have felt powerless and ineffective. Although Americans are less approving of unconventional behaviors, those tactics are sometimes effective in influencing government decisions. The often-violent protests against the Vietnam Conflict discouraged Lyndon Johnson from running for reelection in 1968. In the modern era of the Internet and other forms of "instant news," a single verbal gaffe can cause major problems for a candidate; mistakes by candidates are often quickly spread by supporters of the opposing candidate.

The most common form of political participation in the United States is voting. However, Americans are less likely to vote than citizens of other countries.

Participation Through Voting

Democratic government is "government by the people." In the United States, participation through elections is the basis of the democratic process. According to democratic theory, everyone should be allowed to vote. In practice, however, no nation grants universal suffrage; all nations have requirements for voting.

Expansion of Suffrage

Suffrage is the right to vote. It is a political right that belongs to all those who meet certain requirements set by law. The United States was the first nation to provide for general elections of representatives through mass suffrage. The issue of suffrage is left to the states—the only stipulation found in Article I, Section 2 of the Constitution is that individuals who could vote for "the most numerous branch of the state legislature" could also vote for their Congressional representatives.

The composition of the American **electorate** has changed throughout history. Two major trends have marked the development of suffrage: the elimination of a number of restrictive requirements and the transfer of more and more authority from the states to the federal government.

Changes in voting requirements have included:

- elimination of religious qualifications, property ownership, and tax payments after 1800
- elimination of race disqualifications with the passage of the Fifteenth Amendment in 1870
- elimination of gender disqualifications with the passage of the Nineteenth Amendment in 1920
- elimination of grandfather clauses, white primaries, and literacy requirements with the passage of federal civil rights legislation and court decisions (Civil Rights Acts, Voting Rights Act of 1965)
- allowing residents of Washington, D.C., to vote in presidential elections with the passage of the Twenty-Third Amendment in 1961
- elimination of poll taxes in federal elections with the passage of the Twenty-Fourth Amendment in 1964 (all poll taxes were ruled unconstitutional in *Harper v. Virginia State Board of Elections,* 1966)
- lowering the minimum age for voting in federal elections to 18 with the passage of the Twenty-Sixth Amendment in 1971

Issue or Policy Voting

The Progressive Movement of the early 20th century was a philosophy of political reform that fostered the development of mechanisms for increased direct participation. These included:

- A **direct primary** allows citizens to nominate candidates.
- A **recall** is a special election initiated by petition to allow citizens to remove an official from office before a term expires.
- A **referendum** allows citizens to vote directly on issues called propositions (proposed laws or state constitutional amendments).
- An **initiative** allows voters to petition to propose issues to be decided by qualified voters.

Although the recall, referendum, and initiative do not exist at the national level, several states allow voters to approve or disapprove ballot initiatives on specific issues.

Candidate Voting

Voting for candidates is the most common form of political participation. It allows citizens to choose candidates they think will best serve their interests and makes public officials accountable for their actions. In the United States voters only elect two national office holders—the president and vice president. All remaining candidates represent state or local constituencies.

Low Voter Turnout

Voting has been studied more closely than any other form of political participation in the United States. Studies have shown that voter turnout in the United States has decreased when compared with other nations and when compared with the United States over time. Voter turnout is higher if the election is seen as important; voter turnout is higher in presidential elections than in off-year elections. Several reasons might account for the low voter turnout:

- *expansion of the electorate*—Increase in the number of potential voters (Twenty-Sixth Amendment).
- *failure of political parties to mobilize voters*—Negative campaigning, numerous elections, frequent elections, lack of party identification.
- *no perceived differences between the candidates or parties*—Both parties and their candidates are seen as virtually the same.
- *mistrust of government*—A belief that all candidates are untrustworthy or unresponsive, due in part to the Watergate and Iran-Contra scandals.
- *apathy*—A lack of interest in politics; a belief that voting is not important.
- *satisfaction with the way things are*—A belief that not voting will keep the status quo.
- *lack of **political efficacy***—People do not believe their vote out of millions of votes will make a difference.
- *mobility of electorate*—Moving around leads to a lack of social belonging.
- *registration process*—Differences in registration procedures from state to state may create barriers; the National Voter Registration Act of 1995 (**Motor Voter Law**) was designed to make voter registration easier by allowing people to register at driver's license bureaus and some public offices.

Who Votes?

Several factors affect the likelihood of voting:

- *education*—The higher the level of education, the more likely a person is to vote. This is the most important indicator of voting behavior.
- *occupation and income*—These often depend on education level. Those with white-collar jobs and higher levels of income are more likely to vote than those with blue-collar jobs or lower levels of income.
- *age*—Older people are more likely to vote than younger people.
- *race*—Minorities such as African Americans and Hispanics are less likely to vote than whites, unless they have similar socioeconomic status.
- *gender*—At one time, gender was not a major predictor, but today women are more likely to vote than men.
- *religion*—Those who are more active within their religion are more likely to vote than those who do not attend religious services, or rarely attend.
- *marital status*—Married people are more likely to vote than those who are not married.
- *union membership*—Unions encourage participation, and union members tend to vote regularly.
- *community membership*—People who are well integrated into community life are more likely to vote than those who have moved recently.
- *party identification*—Those who have a strong sense of party identification are more likely to vote.
- *geography*—Residents of states with interparty competition and close elections may be more likely to vote than those who live in states with one-party domination.

Types of Elections

- **Primary elections** are nominating elections in which voters choose the candidates from each party who will run for office in the general election. There are several major types of primaries:
  - **closed primary**—Only voters who are registered in the party may vote to choose the candidate. Separate primaries are held by each political party, and voters must select a primary in advance.
  - **open primary**—Voters may vote to choose the candidates of either party, whether they belong to that party or not. Voters make the decision of which party to support in the voting booth.
  - **blanket primary**—Voters may vote for candidates of either party, choosing a Republican for one office and a Democrat for another; used only in Alaska and Washington.
  - **runoff primary**—When no candidate from a party receives a majority of the votes, the top two candidates face each other in a runoff.
- **General elections** are elections in which the voters choose from among all the candidates nominated by political parties or running as independents.
- Special elections are held whenever an issue must be decided by voters before a primary or general election is held, for example, to fill a vacancy in the Senate.

When Elections Are Held

Local, state, and federal laws determine when elections are held. Congress has established that congressional and presidential elections will be held on the first Tuesday after the first

Monday in November. Congressional elections are held every even-numbered year, and presidential elections are held every fourth year.

Congressional Elections

Since congressional elections are held every even-numbered year, **off-year elections** (mid-term elections) occur during the year when no presidential election is held. Voter turnout in off-year elections is generally lower than during presidential election years. During presidential election years, the popularity of a presidential candidate may create a **coattail effect**, allowing lesser-known or weaker candidates from the presidential candidate's party to win by riding the "coattails" of the nominee.

Presidential Elections

The road to the White House and the presidency begins months and even years prior to the election. Some candidates begin the process as soon as the previous election is over. Phases of a candidacy include:

- *exploration*—In deciding whether to run for president, individuals must determine whether they have enough political and financial support to win against other possible candidates. Often a possible nominee will form an exploratory committee to begin lining up support and finances, as well as to attract media coverage and gain widespread recognition.
- *announcement*—Once a candidate has decided to run, an announcement is generally made in a press conference. This announcement is a formal declaration that the candidate is seeking the party's nomination.
- *presidential primaries and caucuses*—In the past, state party officials would meet in a **caucus** to endorse the party candidate prior to presidential primaries. Abuses of the caucus system led to many states abandoning its use. Iowa still uses caucuses to nominate presidential candidates; however, today they are open to all members of the party. Most states today use the **presidential preference primary** to determine whom the state delegates to the national party convention will support. Voters vote in a primary election, and party delegates to the conventions support the winner of the primary election.
- *nominating conventions*—Each political party holds a national nominating convention in the summer prior to the general election. The convention is composed of delegates from each state, with each party determining its method of selecting delegates. The purpose of the nominating convention is to choose the party's presidential and vice-presidential nominees, write the party platform, and bring unity to the party in support of their chosen nominees.
- *campaigning and the general election*—After the conventions are over, each candidate begins campaigning for the general election. Generally, candidates travel to swing states (those in which neither major party has overwhelming support) and often appear more moderate in an effort to win the largest possible number of votes. Since 1960, the candidates have faced each other in televised debates. The general election is then held to determine which candidate wins the electoral college vote for that state.
- *electoral college*—When voters go to the polls on election day they are casting the popular vote. This vote is actually for electors. Each state has a number of electors equal to its senators and representatives in Congress. Also, Washington, D.C., has three electoral votes. The entire group of 538 electors is known as the electoral college. After the general election, the electors meet in their respective state capitals on the first Monday after the second Wednesday in December. The candidate who wins a majority of popular votes in a state in the general elec-

KEY IDEA

tion wins all the state's electoral votes in the electoral college (winner-take-all). Although the electors are not required to vote for their party's candidate, only rarely do they cast a vote for someone else. The votes cast in the electoral college are then sent to Congress, where they are opened and counted before a joint session. The candidate who receives a majority (270) of electoral votes is declared the winner. If no candidate for president receives a majority of electoral votes, the House of Representatives chooses the president from the top three candidates. If no candidate for vice president receives a majority of electoral votes, the Senate chooses the vice president from the top two candidates.

Partisanship in Elections

- **Maintaining elections** occur when the traditional majority power maintains power based on the party loyalty of voters.
- **Deviating elections** occur when the minority party is able to win with the support of majority-party members, independents, and new voters; however, the long-term party preferences of voters do not change.
- **Critical elections** indicate sharp changes in existing patterns of party loyalty due to changing social and economic conditions; for example, elections of 1860, 1896, and 1932.
- **Realigning elections** occur when the minority party wins by building a new coalition of voters that continues over successive elections. This is usually associated with a national crisis such as the Great Depression, when Franklin D. Roosevelt was able to create a new coalition of southerners, African Americans, the poor, Catholics and Jews, labor union members, and urban dwellers.
- **Dealigning elections** occur when party loyalty becomes less important to voters, as may be seen with the increase in independents and **split-ticket voting**.

Campaign Finance

Campaigning for political office is expensive. For the 2000 elections the Republican and Democratic parties raised more than $1.1 billion.

Campaign Finance Regulations and Reforms

Prior to the 1970s candidates for public office received donations from businesses, labor organizations, and individuals to finance campaigns.

Congress passed the Federal Election Campaign Act (FECA) in 1971, restricting the amount of campaign funds that can be spent on advertising, requiring disclosure of campaign contributions and expenditures, and limiting the amounts candidates and their families can donate to their own campaigns. It also allowed taxpayers to designate a donation on their tax return to the major political party candidates, beginning in the 1976 presidential election.

In 1974, after the **Watergate** scandal, Congress amended the Federal Election Campaign Act to establish a Federal Election Commission (FEC) to enforce the Act, and established public financing for presidential candidates in primaries and the general election. The measure also restricted contributions by prohibiting foreign contributions, limiting individual contributions, and restricting the formation of PACs and their contributions. It was further amended in 1976 and 1979.

In 1976 the Supreme Court ruled in *Buckley v. Valeo* that spending limits established by the FECA Amendments of 1974 were unconstitutional, finding that those restrictions were in violation of the First Amendment's guarantees of **freedom of expression**. *Buckley v. Valeo* also declared that the FECA ban on self-financed campaigns was unconstitutional.

In 1996 new questions arose over the use of "**soft money**," donations to political parties that could be used for general purposes. Originally, the money was supposed to be used for voter registration drives, national party conventions, and issue ads. Political parties were allowed to raise unlimited amounts of money because it was not to be used for campaigning. However, soft money has generally been spent in ways that ultimately help individual candidates. By the 2000 election, soft money donations had exceeded $400 million between the two major parties.

Campaign finance reform has been a major issue in Congress. In 2002 Congress passed the Bipartisan Campaign Reform Act (BCRA), banning the use of soft money in federal campaigns and increasing the 1974 limits on individual and group contributions to candidates. A result of the BCRA in the campaign of 2004 was the formation of "527" political organizations. A 527 political organization is a largely unregulated interest group that focuses on a single policy and attempts to influence voters. After the 2004 election, new rules governing 527 organizations regulated their use of soft money and allowed the FEC to examine their expenditures. In *Citizens United v. FEC* (2010), the Supreme Court ruled that limiting the ability of businesses, unions, and other groups to fund their own efforts to elect or defeat candidates for office is unconstitutional. Critics of the decision worried that the financial influence of big corporations on campaigns would be able to overpower the influence of the citizenry.

> Review Questions

1. Which of the following would NOT be a form of political participation?
   (A) voting in elections
   (B) contacting public officials
   (C) paying taxes
   (D) forming an interest group
   (E) protesting government decisions

2. What is the most common form of political participation in America?
   (A) voting
   (B) contributing money for candidates
   (C) working for a political party
   (D) running for office
   (E) forming interest groups

3. Which of the following best defines a recall?
   (A) Recall allows voters to petition proposed issues presented before them.
   (B) Recall is a form of direct primary.
   (C) Recall is a form of indirect primary.
   (D) Recall is a special election allowing the voters to remove public officials from office before the end of their term.
   (E) Recall allows the voter to vote directly on issues and propositions.

4. Which of the following factors are most likely to affect voter participation?
   I.   age
   II.   health status
   III. degree of religious participation
   IV.   number of children
   V.   gender
      (A) I and III only
      (B) I, III, and V only
      (C) II, III, and IV only
      (D) II, IV, and V only
      (E) I, II, III, IV, and V

5. Which of the following primaries is used by the fewest number of states?
   (A) closed primary
   (B) open primary
   (C) blanket primary
   (D) presidential preference primary
   (E) runoff primary

6. Which of the following is NOT true concerning the expansion of suffrage in the United States?
   (A) Religious qualifications and property ownership requirements were abolished after the Civil War.
   (B) The Fifteenth Amendment eliminated race disqualifications in voting.
   (C) The Nineteenth Amendment eliminated gender disqualifications.
   (D) The Twenty-Sixth Amendment lowered the voting age in federal elections to 18.
   (E) The Voting Rights Act of 1965 eliminated literacy tests.

7. Which of the following is a false statement?
   (A) The first step in running for president of the United States is to explore the possibility of political and financial support.
   (B) Most candidates running for president of the United States make formal announcements as to the seeking of their party's nomination.
   (C) After the national convention, candidates begin campaigning for the general election.
   (D) The purpose of a national nominating convention is to select a party's presidential candidate and write a party platform.
   (E) Presidential primaries provide little help for the American voter in determining a party's political candidate.

8. The electoral college, along with the popular vote of the people determines the winner of a presidential election. What majority of the electoral vote is needed in order to be declared the winner?
   (A) 538
   (B) 435
   (C) 100
   (D) 270
   (E) 271

9. The Federal Election Campaign Act of 1971
   (A) limited the number of candidates who could run for any one office
   (B) restricted the amount of campaign funds that could be spent on a single election
   (C) restricted the amount of campaign donations to $1 per person
   (D) restricted the amount of campaign contributions to $400 million for the major political parties
   (E) allowed for soft money contributions

10. In 1976, the Supreme Court ruled that spending limits established by the Federal Election Campaign Act were unconstitutional. Which Supreme Court case validated this ruling?
   (A) *U.S. v. Nixon*
   (B) *Gibbons v. Ogden*
   (C) *Buckley v. Valeo*
   (D) *McCulloch v. Maryland*
   (E) *Harper v. Virginia State Board of Elections*

› Answers and Explanations

1. **C.** Paying taxes is not a method of political participation.

2. **A.** Voting is the most common form of political participation in the United States. The remaining answer choices are forms of political participation in which fewer party members participate.

3. **D.** A recall is an election that allows voters the opportunity to remove a public official from office prior to the end of a term.

4. **B.** Age, degree of religious participation, and gender are characteristics that may determine whether someone is more likely to vote.

5. **C.** The blanket primary is used only in Washington and Alaska. Closed primaries (A), open primaries (B), and presidential preference primaries (D) are used by many states. Runoff primaries (E) occur only when no party candidate receives a majority of the votes.

6. **A.** Religious qualifications and property ownership requirements were abolished after 1800. The other answer choices are correct.

7. **E.** Presidential primaries are often preference primaries where voters may choose which candidate their party should support at the nominating convention. The other answer choices are correct.

8. **D.** Candidates must win at least 270 electoral votes to win a majority and, therefore, election as president or vice president.

9. **B.** The Federal Election Campaign Act of 1971 limited the amount of money that could be spent in federal election campaigns. The remaining answer choices were not provisions of the FECA.

10. **C.** In *Buckley v. Valeo* the Supreme Court declared spending limits established by the Federal Election Campaign Act unconstitutional. *U.S. v. Nixon* (A) declared that President Nixon did not have executive privilege over information in a criminal proceeding. *Gibbons v. Ogden* (B) expanded the powers of Congress over interstate commerce. *McCulloch v. Maryland* (D) upheld the Supremacy Clause. *Harper v. Virginia State Board of Elections* (E) ruled that all poll taxes were unconstitutional.

› Rapid Review

- Political participation includes all the actions people use in seeking to influence or support government and politics.
- Voting is the most common form of political participation in the United States.
- According to democratic theory, everyone should be allowed to vote.
- Suffrage is the right to vote. The expansion of suffrage has allowed a larger number of voters.
- In the early 20th century the Progressive Movement helped bring about an increase in direct participation.
- The president and vice president are the only two nationally elected office holders.
- Voter turnout in the United States has been decreasing for numerous reasons.
- Various characteristics have been attributed to those who are more likely to vote.
- Primary elections are intraparty elections held to narrow down the field of candidates.
- General elections are interparty elections where voters choose the office holders.
- Federal, state, and local laws determine the holding of elections.
- Congressional elections that take place in years when no presidential election is occurring are called off-year or mid-term elections.
- The presidential election process includes exploration, announcement, primaries, nominating conventions, campaigning, the general election, and the electoral college vote.
- An electoral college elects the president and vice president.
- Partisanship allows for elections to be maintaining, deviating, critical, realigning, or dealigning in scope.
- The Federal Election Campaign Act and its amendments regulate campaign finances. Reforms of campaign financing include the passage of the Bipartisan Campaign Reform Act that bans the use of "soft money" in federal campaigns. The Supreme Court ruled in *Citizens United v. FEC* (2010) that limiting the ability of businesses, unions, and other groups to fund their own efforts to elect or defeat candidates for office is unconstitutional.

CHAPTER 11

Interest Groups and the Mass Media

IN THIS CHAPTER

Summary: People form and join groups to take their concerns before public officials at all levels of government. Interest groups are different from a political party in that they have no legal status in the election process. They do not nominate candidates for public office; however, they may actively support candidates who are sympathetic to their cause. While political parties are interested in controlling government, **interest groups** are concerned with influencing the policies of government, usually focusing on issues that directly affect their membership. Membership in interest groups may be restricted or open to all who are interested. Not all interested people belong to interest groups. Many people belong to various interest groups at the same time.

Key Terms

interest groups
political action
   committees (PACs)

lobbying
grassroots
mass media

gatekeepers
media events

Interest Groups

Historical Background of Interest Groups

Interest groups have often been viewed with suspicion. In *Federalist #10*, James Madison warned against the dangers of "factions." Although Madison was opposed to the elimination of factions, he believed that the separation of powers under the Constitution would moderate their effect.

Functions of Interest Groups

Interest groups serve several important functions. They:

- raise awareness and stimulate interest in public affairs by educating their members and the public
- represent their membership, serving as a link between members and government
- provide information to government, especially data and testimony useful in making public policy
- provide channels for political participation that enable citizens to work together to achieve a common goal

Types of Interest Groups

Economic Interest Groups

Most interest groups are formed on the basis of economic interests.

- Labor groups promote and protect the interest of organized labor. Examples include the AFL-CIO and the Teamsters Union.
- Business groups promote and protect business interests in general. The Chamber of Commerce of the United States and the National Association of Manufacturers are examples.
- Professional groups maintain standards of the profession, hold professional meetings, and publish journals. Some examples are the National Education Association (NEA), the American Medical Association (AMA), and the American Bar Association (ABA).
- Agricultural groups, such as the National Grange and the National Farmers' Union, promote general agricultural interests.

Groups That Promote Causes

- specific causes
  — American Civil Liberties Union (ACLU)
  — National Rifle Association (NRA)
- welfare of specific groups of individuals
  — American Association of Retired Persons (AARP)
  — National Association for the Advancement of Colored People (NAACP)
  — Veterans of Foreign Wars (VFW)
- religion-related causes
  — National Council of Churches
  — American Jewish Congress

Public Interest Groups

Public interest groups are concerned with issues such as the environment, consumer protection, crime, and civil rights.

- public interests
  — Common Cause
  — League of Women Voters
  — Mothers Against Drunk Driving (MADD)

Strategies of Interest Groups

- *influencing elections*—encouraging members to vote for candidates who support their views, influencing party platforms and the nomination of candidates, campaigning and contributing money to parties and candidates through **political action committees (PACs)**

- *lobbying*—attempting to influence policymakers, often by supplying data to government officials and their staffs to convince these policymakers that their case is more deserving than another's
  - — direct lobbying—using personal contacts between lobbyists and policymakers
  - — **grassroots** lobbying—interested group members and others outside the organization write letters, send telegrams, e-mails, and faxes, and make telephone calls to influence policymakers
  - — coalition lobbying—several interest groups with common goals join together to influence policymakers
- *litigation*—groups often take an issue to court if they are unsuccessful in gaining the support of Congress; this strategy was used successfully by the NAACP to argue against segregation during the 1950s
- *going public*—appealing to the public for support by bringing attention to an issue or using public relations to gain support for the image of the interest group itself

Political Action Committees (PACs)

KEY IDEA

The campaign finance reforms of the 1970s prohibited corporations and labor unions from making direct contributions to candidates running for federal office. Political action committees (PACs) were formed as political arms of interest groups. Federal law regulates PACs; they must register with the federal government, raise money from multiple contributors, donate to several candidates, and follow strict accounting rules.

Regulation of Interest Groups

The first major attempt to regulate lobbying came in 1946 with the passage of the Federal Regulation of Lobbying Act, requiring lobbyists to register with the clerk of the House of Representatives and the secretary of the Senate if their principal purpose was to influence legislation. This law was directed only at those who tried to influence members of Congress. In 1995 Congress passed the Lobbying Disclosure Act, creating much stricter regulations by requiring registration if lobbying was directed at members of Congress, congressional staff, or policymakers within the executive branch. It also required the disclosure of more information concerning the activities and clients of lobbyists.

Mass Media

Mass media refers to all forms of communication that transmit information to the general public. Although the mass media are not the only means of communication between citizens and government (political parties, interest groups, and voting are other means), they are the only linkage mechanism that specializes in communication.

Development of the Modern Media

The development of the mass media in the United States reflects the growth of the country, new inventions and technology, and changing attitudes about the role of government.

Newspapers

The earliest American newspapers, operating during colonial times, were expensive, had small circulations, and were often prepared or financed by political organs or those advocating a particular cause. Improvements in printing, the telegraph, and the rotary press led to the growth of newspapers and newspaper circulations. By the 1890s almost every major city in the United States had one or more daily papers. Circulation wars led to "yellow journalism" and political consequences resulted. Since the 1950s newspaper competition has decreased. By 2009, many newspapers in the United States had gone out of business and the very future of the newspaper was being called into question.

Magazines

Magazines tended to have smaller circulations with less frequent publication. The earliest public affairs magazines were published in the mid-1800s. They often exposed political corruption and business exploitation with the writings of muckrakers such as Ida Tarbell, Lincoln Steffens, and Sinclair Lewis. In the 1920s and 1930s, three weekly news magazines, *Time, Newsweek,* and *U.S. News and World Report* attracted mass readership. Today, they often substitute for daily newspapers. Liberal and conservative magazines have smaller circulations but are read by supporters on both sides.

Radio

The wide use of radio began in the 1920s and made celebrities of news personalities. Franklin Roosevelt successfully used radio to broadcast his "fireside chats" to the American people.

Television

Today, television claims the largest audience of the mass media. After World War II television increased the visibility of broadcast journalists, making them celebrities. Television promoted the careers of politicians such as Joe McCarthy, during hearings of the House Unamerican Activities Committee, and John Kennedy, during his campaign debates against Richard Nixon. The recent growth of cable TV news and the 24/7 news cycle have greatly changed the coverage of the American political system.

Internet as Media

The rapid growth of Internet usage has led to media organizations using the Internet as a way to convey information. Newspapers, magazines, blogs, and radio and television stations have sites on the World Wide Web. More and more Americans are receiving their news from the Internet. Critics note that Internet news has less "fact-checking" associated with it than does news from the more traditional forms of media; they claim that rumor and unsubstantiated allegations make up a large portion of Internet "news."

Roles of the Media

The media perform several important functions:

- informing the public
- shaping public opinion
- providing a link between citizens and government
- serving as a watchdog that investigates and examines personalities and government policies
- agenda setting by influencing what subjects become national political issues; protests against the Vietnam Conflict are an example

Media Ownership and Government Regulation

The mass media are privately owned in the United States, giving them more political freedom than in most other countries, where they are publicly owned, but also making them more dependent on advertising profits. Government regulation of the media affects the broadcast media (radio and television) more than the print media (newspapers and magazines) and the Internet. Government regulation of the broadcast media falls into three categories:

- *technical regulations*—The Federal Communications Act of 1934 created the Federal Communications Commission (FCC) as an independent regulatory agency to regulate interstate and foreign communication by radio, television, telephone, telegraph, cable, and satellite.
- *structural regulations*—These control the organization and ownership of broadcasting companies; in 1996 the Telecommunications Act broadened competition.
- *content regulations*—Although the mass media are protected by the First Amendment, the broadcast media have been subject to regulation of content.

What Is News? Reporting the News

"News" is any important event that has happened within the past 24 hours. The media decide what is news by deciding what to report. News is generally directed through **gatekeepers**—media executives, news editors, and prominent reporters—who decide which events to present and how to present them. Time limitations and the potential impact of the story are major elements in selecting what is news. In political coverage, "horse-race journalism" often focuses on which candidate is winning or losing, rather than the issues of the election.

Media and the President

The major news organizations maintain journalists in major cities and government centers to report political events firsthand. Washington, D.C., has the largest press corps of any city in the United States, with one-third of the press assigned to cover the White House. News events may be staged as **media events**. The White House allows special access to the president, with the press receiving information through the Office of the Press Secretary.

Some ways that journalists receive information are:

- *news releases*—prepared texts to be used exactly as written
- *news briefings*—announcements and daily questioning of the press secretary about news releases
- *news conferences*—questioning of high-level officials, often rehearsed
- *leaks*—information released by officials who are guaranteed anonymity; may be intentional to interfere with the opposition or to "float" an idea and measure reaction

Reporters are expected to observe "rules" when talking to officials:

- *on the record*—the official may be quoted by name
- *off the record*—what the official says cannot be printed
- *on background*—what the official says can be printed but may not be attributed to the official by name
- *on deep background*—what the official says can be printed, but it cannot be attributed to anybody

Media and Congress

Fewer reporters regularly cover Congress, which does not maintain as tight a control over news stories as the White House. Most of the coverage of Congress concerns the House of Representatives, the Senate, or Congress as an organization, rather than individual members. News about Congress may cover confirmation hearings, oversight investigations, or scandals among members.

C-SPAN (Cable-Satellite Public Affairs Network) was created to increase coverage of Congressional activities. The floor and some committee proceedings of the House of Representatives and Senate are now broadcast on C-SPAN and C-SPAN II. Members of Congress may also record radio and television messages to their constituents.

Biases in the Media

Critics of the media contend the media are biased in reporting. Reporters are said to have a liberal bias, while media owners, publishers, and editors are said to be more conservative. Studies confirm that reporters have a liberal orientation; however, the bias tends to be against incumbents and frontrunners. There is also a tendency for "pack journalism," with journalists adopting the viewpoints of other journalists with whom they spend time and exchange information. This bias often extends to viewers, listeners, and readers because individuals often read, watch, or listen to news outlets that support political views that they already have.

❯ Review Questions

1. How is an interest group different from a political party?
   (A) Interest groups often support political candidates for office.
   (B) Membership in an interest group is nonrestrictive.
   (C) Interest groups have no legal status in the election process.
   (D) Interest groups control government.
   (E) Only interested people belong to interest groups.

2. Which of the following is not a function of an interest group?
   (A) represent a broad range of interests
   (B) raise awareness and stimulate interest in public affairs
   (C) serve as a link between its members and government
   (D) provide information to the government
   (E) provide a channel for public political participation for the achievement of common goals

3. An example of an interest group that would promote a specific cause is
   (A) the National Grange
   (B) the Teamsters Union
   (C) the American Bar Association
   (D) the National Education Association
   (E) the National Rifle Association

4. An example of a public interest group is
   (A) the League of Women Voters
   (B) the American Association of Retired Persons
   (C) the American Bar Association
   (D) the National Council of Churches
   (E) the American Jewish Congress

5. A method of lobbying by which interest group members and others outside the organization write letters, send telegrams, and make telephone calls to influence policymakers is known as
   (A) litigation lobbying
   (B) grassroots lobbying
   (C) direct lobbying
   (D) coalition lobbying
   (E) influential lobbying

6. Which of the following is true regarding the regulation of lobbying?
   (A) The Federal Regulation of Lobbying Act was directed at those who tried to influence members of the executive branch.
   (B) The first major attempt to regulate lobbying came during the Progressive Era in the early years of the 20th century.
   (C) In the second half of the 20th century, laws regulating lobbying became more lenient.
   (D) The Lobbying Disclosure Act did not apply to lobbyists who attempted to influence congressional staff members.
   (E) Both the Federal Regulation of Lobbying Act and the Lobbying Disclosure Act required lobbyists to register.

7. Which is true of government regulation of the media?
   (A) Government regulation of the media affects the print media more than the broadcast media.
   (B) Structural regulations deal with issues affecting the organization of broadcasting companies.
   (C) The Telecommunications Act (1996) restricted competition among broadcasting companies.
   (D) The Federal Communications Commission is restricted to the regulation of interstate commerce.
   (E) The First Amendment protects the broadcast media from the regulation of content.

8. In the history of radio as a mode of mass media, which American president was first to make the medium a regular feature of his administration as a method of informing the people?
   (A) Ronald Reagan
   (B) Franklin Roosevelt
   (C) Bill Clinton
   (D) George H. W. Bush
   (E) Harry Truman

9. Which of the following has been an important function in the role of the mass media?
   I. directing government
   II. agenda setting
   III. informing the public
   IV. shaping public opinion
   (A) II, III, and IV only
   (B) I, II, and III only
   (C) I only
   (D) II and IV only
   (E) II and IV only

10. Those media executives and news editors who decide which events to present and how to present the news are called
    (A) content regulators
    (B) gatekeepers
    (C) technical regulators
    (D) telecommunication regulators
    (E) media representatives

❯ Answers and Explanations

1. **C.** Interest groups have no legal status in the election process, whereas political parties fulfill many roles in the election process. Interest groups may support political candidates for office; only political parties nominate candidates for office (A). Membership in an interest group may be restricted (B). Interest groups influence governmental policies, whereas political parties control government (D). Not all interested people belong to interest groups (E).

2. **A.** Interest groups focus on issues that directly affect their membership. The other answer choices reflect the functions of an interest group.

3. **E.** The National Rifle Association promotes gun ownership as a right of citizens. The National Grange (A) promotes general agricultural interests. The Teamsters Union (B) advocates and protects the interests of organized labor. The American Bar Association (C) and the National Education Association (D) are professional groups.

4. **A.** The League of Women Voters is a public interest group created to encourage voter participation. The AARP (B), the National Council of Churches (D), and the American Jewish Congress (E) are groups that promote causes. The American Bar Association (C) is a professional group.

5. **B.** Grassroots lobbying attempts to reach the average voter at the local level. Litigation lobbying involves taking an issue to court (A). Direct lobbying (C) uses personal contacts between lobbyists and policymakers. Coalition lobbying (D) brings together several interest groups with common goals. Influential lobbying influences elections (E).

6. **E.** Both laws require the registration of lobbyists, with the Lobbying Disclosure Act requiring registration under more circumstances than the Federal Regulation of Lobbying Act. The Federal Regulation of Lobbying Act was directed at those trying to influence members of Congress (A). The first major attempt to regulate lobbying came in 1976 (B). Laws regulating lobbying became stricter and more comprehensive (C). The Act applied to lobbying of members of Congress, congressional staff, or policymakers in the executive branch (D).

7. **B.** Structural regulations control the organization and ownership of broadcasting companies. Government regulation affects radio and television more than newspapers and magazines (A). The Telecommunications Act broadened competition (C). The FCC regulates interstate and foreign communication (D). The broadcast media have been subject to regulation of content (E).

8. **B.** Franklin Roosevelt used the radio to deliver his "fireside chats" to the American people as a method of informing them about the economy and the war.

9. **A.** Agenda setting, informing the public, and shaping public opinion are functions of the mass media. The mass media investigate government policies, but do not direct government.

10. **B.** News is generally directed through gatekeepers (media executives, news editors, and prominent reporters who decide which events to present and how to present them).

❯ Rapid Review

- Interest groups are different from political parties.
- James Madison warned against the dangers of "factions" in *Federalist #10.*
- Interest groups perform many functions: creating awareness among the public, linking the public and government, providing information, and creating avenues for political participation.
- There are three major types of interest groups: economic, cause-related, and public interest.
- Strategies used by interest groups may include influencing elections, lobbying, litigation, and going public.
- PACs, or political action committees, are political arms of interest groups that raise money for political candidates.
- Federal, state, and local laws regulate interest group activities and fundraising.
- Mass media refers to all the forms of communication that transmit information to the general public. Mass media include newspapers, magazines, radio, television, and the Internet.
- One of the major roles of the media is agenda setting.
- The mass media are privately owned in the United States.
- Government regulation of broadcast media includes technical, structural, and content regulation.
- Gatekeepers are the media executives, news editors, and prominent reporters who decide which events to present and how to present them.
- The Office of the Press Secretary allows the press to have greater access to the president through new releases, briefings, and conferences.
- Media coverage of Congress often centers on the institution rather than individual members.
- Criticism of the media's influence often refers to bias in reporting.
- More and more Americans are receiving their news from the Internet rather than from traditional news outlets; some critics note the potential unreliability of news reported in the Internet age.

CHAPTER 12

The Legislative Branch

IN THIS CHAPTER

Summary: Article I of the United States Constitution creates a **bicameral**, or two-house, legislature consisting of the House of Representatives and the Senate. The current structure of the Congress was the result of the Connecticut (Great) Compromise, reached at the Constitutional Convention. The Founding Fathers based their compromise in part on the belief that each house would serve as a check on the power of the other house. The House of Representatives was to be based on the population in the states, representative of the people, with its members chosen by popular vote. The Senate was to represent the states, with each state having the same number of senators, chosen by the state legislatures.

Key Terms

bicameral
apportionment
reapportionment
congressional districting
gerrymandering
incumbency effect
casework
constituents
Speaker of the House
majority leader
president *pro tempore*

floor leaders
seniority system
standing committee
select committee
joint committee
conference committee
caucuses
trustee
franking privilege
oversight
bills

rules committee
filibuster
cloture
pork barrel legislation
logrolling
riders
amendments
lobbying
legislative veto

Structure of Congress

Figure 12-1 shows the structure of the two arms of Congress.

Structure of Congress: A Comparison of the House and Senate

	House of Representatives	**Senate**
Membership	435 members (apportioned by population)	100 members (two from each state)
Term of office	2 years; entire House elected every 2 years	6 years; staggered terms with one-third of the Senate elected every 2 years
Qualifications	At least 25 years of age; citizen for 7 years; must live in state where district is located	At least 30 years of age; citizen for 9 years; must live in state
Constituencies	Smaller, by districts	Larger, entire state
Prestige	Less prestige	More prestige

Figure 12-1

Organization of Congress

- Two houses meet for terms of two years beginning on January 3 of odd-numbered years; each term is divided into two one-year sessions
- The president may call special sessions in cases of national emergency
- Each house of Congress chooses its own leadership and determines its own rules

Election to Congress

Getting Elected to the House of Representatives

The Constitution guarantees each state at least one representative. Members are chosen from districts within each state. Some practices related to determining congressional representation are:

- *apportionment*—distribution among the states based on the population of each of the states
- *reapportionment*—the redistribution of Congressional seats after the census determines changes in population distribution among the states
- *congressional districting*—the drawing by state legislatures of congressional districts for those states with more than one representative
- *gerrymandering*—drawing congressional districts to favor one political party or group over another

Getting Elected to the Senate

The Constitution guarantees that "no state, without its consent, shall be deprived of its equal suffrage in the Senate" (Article V).

- Members were originally chosen by the state legislatures in each state.
- Since 1913, the Seventeenth Amendment allows for the direct election of senators by the people of the state.

Incumbency Effect

The **incumbency effect** is the tendency of those already holding office to win reelection. The effect tends to be stronger for members of the House of Representatives and weaker for the Senate. Advantages may include:

- *name recognition*—Voters are more likely to recognize the office holder than the challenger.
- *credit claiming*—The office holder may have brought government projects and money into the state or district.
- ***casework** for **constituents***—Office holders may have helped constituents solve problems involving government and the bureaucracy.
- *more visible to constituents*—Members can use the "perks" of the office to communicate with constituents. Franking, the privilege of sending official mail using the incumbent's signature as postage, provides communication with constituents.
- *media exposure*—Incumbents are more likely to gain "free" publicity during a campaign through the media.
- *fundraising abilities*—It is generally greater for incumbents.
- *experience in campaigning*—Incumbents have already experienced the campaign process.
- *voting record*—Voters can evaluate their performance based on their record.

Term Limits

Although several states have passed legislation establishing term limits for members of Congress, the Supreme Court has ruled that neither the states nor Congress may impose term limits without a constitutional amendment. Therefore, today, there are no limitations on the number of terms a member of Congress may serve.

Leadership of Congress

The majority political party in each house controls the leadership positions of Congress.

House of Representatives

- The **Speaker of the House** is the presiding officer and most powerful member of the House. Major duties include assigning bills to committee, controlling floor debate, and appointing party members to committees. The Speaker is elected by members of his or her political party within the House.
- Majority and minority leaders
  - The **majority leader** serves as the major assistant to the speaker, helps plan the party's legislative program, and directs floor debate.
  - The minority floor leader is the major spokesperson for the minority party and organizes opposition to the majority party.
- Whips help floor leaders by directing party members in voting, informing members of impending voting, keeping track of vote counts, and pressuring members to vote with the party.

Senate

- The U.S. vice president, although not a Senate member, is the presiding officer of the Senate, according to the Constitution. The vice president may not debate and only votes to break a tie.

- The **president** *pro tempore* is a senior member of the majority party chosen to preside in the absence of the Senate president. This is a mostly ceremonial position lacking real power.
- Majority and minority **floor leaders**
  — The majority floor leader is the most influential member of the Senate and often the majority party spokesperson.
  — The minority floor leader performs the same role as the House minority leader.
- Whips serve the same role as whips in the House of Representatives.

The Committee System

Most of the work of Congress is accomplished through committees. Committees permit Congress to divide the work among members, thus allowing for the study of legislation by specialists and helping speed up the passage of legislation.

Leadership of Committees

Committee chairpersons are members of the majority party in each house chosen by party caucus. They set agendas, assign members to subcommittees, and decide whether the committee will hold public hearings and which witnesses to call. They manage floor debate of the bill when it is presented to the full House or Senate. Traditionally chairpersons were chosen based on the **seniority system**, with the majority party member having the longest length of committee service chosen as chairperson. Today, reforms allow for the selection of chairpersons who are not the most senior majority-party member on the committee. However, most are long-standing members of the committee.

Membership on Committees

The percentage of each committee's membership reflects the overall percentage of Democrats and Republicans in each house. Members try to serve on committees where they can influence public policy relating to their district or state (for example, a Kansas senator on the agriculture committee) or influence important national public policy.

Types of Committees

- A **standing committee** is a permanent committee that deals with specific policy matters (agriculture, energy and natural resources, veterans' affairs).
- A **select committee** is a temporary committee appointed for a specific purpose. Most are formed to investigate a particular issue, such as the Senate Watergate Committee.
- A **joint committee** is made up of members of both houses of Congress. It may be a select committee (Iran-Contra Committee) or perform routine duties (Joint Committee on the Library of Congress).
- A **conference committee** is a temporary committee of members from both houses of Congress, created to resolve the differences in House and Senate versions of a bill. It is a compromise committee.

Caucuses

Legislative **caucuses** are informal groups formed by members of Congress who share a common purpose or set of goals (Congressional Black Caucus, Women's Caucus, Democratic or Republican Caucus).

Congressional Staff and Support

- Personal staff work directly for members of Congress in Washington, D.C., and their district offices in their home states.
- Committee staff work for committees and subcommittees in Congress, researching problems and analyzing information.
- Support agencies provide services to members of Congress (Library of Congress, Government Printing Office).

Roles of Members of Congress

Members of Congress have several roles:

- *policymaker*—make public policy through the passage of legislation
- *representative*—represent constituents
  - **delegate**—members vote based on the wishes of constituents, regardless of their own opinions
  - **trustee**—after listening to constituents, members vote based on their own opinions
- *constituent servant*—help constituents with problems
- *committee member*—serve on committees
- *politician/party member*—work to support their political party platform and get reelected

Privileges of Members of Congress

Members of Congress enjoy several privileges, including:

- allowances for offices in their district or home state
- travel allowances
- the **franking privilege** allows members of Congress to send mailings to constituents postage free
- immunity from arrest while conducting congressional business
- immunity from libel or slander suits for their speech or debate in Congress

Powers of Congress

Congress has legislative and nonlegislative powers.

1. Legislative powers—power to make laws

   - *expressed powers*—powers specifically granted to Congress, mostly found in Article I, Section 8 of the Constitution
   - *implied powers*—powers that may be reasonably suggested to carry out the expressed powers; found in Article I, Section 8, Clause 18; "necessary and proper" or elastic clause; allows for the expansion of Congress's powers (expressed power to raise armies and navy implies the power to draft men into the military)
   - *limitations on powers*—powers denied Congress by Article I, Section 9 and the Tenth Amendment

2. Nonlegislative powers—duties other than lawmaking

   - *electoral powers*—Selection of the president by the House of Representatives and/or vice president by the Senate upon the failure of the electoral college to achieve a majority vote.

- *amendment powers*—Congress may propose amendments by a two-thirds vote of each house or by calling a national convention to propose amendments if requested by two-thirds of the state legislatures.
- *impeachment*—The House may bring charges, or impeach, the president, vice president, or any civil officer; case is tried in the Senate with the Senate acting as the jury (Andrew Johnson and Bill Clinton were both impeached by the House but not convicted by the Senate).
- *executive powers of Senate*—The Senate shares the appointment and treaty-making powers with the executive branch; the Senate must approve appointments by majority vote and treaties by two-thirds vote.
- *investigative/**oversight** powers*—Investigate matters falling within the range of its legislative authority; often involves the review of policies and programs of the executive branch.

The Lawmaking Process

Figure 12-2 shows the steps involved for a bill to become a law.

How a Bill Becomes a Law

> **Bills**, or proposed laws, may begin in either house, except revenue bills, which must begin in the House of Representatives.

HOUSE OF REPRESENTATIVES	SENATE
A bill is introduced, numbered, and assigned to a committee.	A bill is introduced, numbered, and assigned to a committee.
The bill may be assigned to a subcommittee for further study.	The bill may be assigned to a subcommittee for further study.
The bill is returned to committee, where it is approved or rejected.	The bill is returned to committee, where it is approved or rejected.
The **rules committee** sets terms of debate for the bill.	No rules committee!
The bill is debated by the House.	The bill is debated by the Senate.
A vote is taken, where the bill is passed or defeated. Bills that pass the House are sent to the Senate.	A vote is taken, where the bill is passed or defeated. Bills that pass the Senate are sent to the House.

↓ ↓

> Conference committee resolves differences between House and Senate versions of a bill. Compromise versions may not contain any new material.

↓ ↓

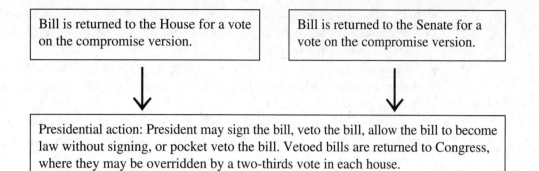

| Bill is returned to the House for a vote on the compromise version. | Bill is returned to the Senate for a vote on the compromise version. |

Presidential action: President may sign the bill, veto the bill, allow the bill to become law without signing, or pocket veto the bill. Vetoed bills are returned to Congress, where they may be overridden by a two-thirds vote in each house.

Figure 12-2

Legislative Tactics

Legislative tactics are the strategies and devices used by Congress and others in an attempt to block legislation or to get legislation passed.

- *caucuses*—May form voting blocs.
- the *committee system*—Plays a major role in the passage of legislation; bills may die if committees fail to act upon them or reject them.
- *filibuster* and *cloture*—Filibuster is unlimited debate in an attempt to stall action on a bill. It occurs in the Senate only, and is possible because the Senate's rules for debate are almost unrestricted. Cloture is the method by which the Senate limits a filibuster. It involves a petition to end debate and requires the vote of at least 60 senators.
- **pork barrel legislation**—An attempt to provide funds and projects for a member's home district or state.
- *logrolling*—An attempt by members to gain the support of other members in return for their support on the member's legislation; "I'll support your bill, if you will support mine."
- *riders*—Additions to legislation which generally have no connection to the legislation; generally legislation that would not pass on its own merit; when a bill has lots of riders it becomes a "Christmas tree bill."
- *amendments*—Additions or changes to legislation that deal specifically with the legislation.
- *lobbying*—Trying to influence members of Congress to support or reject legislation.
- *conference committees*—May affect the wording and therefore the final intent of the legislation.
- *legislative veto*—The rejection of a presidential or executive branch action by a vote of one or both houses of Congress, used mostly between 1932 and 1980 but declared unconstitutional by the Supreme Court in 1983 (*Immigration and Naturalization Service v. Chadha*) stating that Congress cannot take any actions having the force of law unless the president agrees.

Influences on Congress

Various individuals and groups influence Congress members.

- *constituents*—Members, especially those who hope to win reelection, often take into consideration the opinions of their constituents and voters back home in their district or state.
- *other lawmakers and staff*—More senior members often influence newer members; committee members who worked on legislation often influence other members; and staff often research issues and advise members.

- *party influences*—Each party's platform takes a stand on major issues, and loyal members often adhere to the "party line." Members in the House are more likely to support the party position than are Senators.
- *president*—Presidents often lobby members to support legislation through phone calls, invitations to the White House, or even appeals to the public to gain support from voters to bring pressure on members.
- *lobbyists and interest groups*—Often provide members with information on topics relating to their group's interest or possible financial support in future campaigns.

› Review Questions

1. After a national census has been taken, changes in population distribution cause the changing of congressional seats among the states. This effect is commonly called
   (A) congressional districting
   (B) apportionment
   (C) gerrymandering
   (D) reapportionment
   (E) census apportionment

2. Which of the following is NOT true of the Congress?
   (A) Each house determines its own leadership and rules.
   (B) Terms of Congress last for two years.
   (C) Congress is unicameral in nature.
   (D) Only the president may call special sessions of Congress.
   (E) A session of Congress begins on January 3 of odd-numbered years.

3. Which of the following is true about the officers of the House of Representatives?
   (A) It is the responsibility of the party whip to keep track of vote counts and pressure members to vote with the party.
   (B) The presiding officer is the majority leader.
   (C) Minority leaders direct floor debates.
   (D) The major duty of the majority leader is to assign bills to committee.
   (E) The whip serves as the major assistant to the speaker in determining the party's legislative program.

4. Temporary committees appointed for the specific purpose of investigating a particular issue are called
   (A) joint committees
   (B) select committees
   (C) standing committees
   (D) investigating committees
   (E) compromise committees

5. Which of the following is NOT true of members of Congress?
   (A) Members of Congress act as policymakers and make public policy through the passage of legislation.
   (B) Members of Congress are constituent servants.
   (C) Members of Congress work to support their political party platform.
   (D) After listening to constituents, members vote based on the opinions of those constituents, that is, they become the trustee of the constituent.
   (E) Members of Congress serve on committees.

6. Which of the following best describes a nonlegislative power of Congress?
   (A) power to declare war
   (B) power to tax
   (C) impeachment power
   (D) power to regulate commerce
   (E) power to make all laws which are necessary and proper

7. Which of the following would not be a step that a proposed bill would encounter on its journey through Congress?
   (A) The bill is debated.
   (B) The bill is voted on, at which time it may pass or be defeated.
   (C) The bill may be assigned to a subcommittee.
   (D) The bill is numbered.
   (E) The bill is introduced by a member of the Congress or by a member of the executive department.

8. After receiving a bill the president may
   I. sign the bill
   II. veto the bill
   III. return the bill to Congress for clarification on some point within the bill
   IV. allow the Congress to pocket veto the bill, thereby allowing the bill to become law without his signature
   (A) I only
   (B) II only
   (C) I and II only
   (D) I, II, III only
   (E) I, II, III, and IV

9. Which legislative tactic is most effectively used only in the Senate?
   (A) filibustering
   (B) logrolling
   (C) caucuses
   (D) riders
   (E) pork barrel legislation

10. Which of the following is not considered to be a contributing factor to the incumbency effect?
    (A) name recognition
    (B) voting record
    (C) educational background
    (D) experience in campaigning
    (E) visibility to constituents

› Answers and Explanations

1. **D.** Reapportionment is the change in the number of congressional seats per state based on state population changes. Gerrymandering (C) is the drawing of congressional electoral districts in order to give an advantage to a group or party.

2. **C.** Congress is a bicameral legislature composed of the House of Representatives and the Senate. The other responses are correct descriptions of Congress.

3. **A.** The minority and majority whips are responsible for keeping track of vote counts and pressuring members to support the party vote. The presiding officer is the speaker of the House (B). The speaker directs floor debates (C) and largely controls the assignment of bills to committee (D). The majority leader serves as the major assistant to the speaker (E).

4. **B.** Select committees are temporary committees responsible for investigating specific issues. Some select committees investigate issues (D). Joint committees (A) are those made up of members of both houses of Congress. Standing committees (C) are permanent committees that deal with specific policy matters. A compromise committee (E) is a description of a conference committee.

5. **D.** Members of Congress who vote according to constituent wishes are delegates of the constituents. The remaining answer choices accurately reflect the duties of members of Congress.

6. **C.** The impeachment power of Congress is a nonlegislative power, having nothing to do with the passage of legislation. The powers to declare war (A), to tax (B), to regulate commerce (D), and to make all laws that are necessary and proper (E) deal with the passage of legislation. They are, therefore, among the legislative powers of Congress.

7. **E.** Although bills may be suggested by members of the executive branch, they may be introduced only by members of Congress. The remaining answer choices are correct and occur in the following order: (D), (C), (A), (B).

8. **C.** The president may not return bills to Congress for clarification. Only the president has the power of the pocket veto.

9. **A.** Filibustering is a stalling tactic used only in the Senate. Logrolling (B), caucuses (C), riders (D), and pork barrel legislation (E) are used in both houses of Congress.

10. **C.** The incumbency effect is the tendency of those already holding office to win reelection because of advantages of holding that office. A candidate's educational background does not contribute to the incumbency effect. Name recognition (A), voting record (B), campaign experience (D), and visibility to constituents (E) are factors that contribute to the incumbency effect.

› Rapid Review

- Congress is bicameral in nature.
- Members of the House of Representatives are chosen from districts within a state. The number of representatives per state is based on state population.
- Members of the Senate are elected from the state. States are equally represented, with two senators from each state.
- Reelection to Congress is often a consequence of the incumbency effect. Several factors may contribute to the incumbency effect.
- There are no term limits in Congress.
- Leaders of the House of Representatives include the speaker of the House, the floor leaders, and the whips. Leaders of the Senate include the president of the Senate (vice president), the president *pro tempore*, the floor leaders, and the whips.
- Most of the legislative work of Congress is accomplished through committees. Membership on committees is based on party strength. Types of committees include standing, joint, select, and conference committees.
- Personal staff, committee staff, and support agencies aid members of Congress and the committees.
- Congressmen serve in many roles.
- Congress has both legislative and nonlegislative powers. Legislative powers include expressed, implied, and denied powers. Nonlegislative powers include electoral powers, amendment powers, impeachment powers, executive powers of the Senate, and oversight powers.
- Congress has a specific process for how a bill becomes a law.
- Legislative tactics are used in the process of passing, stopping, or slowing legislation.
- Constituents, other lawmakers, party influences, the president, lobbyists, and interest groups influence members of Congress.

CHAPTER 13

The Executive Branch and the Bureaucracy

IN THIS CHAPTER

Summary: The office of the president is the most important single position in the government of the United States. The president of the United States has many responsibilities and functions originating in Article II of the Constitution. From the time of George Washington to the present, holders of the office of the president have striven to be more than just a ceremonial head of state. The American president is not just a figurehead but also a personality who commands power and respect.

Key Terms

impeachment
executive orders
electoral college
executive agreements
pardons

impoundment
War Powers Act
legislative vetoes
bureaucracy
Hatch Act

cabinet
iron triangles
issue networks

Constitutional Origins of the Presidency

Delegates to the constitutional convention studied the writings of philosophers Montesquieu and Locke, analyzed the powers of the British monarchs, and studied the role of governors in the American colonial governments. The delegates decided they did not want a king; they wanted power to rest with the people. Debate arose over a single versus a plural executive, and a weak executive appointed by Congress versus a strong executive independent of the legislature. The final compromise created a single executive with powers limited by the checks and balances of the legislative and judicial branches.

Qualifications

Article II of the Constitution establishes the formal qualifications of the president:

- natural-born citizen
- at least 35 years of age
- resident of United States for 14 years prior to election

Historically, many candidates who have run for the office of the president have also shared several characteristics:

- political or military experience
- political acceptability
- married
- white male
- protestant
- northern European ancestry

In the 2008 presidential election, Barack Obama presented himself as a new type of presidential candidate.

Term and Tenure

The concept of a popularly elected president is an American invention. After much debate and compromise, the Founding Fathers created a single executive, elected indirectly through an electoral college for a four-year term. Until the addition of the Twenty-Second Amendment in 1951, the number of terms of the president was unlimited. After Franklin D. Roosevelt won the office an unprecedented four times, the Twenty-Second Amendment was added, limiting the president to two elected terms.

Succession and Disability

The Constitution provides that if the president can no longer serve in office, the vice president will carry out the powers and duties of the office. The Constitution does not state that the vice president shall actually become president; that tradition began with the death of W. H. Harrison. After the assassination of John F. Kennedy, the Twenty-Fifth Amendment was added to the Constitution, stating that the vice president becomes president if the office of president becomes vacant. That amendment also provides for the new president to nominate a new vice president, with the approval of a majority of both houses of Congress. The first use of the Twenty-Fifth Amendment occurred when Spiro Agnew resigned the vice presidency and was replaced by Gerald Ford in 1973. The following year it was used again when President Richard Nixon resigned; Vice President Gerald Ford became president; and Ford nominated, and Congress confirmed, Nelson Rockefeller as his new vice president.

The Twenty-Fifth Amendment also provides for presidential disability. If the president is unable to perform the duties of his office, the vice president may become "acting president" under one of the following conditions:

- The president informs Congress of the inability to perform the duties of president.
- The vice president and a majority of the cabinet inform Congress, in writing, that the president is disabled and unable to perform those duties.

The president may resume the duties of office upon informing Congress that no disability exists. If the vice president and a majority of the cabinet disagree, Congress has 21 days to decide the issue of presidential disability by a two-thirds vote of both houses.

Impeachment and Removal

The Constitution allows for the removal of a president from office through the impeachment process. **Impeachment** involves bringing charges of wrongdoing against a government official. The United States Constitution gives the House of Representatives the authority to impeach the president or vice president for "Treason, Bribery or other High Crimes and Misdemeanors." Once charges of impeachment have been levied against the president or vice president, the Senate then sits in judgment of the charges. The chief justice of the Supreme Court presides over the trial. If found guilty of the charges, the official may be removed from office. Conviction requires a two-thirds vote of the Senate.

The Road to the White House

There are two basic methods of becoming president: succeed to the office or win election to the office. Most presidents have been elected to the office. Many nominees seeking the office have gained political experience through elected or appointed offices—in Congress (mostly the Senate), as state governors, as vice president, or as a cabinet member. Several nominees gained recognition as military leaders.

The Electoral College System

According to the Constitution and the Twelfth Amendment, an **electoral college** elects the president and vice president. Each state chooses a number of electors equal to its number of members in the House of Representatives and Senate in a method set by the state legislatures. In the general election, voters go to the polls and vote for the candidates of their choice. In December, the electors of the respective candidates meet in each state capital to cast ballots for president and vice president. The electoral college then sends the ballots to the president of the Senate, where they are opened before a joint session of Congress and counted. To win the election, a candidate must receive a majority of electoral votes (270). If no candidate for president receives a majority of electoral votes, the House of Representatives chooses the president from among the top three candidates. If no candidate for vice president receives a majority of electoral votes, the Senate chooses the vice president from the top two candidates.

The Vice Presidency

During much of American history, the office of the vice president has been seen as one to be avoided by ambitious politicians. Constitutionally, the vice president has two duties:

- preside over the Senate, casting tie-breaking votes if necessary
- help determine presidential disability under the Twenty-Fifth Amendment and take over the presidency if necessary

Because the vice president may some day become president, the formal qualifications for vice president are the same as those for the president. The vice president serves a four-year term; however, the number of terms a vice president may serve is not limited. The selection of the nominee for vice president occurs at the national convention when the presidential nominee selects a "running mate." Often the choice of nominee is influenced by the party's desire to balance the ticket; that is, to improve a candidate's chances of winning the election by choosing someone from a different faction of the party or from a different geographic section of the country. With the assassination of Kennedy and attempts on the lives of Ford and Reagan, more attention has focused on the vice president. Today, the vice president is often given a larger role in government, taking part in cabinet meetings, serving on the National Security Council, and acting as the president's representative on diplomatic missions. More consideration is also given to the background, health, and other qualifications of vice presidents.

Presidential Powers

Article II of the Constitution outlines the powers of the president. The checks and balances of the other branches of government limit them. The power of the modern presidency comes from the men who have held the office and have shaped the use of these powers. Historians have often rated presidents as strong or weak. After the 1960s and 1970s, Arthur Schlesinger, Jr., argued that the presidency had become so powerful that an "imperial presidency" existed, applying the term to Richard Nixon and his administration in particular. Richard Neustadt contended that the president's powers lie in the ability to persuade others through negotiation, influence, and compromise. From 2002 to 2008 President George W. Bush and Vice President Dick Cheney argued for greatly expanded powers for the presidency in both domestic and foreign affairs.

Presidential powers can be categorized as executive, legislative, diplomatic, military, judicial, and party powers.

Executive Powers

- enforces laws, treaties, and court decisions
- issues **executive orders** to carry out policies
- appoints officials; removes officials
- assumes emergency powers
- presides over the cabinet and executive branch

Legislative Powers

- Gives annual State of the Union message (constitutionally required) identifying problems, recommending policies, and submitting specific proposals (president's legislative agenda). Expectations are that the president will propose a comprehensive legislative program to deal with national problems (the Budget and Accounting Act of 1921 requires the president to prepare and propose a federal budget).
- Issues annual budget and economic reports.
- Signs or vetoes bills.
- Proposes legislation and uses influence to get it passed.
- Calls for special sessions of Congress.

Diplomatic Powers

- appoints ambassadors and other diplomats
- negotiates treaties and **executive agreements**
- meets with foreign leaders in international conferences
- accords diplomatic recognition to foreign governments
- receives foreign dignitaries

Military Powers

- serves as commander-in-chief of the armed forces
- has final decision-making authority in matters of national and foreign defense
- provides for domestic order

Judicial Powers
- appoints members of the federal judiciary
- grants reprieves, **pardons**, and amnesty

Party Powers
- is the recognized leader of the party
- chooses vice-presidential nominee
- strengthens the party by helping members get elected (coattails)
- appoints party members to government positions (patronage)
- influences policies and platform of the party

Limitations on Presidential Powers

In order to avoid the possibility of abuses by the executive, the Founding Fathers provided for checks upon the powers of the executive.

- Congressional checks
  — Override presidential vetoes; requires a two-thirds vote of both houses of Congress.
  — Power of the purse; agency budgets must be authorized and appropriated by Congress. In 1974 Congress passed the Congressional Budget and **Impoundment** Control Act, which denied the president the right to refuse to spend money appropriated by Congress and gave Congress a greater role in the budget process.
  — Power of impeachment.
  — Approval powers over appointments.
  — Legislation that limits the president's powers (for example, the **War Powers Act** limited the president's ability to use military force).
  — **Legislative vetoes** to reject the actions of the president or executive agency by a vote of one or both houses of Congress without the consent of the president; declared unconstitutional by the Supreme Court in 1983.
- Judicial checks—Judicial review of executive actions
- Political checks
  — public opinion
  — media attention
  — popularity

Presidential Character

Political scientist James David Barber examined the importance of a president's personality and character, classifying presidents into four distinct types based on their childhood and other experiences. Barber measured each president's assertiveness in office as active or passive, and how positive or negative his feelings were about the office itself. His classifications were:

- *active-positive*—takes pleasure in the work of the office, easily adjusts to new situations and is confident in himself (FDR, Truman, Kennedy, Ford, Carter, Bush)
- *active-negative*—hard worker but doesn't enjoy the work, insecure in the position, may be obsessive or antagonistic (Wilson, Hoover, LBJ, Nixon)

- *passive-positive*—easygoing, wanting agreement from others with no dissent, may be overly confident (Taft, Harding, Reagan)
- *passive-negative*—dislikes politics and tends to withdraw from close relationships (Coolidge, Eisenhower)

The Bureaucracy

A **bureaucracy** is a systematic way of organizing a complex and large administrative structure. The bureaucracy is responsible for carrying out the day-to-day tasks of the organization. The bureaucracy of the federal government is the single largest in the United States, with 2.8 million employees. Bureaucracies generally follow three basic principles:

- *hierarchical authority*—similar to a pyramid, with those at the top having authority over those below
- *job specialization*—each worker has defined duties and responsibilities, a division of labor among workers
- *formal rules*—established regulations and procedures that must be followed

History and Growth

- *beginnings*—standards for office included qualifications and political acceptability
- *spoils system*—practice of giving offices and government favors to political supporters and friends
- *reform movement*—competitive exams were tried but failed due to inadequate funding from Congress
- *Pendleton Act*—Civil Service Act of 1883, passed after the assassination of Garfield by a disappointed office-seeker; replaced the spoils system with a merit system as the basis for hiring and promotion
- **Hatch Act** *of 1939, amended in 1993*—prohibits government employees from engaging in political activities while on duty or running for office or seeking political funding while off duty; if in sensitive positions, may not be involved with political activities on or off duty
- *Civil Service Reform Act of 1978*—created the Office of Personnel Management (replaced the Civil Service Commission) to recruit, train, and establish classifications and salaries for federal employees

Organization

The federal bureaucracy is generally divided into four basic types:

- **cabinet** *departments*—15 executive departments created to advise the president and operate a specific policy area of governmental activity (Department of State, Department of Labor, Department of the Interior); each department is headed by a secretary, except the Department of Justice, which is headed by the attorney general
- *independent executive agencies*—similar to departments but without cabinet status (NASA, Small Business Administration)
- *independent regulatory agencies*—independent from the executive; created to regulate or police (Securities and Exchange Commission, Nuclear Regulatory Commission, Federal Reserve Board)

- *government corporations*—created by Congress to carry out business-like activities; generally charge for services (Tennessee Valley Authority, National Railroad Passenger Corporation [AMTRAK], United States Postal Service)

Influences on the Federal Bureaucracy

- *executive influences*—appointing the right people, issuing executive orders, affecting the agency's budget, reorganization of the agency
- *Congressional influences*—influencing appointments, affecting the agency's budget, holding hearings, rewriting legislation or making legislation more detailed
- **iron triangles** *(subgovernments)*—iron triangles are alliances that develop between bureaucratic agencies, interest groups, and congressional committees or subcommittees. Because of a common goal, these alliances may work to help each other achieve their goals, with Congress and the president often deferring to their influence.
- **issue networks**—individuals in Washington—located within interest groups, congressional staff, think tanks, universities, and the media—who regularly discuss and advocate public policies. Unlike iron triangles, issue networks continually form and disband according to the policy issues.

The Executive Office of the President (EOP)

The Executive Office of the President includes the closest advisors to the president. Although it was established in 1939, every president has reorganized the EOP according to his style of leadership. Within the executive office are several separate agencies.

- *White House Office*—personal and political staff members who help with the day-to-day management of the executive branch; includes the chief of staff, counsel to the president, press secretary
- *National Security Council*—established by the National Security Act of 1947; advises the president on matters of domestic and foreign national security
- *Office of Management and Budget*—helps the president prepare the annual federal budget
- *Office of Faith-Based and Community Initiatives*—created by George W. Bush to encourage and expand private efforts to deal with social problems
- *Office of National Drug Control Policy*—advisory and planning agency to combat the nation's drug problems
- *Office of Policy Development*—gives the president domestic policy advice
- *Council of Economic Advisors*—informs the president about economic developments and problems
- *Office of U.S. Trade Representative*—advises the president about foreign trade and helps negotiate foreign trade agreements
- *Office of Administration*—provides administrative services to personnel of the EOC and gives direct support services to the president
- *Council on Environmental Quality*—coordinates federal environmental efforts and analyzes environmental policies and initiatives
- *Office of Science and Technology Policy*—advises the president on the effects of science and technology on domestic and international affairs; it also works with the private sector and state and local governments to implement effective science and technology policies
- *Office of the Vice President*—consists of the vice president's staff

Executive Departments

- *State (1789)*—advises the president on foreign policy, negotiates treaties, represents the United States in international organizations
- *Treasury (1789)*—collects federal revenues; pays federal bills; mints coins and prints paper money; enforces alcohol, tobacco and firearm laws
- *Defense (1789)*—formed from the Department of War and the Department of the Navy (1789) but changed to the Department of Defense in 1947; manages the armed forces, operates military bases
- *Interior (1849)*—manages federal lands, refuges, and parks; operates hydroelectric facilities; manages Native American affairs
- *Justice (1870)*—provides legal advice to the president, enforces federal laws, represents the United States in court, operates federal prisons
- *Agriculture (1889)*—provides agricultural assistance to farmers and ranchers, inspects food, manages national forests
- *Commerce (1903)*—grants patents and trademarks; conducts the national census; promotes international trade
- *Labor (1913)*—enforces federal labor laws (child labor, minimum wage, safe working conditions); administers unemployment and job training programs
- *Health and Human Services (1953)*—administers Social Security and Medicare/Medicaid programs; promotes health care research; enforces pure food and drug laws
- *Housing and Urban Development (1965)*—provides home financing and public housing programs, enforces fair housing laws
- *Transportation (1967)*—promotes mass transit programs and programs for highways, railroads, and air traffic; enforces maritime law
- *Energy (1977)*—promotes development and conservation of fossil fuels, nuclear energy, research programs
- *Education (1979)*—administers federal aid programs to schools; engages in educational research
- *Veterans' Affairs (1989)*—promotes the welfare of veterans of the armed forces
- *Homeland Security (2002)*—prevents terrorist attacks within the United States, reduces America's susceptibility to terrorism, and minimizes damage and helps recovery from attacks that do occur; includes Coast Guard, Secret Service, Border Patrol, Immigration and Visa Services, and Federal Emergency Management Agency (FEMA)

❯ Review Questions

1. The office of the president of the United States can best be described as an office
   (A) of great responsibility and function
   (B) created as a mere ceremonial head of state
   (C) full of conflict and by nature difficult to understand
   (D) untouched by the power and experience of the person holding it
   (E) dedicated to the service of the government beyond the will of the people

2. Which of the following amendments provides for presidential succession and disability?
   (A) Twenty-Second
   (B) Twentieth
   (C) Twenty-Fifth
   (D) Twenty-Third
   (E) Twenty-Seventh

3. When the Founding Fathers finally decided on the length of the presidential term of office, they established a term
   (A) of 8 years
   (B) of 4 years
   (C) not to exceed 10 years
   (D) that could not be renewed after 4 years
   (E) that could extend indefinitely if reviewed by Congress

4. Which of the following is a constitutional qualification for being president?
   I.   must be at least 35 years old
   II. must be a natural-born citizen
   III. must have lived in the United States for at least 14 years
   IV. must be a naturalized citizen within the first five years of birth
   (A) I and II only
   (B) II and III only
   (C) II, III, and IV only
   (D) I, II, III only
   (E) I, II, III, and IV

5. If the president becomes disabled and cannot perform his duties, how may the vice president take over the office of the president?
   I.   The president may write a letter to the leaders of Congress stating lack of ability to perform the duties of office.
   II. Congress removes the president.
   III. The vice president and a majority of the cabinet may remove the president.
   (A) I only
   (B) II only
   (C) I and II only
   (D) II and III only
   (E) I and III only

6. Which of the following is NOT considered to be a part of the Executive Office of the President?
   (A) National Security Council
   (B) White House Office
   (C) Office of Management and Budget
   (D) Office of Personnel Management
   (E) Council of Economic Advisors

7. Members of the president's cabinet are usually individuals of great ability but little or no political power. Which of the following best describes this statement?
   (A) The Senate must approve all appointments made by the president.
   (B) The primary functions of cabinet members are to effectively run a department of government and advise the president.
   (C) Cabinet members serve as long as the president remains in office.
   (D) Cabinet members serve as an informal advisory body.
   (E) Only the president may appoint and remove members of the cabinet.

8. Which of the following was NOT an original cabinet position?
   (A) secretary of state
   (B) secretary of war
   (C) attorney general
   (D) secretary of the interior
   (E) secretary of the treasury

9. Which of the following powers is used by the president for the purpose of enforcing federal law?
   (A) general administrative power
   (B) veto power
   (C) executive agreements
   (D) patronage
   (E) judicial power

10. The partisan power of the president is most recognizable in the fact that the president
    (A) is an elected leader
    (B) checks the power of the party controlling Congress
    (C) is the head of a political party
    (D) alone must write the party platform
    (E) appoints all party members

› Answers and Explanations

1. **A.** The presidency is the most important single office in the United States, and the powers of the president extend beyond just ceremonial duties (B). The roles and powers of the presidency are clearly defined by Article II of the Constitution (C, E). The power and experience of the president contributes to the prestige of the office (D).

2. **C.** The Twenty-Fifth Amendment provides for succession and disability. The Twenty-Second Amendment (A) deals with presidential tenure. The Twentieth Amendment (B) sets the beginning dates of the terms for the president, vice president, and members of Congress. The Twenty-Third Amendment (D) provides presidential electors for the District of Columbia. The Twenty-Seventh Amendment (E) deals with salary increases for members of Congress.

3. **B.** The term of office for the president is four years.

4. **D.** There are three formal qualifications for president outlined in the Constitution: he or she must be at least 35 years of age, must be a natural-born citizen of the United States, and must have lived in the United States for at least 14 years.

5. **E.** Either the president may inform Congress of his or her inability to perform the duties of office, or the vice president and a majority of the cabinet may inform Congress of the president's inability to perform his or her duties.

6. **D.** The Office of Personnel Management is an independent agency that is not a part of the EOC. The other answer choices are offices in the EOC.

7. **B.** Cabinet members must possess the administrative skills necessary to run a cabinet-level department as well as to advise the president. At the same time, they serve largely at the request of the president (C, D, E) and by approval of the Senate (A).

8. **D.** The secretary of the interior was not added to the cabinet until 1849. Washington's cabinet was composed of secretaries of state (A), war (B), and the treasury (E) in addition to an attorney general (C).

9. **A.** The president uses administrative powers to enforce federal laws. The president's veto power (B) is a legislative power; executive agreements (C) are included in the president's diplomatic powers. Patronage (D) is the practice of offering political positions or jobs to friends and supporters. The president's judicial power (E) includes appointing members of the federal judiciary and granting pardons, reprieves, and amnesty.

10. **C.** The president serves as the elected leader of his or her political party (A).

> Rapid Review

- Article II of the Constitution establishes the office of the president and outlines the powers and duties of the office.
- The presidency was a compromise creating a single executive with limited powers.
- There are both formal and informal qualifications for the president.
- The Twenty-Fifth Amendment provides for the succession and disability of the president.
- The House of Representatives impeaches and the Senate tries cases of impeachment of the president. Only two presidents have been impeached, and none has been removed from office.
- To become president one must succeed to the office or win election to the office.
- The electoral college is an indirect method of electing the president.
- The constitutional duties of the vice president include presiding over the Senate and determining presidential disability.
- Presidents have numerous powers: executive, legislative, diplomatic, military, judicial, and party.
- The powers of the president may be limited by congressional, judicial, and political checks.
- James David Barber described presidential personality and character by classifying presidents as one of four distinct types: active-positive, passive-positive, active-negative, and passive-negative.
- The bureaucracy is a systematic way of organizing government.
- The development of the current bureaucracy has undergone several changes and reforms.
- The organization of the bureaucracy may be divided into four major types: cabinet departments, independent executive agencies, independent regulatory agencies, and government corporations.
- The executive, Congress, iron triangles, and issue networks may influence the federal bureaucracy.
- There are currently 15 executive departments in the executive branch of government.

CHAPTER 14

The National Judiciary

IN THIS CHAPTER

Summary: The United States has a dual system of courts—a federal court system and the court systems of each of the 50 states. Under the Articles of Confederation, there was no national court system. State courts had the sole power to interpret and apply laws. This weakness led to Article III of the Constitution, which states that there shall be one Supreme Court and that Congress may establish a system of inferior courts.

Key Terms

jurisdiction	senatorial courtesy	concurring opinion
original jurisdiction	rule of four	dissenting opinion
appellate jurisdiction	brief orders	precedents
concurrent jurisdiction	*writ of certiorari*	executive privilege
constitutional courts	certificate	judicial activism
district courts	brief	judicial restraint
Courts of Appeals	*amicus curiae* briefs	strict constructionist
legislative courts	majority opinion	loose constructionist

The Federal Court System

Jurisdiction

Jurisdiction is the authority of the courts to hear certain cases. Under the Constitution, federal courts have jurisdiction in cases involving federal law, treaties, and the interpretation of the Constitution.

- ***original jurisdiction***—Lower courts have the authority to hear cases for the first time; in the federal system district courts and the Supreme Court (in a limited number of cases) have original jurisdiction where trials are conducted, evidence is presented, and juries determine the outcome of the case.

- *appellate jurisdiction*—Courts that hear reviews or appeals of decisions from the lower courts; Courts of Appeals and the Supreme Court have appellate jurisdiction.
- *concurrent jurisdiction*—Allows certain types of cases to be tried in either the federal or state courts.

Structure of the Judicial System

The federal judicial system consists of constitutional courts and legislative courts. **Constitutional courts** are the federal courts created by Congress under Article III of the Constitution and the Supreme Court. Also included are the **district courts**, **Courts of Appeals**, Court of Appeals for the Federal Circuit, and the U.S. Court of International Trade. Congress has created special or **legislative courts** (Territorial Courts, U.S. Tax Court, U.S. Court of Appeals for the Armed Forces) to hear cases arising from the powers given to Congress under Article I. These legislative courts have a narrower range of authority than the constitutional courts.

District Courts

Congress, under the Judiciary Act of 1789, created the district courts to serve as trial courts at the federal level. Every state has at least one district court; larger states may have several, with Washington D.C., and Puerto Rico each having one court. There are currently 94 districts. The district courts have original jurisdiction; they do not hear appeals. District courts decide civil and criminal cases arising under the Constitution and federal laws or treaties. More than 80% of all federal cases are heard in the district courts.

Courts of Appeals

Congress created the Courts of Appeals in 1891 to help lessen the work load of the Supreme Court. The Courts of Appeals decide appeals from United States district courts and review decisions of federal administrative agencies. There are 13 United States Courts of Appeals. The states are divided into circuits, or geographic judicial districts. There is also a circuit for Washington, D.C., and a Federal Circuit, which hears cases involving federal agencies. The Courts of Appeals have appellate jurisdiction only; they may only review cases already decided by a lower court. A panel of judges decides cases in the Courts of Appeals.

Supreme Court

The only court actually created directly by the Constitution is the Supreme Court. It is the highest court in the federal judicial system. It is the final authority in dealing with all questions arising from the Constitution, federal laws, and treaties. The Supreme Court has both original and appellate jurisdiction. Most of the cases heard in the Supreme Court are on appeal from the district and appellate courts of the federal judicial system; however, cases may come to the Supreme Court from state Supreme Courts, if a federal law or the Constitution is involved. The United States Supreme Court may also hear cases of original jurisdiction if the cases involve representatives of a foreign government, or certain types of cases where a state is a party.

The decisions of the Supreme Court may have a strong impact on social, economic, and political forces in our society. Congress establishes the size of the Supreme Court, having the power to change the number of justices. The current size of the Supreme Court was set in 1869. Today, the Supreme Court consists of nine judges—eight associate justices and one chief justice. They are all nominated by the president and confirmed by the Senate.

Judicial Selection

The president appoints federal judges, with confirmation by the Senate. Under the Constitution, there are no formal qualifications for federal judges. Federal judges serve "during good behavior," which generally means for life. The notion of the life term was to allow judges to be free from political pressures when deciding cases. Federal judges may be removed from office through impeachment and conviction.

Lower Courts

Because of the large number of appointments made to the lower courts, the Department of Justice and White House staff handle most of these nominations. **Senatorial courtesy**, the practice of allowing individual senators who represent the state where the district is located to approve or disapprove potential nominees, has traditionally been used to make appointments to the District Courts. Because the circuits for the Courts of Appeals cover several states, individual senators have less influence and senatorial courtesy does not play a role in the nomination process. The Senate tends to scrutinize appeals court judges more closely, since they are more likely to interpret the law and set precedent.

Supreme Court

The higher visibility and importance of the Supreme Court demands that the president give greater attention to the nomination of Supreme Court justices. Presidents only make appointments to the Supreme Court if a vacancy occurs during their term of office. When making appointments, presidents often consider:

- *party affiliation*—choosing judges from their own political party
- *judicial philosophy*—appointing judges who share their political ideology
- *race, gender, religion, region*—considering these criteria may help bring balance to the court or satisfy certain segments of society
- *judicial experience*—previous judicial experience as judges in district courts, courts of appeals, state courts
- *"litmus test"*—a test of ideological purity toward a liberal or conservative stand on certain issues such as abortion
- *acceptability*—noncontroversial and therefore acceptable to members of the Senate Judiciary Committee and the Senate
  - American Bar Association—The largest national organization of attorneys; often consulted by presidents; rates nominees' qualifications.
  - interest groups—May support or oppose a nominee based on his or her position on issues of importance to the interest group; use lobbyists to pressure senators.
  - Justices—Endorsements from members of the Supreme Court may help a nominee.

Background of Judges

Almost all federal judges have had some form of legal training, have held positions in government, or have served as lawyers for leading law firms, as federal district attorneys, or as law school professors. Some federal judges have served as state court judges. Until recently, few African Americans, Hispanics, or women were appointed as judges to the lower federal courts. Lyndon Johnson appointed the first African American, Thurgood Marshall, to the Supreme Court; Ronald Reagan appointed the first woman, Sandra Day O'Connor.

The Court at Work

The term of the Supreme Court begins on the first Monday in October and generally lasts until June or July of the following year.

Accepting Cases

Thousands of cases are appealed to the Supreme Court every year; only a few hundred cases are actually heard. Most of the cases are denied because the justices either agree with the lower court decision or believe that the cases does not involve a significant point of law. Cases that are accepted for review must pass the **rule of four**—four of the nine justices must agree to hear the case. Many of the cases accepted may be disposed of in **brief orders**— returned to the lower court for reconsideration because of a related case that was recently decided. Those cases presented to the Supreme Court for possible review may be appealed through:

- *writ of certiorari*—An order by the Court (when petitioned) directing a lower court to send up the records of a case for review; usually requires the need to interpret law or decide a constitutional question.
- *certificate*—A lower court may ask the Supreme Court about a rule of law or procedures in specific cases.

Briefs and Oral Arguments

Once a case reaches the Supreme Court, lawyers for each party to the case file a written **brief**. A brief is a detailed statement of the facts of the case supporting a particular position by presenting arguments based on relevant facts and citations from previous cases. Interested parties may also be invited to submit *amicus curiae* ("friends of the court") **briefs**, supporting or rejecting arguments of the case.

Oral arguments allow both sides to present their positions to the justices during a 30-minute period. Justices may interrupt the lawyers during this time, raising questions or challenging points of law.

Research and Conferences

Justices use law clerks to research the information presented in oral arguments and briefs. Throughout the term, the justices meet in private conferences to consider cases heard in oral argument, with the chief justice presiding over the conferences. Each justice may speak about the cases under discussion. An informal poll determines how each justice is leaning in the case.

Writing Opinions

Once the Supreme Court has made a decision in a case, the decision is explained in a written statement called an opinion. If voting with the majority, the chief justice selects who will write the opinion; if voting with the minority, the most senior associate justice of the majority selects who will write the opinion.

- *majority opinion*—a majority of the justices agree on the decision and its reasons
- *concurring opinion*—a justice who agrees with the majority opinion but not with the reasoning behind the decision
- *dissenting opinion*—a justice or justices who disagree with the majority opinion

Opinions of the Supreme Court are as important as the decisions they explain. Majority opinions become **precedents**, standards or guides to be followed in deciding similar cases in the future.

Courts as Policymakers

New Deal Era

Controversy surrounded the Supreme Court during the New Deal era, as Congress passed numerous laws designed to end the Depression and the conservative court ruled these laws unconstitutional. In response, Franklin Roosevelt proposed what opponents termed a "court-packing plan" to increase the number of justices, allowing Roosevelt to appoint justices supportive of New Deal legislation. Although Congress did not pass Roosevelt's plan to expand the Court, two justices, Chief Justice Charles Evans Hughes and Associate Justice Owen Roberts, began voting in favor of New Deal legislation (sometimes referred to as "the switch in time to save nine").

The Warren Court (1953–1969)

Often termed "the most liberal court ever," the Warren Court under Chief Justice Earl Warren was especially active in the area of civil rights and civil liberties. This Court heard *Brown v. Board of Education* (1954), declaring segregation in public schools unconstitutional. The Warren Court also expanded the rights of criminal defendants in *Gideon v. Wainwright* (1963) and *Miranda v. Arizona* (1966).

The Burger Court (1969–1986)

Richard Nixon's appointment of Warren Burger as chief justice returned the Supreme Court to a more conservative ideology with regard to narrowing the rights of defendants. The Burger Court permitted abortions in *Roe v. Wade* (1973) and ruled that Nixon did not have **executive privilege** over information in a criminal proceeding in *U.S. v. Nixon* (1974). In *Regents of the University of California v. Bakke* (1978), the Court ruled against the use of quotas in the admissions process. At the same time, the Court upheld the legality of affirmative action.

The Rehnquist and Roberts Courts (1986–present)

The conservative court under Chief Justice William Rehnquist continued to limit, but not reverse, decisions of the earlier more liberal courts in the areas of defendants' rights, abortion (*Planned Parenthood v. Casey*, 1992), and affirmative action. The court of Chief Justice John Roberts (2005–) continued the conservative ideology of the Rehnquist Court. In 2007 the Roberts Court upheld the federal Partial-Birth Abortion Act of 2003. Two new Supreme

Court justices (Sonia Sotomayor and Elena Kagan) were sworn in during the first two years of the Obama administration; the impact of these appointments on the complexion and outlook of the Supreme Court is still to be determined.

Judicial Philosophy

KEY IDEA

Judicial philosophy of activism or restraint is not the same as political philosophy such as liberal or conservative. Although some recent justices who supported an activist philosophy (Warren and T. Marshall) were also more liberal, this has not always been the case. The Marshall Court was activist in establishing judicial review but conservative in protecting property rights.

Judicial Activism

The philosophy of **judicial activism**, or judicial intervention, holds that the Court should play an active role in determining national policies. The philosophy advocates applying the Constitution to social and political questions, especially where constitutional rights have been violated or unacceptable conditions exist.

Judicial Restraint

The philosophy of **judicial restraint** holds that the court should avoid taking the initiative on social and political questions, operating strictly within the limits of the Constitution and upholding acts of Congress unless the acts clearly violate specific provisions of the Constitution. Judicial restraint involves only a limited use of judicial powers and advocates the belief that the court should be more passive, allowing the executive and legislative branches to lead the way in policymaking.

› Review Questions

1. Under the guidelines of the Constitution, which of the following is NOT within the jurisdiction of the federal courts?
   (A) cases involving federal law
   (B) cases involving interpretation of state constitutions
   (C) cases involving interpretation of the federal Constitution
   (D) treaties
   (E) cases involving territories

2. Federal courts created by Congress under Article III of the Constitution include the Supreme Court, district courts, the Courts of Appeals, Court of Appeals for the Federal Circuit, and the U.S. Court of International Trade. These courts can best be described as
   (A) legislative courts
   (B) territorial courts
   (C) constitutional courts
   (D) original courts
   (E) inferior courts

3. What type of jurisdiction does the Supreme Court have?
   I. original
   II. appellate
   III. concurrent
      (A) I only
      (B) II only
      (C) III only
      (D) I and II
      (E) I, II, and III

4. Which of the following best describes the formal qualifications for a federal judge?
   (A) They serve "during good behavior."
   (B) The president appoints them with the approval of the House of Representatives.
   (C) They serve at the discretion of the president.
   (D) They serve at the discretion of the Congress.
   (E) They have no formal qualification other than being a loyal follower of the president.

5. Which of the following has little bearing when the president makes an appointment to the Supreme Court?
   (A) party affiliation
   (B) judicial philosophy
   (C) likability
   (D) "litmus test"
   (E) judicial experience

6. Who was the first president to appoint an African American to the Supreme Court?
   (A) Richard Nixon
   (B) Lyndon Johnson
   (C) Ronald Reagan
   (D) John Kennedy
   (E) Jimmy Carter

7. Which of the following terms best describes the Supreme Court's issuance of an order directing a lower court to send up its record for review?
   (A) certificate
   (B) rule of four
   (C) *amicus curiae*
   (D) *writ of certiorari*
   (E) brief order

8. The majority opinion, issued by the Supreme Court as the final decision of a case, becomes the standard or guide that will be followed in deciding similar cases in the future. This standard or guide is known as a
   (A) precedent
   (B) brief
   (C) argument
   (D) decision
   (E) poll of the court

9. Which of the following courts was first known for narrowing the rights of defendants?
   (A) Warren Court
   (B) Rehnquist Court
   (C) Burger Court
   (D) New Deal Court
   (E) Nixon Court

10. The judicial philosophy that advocates the courts' active role in policymaking is called
    (A) strict constructionist
    (B) judicial activism
    (C) loose constructionist
    (D) judicial restraint
    (E) liberalism

› Answers and Explanations

1. **B.** Cases involving state constitutions are heard in state courts, not federal courts. The other answer choices are within the jurisdiction of the federal courts.

2. **C.** Constitutional courts include the Supreme Court, district courts, the Courts of Appeals, the Court of Appeals for the Federal Circuit, and the U.S. Court of International Trade. Legislative courts (A) hear cases arising from the powers given to Congress under Article I. Territorial courts (B) are a type of legislative court. There are courts with original jurisdiction, but there are no courts termed "original courts" (D). Inferior courts (E) are federal courts below the Supreme Court.

3. **D.** The Supreme Court has both original and appellate jurisdiction.

4. **A.** There are no constitutional (formal) qualifications for federal judges (E). They are appointed by the president with confirmation by the Senate (B) and serve during "good behavior" (A, C, D).

5. **C.** The nominee's personality is not a primary consideration in the nomination process. The president may consider party affiliation (A), judicial philosophy (B), and judicial experience (E) when appointing justices to the Supreme Court. A "litmus test" may also serve as a gauge of the nominee's purity toward a liberal or conservative stand on certain issues (D).

6. **B.** In 1967 Lyndon Johnson appointed Thurgood Marshall, who became the first African American on the Supreme Court.

7. **D.** A *writ of certiorari* is a court order directing a lower court to send up the records of a case for review. A certificate (A) is an appeal in which a lower court asks the Supreme Court about a rule of law or procedures. The rule of four (B) means that, in order for a case to be considered by the Supreme Court, four of the nine justices must agree to hear the case. An *amicus curiae* brief (C) is a statement written by interested parties to a court case. A brief order (E) is a document issued by the Supreme Court that returns a case to a lower court for reconsideration.

8. **A.** A precedent is a standard used by the courts to decide similar cases. A brief (B) is a detailed statement of the facts of a case supporting a particular position. An argument (C) is the presentation of a case before a court. A decision (D) is the final ruling of a court. A poll of the court (E) occurs in conference to determine how each justice is leaning in the case.

9. **C.** The Supreme Court under Chief Justice Warren Burger was the first to narrow the rights of defendants after those rights were broadened under the Warren Court (A). The Rehnquist Court (B) continued to narrow the rights of defendants. The New Deal Court (D) focused on consideration of laws designed to end the Great Depression. There was no Nixon Court (E).

10. **B.** The philosophy of judicial activism advocates policymaking by the courts. A strict constructionist (A) view holds that justices should base decisions on a narrow interpretation of the Constitution. A loose constructionist view (C) believes that judges should have freedom in interpreting the Constitution. Judicial restraint (D) is a philosophy that holds that the court should avoid taking the initiative on social and political questions (D). Liberalism (E) is a political philosophy favoring broad government involvement in business, social welfare, and minority rights.

› Rapid Review

- Article III of the Constitution establishes the Supreme Court and a system of inferior courts.
- Jurisdiction is the authority of the federal courts to hear certain cases. Jurisdiction may be original, appellate, or concurrent.
- The Supreme Court, the Courts of Appeals, and district courts are constitutional courts.
- The Supreme Court was created directly by the Constitution. It is the highest court in the United States, having both original and appellate jurisdiction.
- Federal judges are appointed by the president and confirmed by a majority of the Senate.
- Presidents make appointments to the Supreme Court only when a vacancy occurs during a president's term of office.
- Almost all federal judges have some form of legal training.
- The Supreme Court hears only a few hundred cases each year from the several thousand cases submitted.
- Cases may be presented to the Supreme Court for possible review by *writ of certiorari*, certificate, or the submission of an *amicus curiae* brief.
- Oral arguments allow both sides time to present their arguments to the justices.
- Law clerks research information presented in oral arguments and briefs.
- Supreme Court decisions are explained in written statements known as opinions. Opinions may be majority, concurring, or dissenting.
- Courts are often termed liberal or conservative, depending on the decisions of the court and the guidance of the chief justice.
- Judicial philosophy may follow the lines of judicial activism or judicial restraint.

CHAPTER 15

Civil Liberties and Civil Rights

IN THIS CHAPTER

Summary: In the Declaration of Independence, Thomas Jefferson wrote that all people "are endowed by their creator with certain unalienable rights." **Civil liberties** are those rights that belong to everyone; they are protections against government and are guaranteed by the Constitution, legislation, and judicial decisions. **Civil rights** are the positive acts of government, designed to prevent discrimination and provide equality before the law.

Key Terms

civil liberties
civil rights
writ of habeas corpus
bills of attainder
ex post facto laws
self-incrimination
double jeopardy
incorporation
symbolic speech

Establishment Clause
Free Exercise Clause
Lemon Test
pure speech
speech plus
prior restraint
substantive due process
procedural due process
eminent domain

exclusionary rule
Miranda v. Arizona
Plessy v. Ferguson
*Brown v. Board of
   Education*
Equal Protection Clause
affirmative action

Civil Liberties

- *Constitution*—The original Constitution mentions specific rights considered to be fundamental freedoms by the Founding Fathers:
  - **writ of habeas corpus**—You must be brought before the court and informed of charges against you.
  - no **bills of attainder**—You cannot be punished without a trial.

— no **ex post facto laws**—Laws applied to acts committed before the laws' passage are unconstitutional.

— trial by jury

- *Bill of Rights*—added in 1791 to the original Constitution to provide specific guarantees by the national government:

  — freedom of religion, speech, press, petition, and assembly

  — no unreasonable searches and seizure

  — protections against **self-incrimination** and **double jeopardy**

  — protections in criminal procedures

- *The Fourteenth Amendment provided for the expansion of individual rights*—The Supreme Court in *Gitlow v. New York* (1925) and subsequent cases has interpreted the Due Process Clause of the Fourteenth Amendment to apply the guarantees of the Bill of Rights to state and local governments (**incorporation**). Today, most guarantees of the Bill of Rights have been incorporated to apply to the state and local governments.
- *Legislative actions are laws that set limits or boundaries on one person's rights over another's or bring balance between the rights of individuals and the interests of society*—For example, false advertising is not protected under the First Amendment guarantee of freedom of speech.
- *Court decisions protect rights through the use of judicial review*—Flag burning (*Texas v. Johnson*, 1989) is protected, but burning a draft card (*United States v. O'Brien*, 1968) is not protected **symbolic speech.**

Freedom of Religion

Two protections for freedom of religion exist: the **Establishment Clause** and the **Free Exercise Clause.**

> *Congress shall make no law respecting an establishment of religion, or prohibiting the free exercise thereof.*—Amendment 1

The Establishment Clause

According to Thomas Jefferson, the Constitution creates a "wall of separation between Church and State." Because the church and government are separate in the United States, Congress cannot establish any religion as the national religion, nor favor one religion over another, nor tax American citizens to support any one religion. Controversy concerning the exact meaning and extent of the Establishment Clause has led to actions by the Supreme Court in defining the parameters of the clause, including:

- *Everson v. Board of Education (1947)*—The Court upheld a New Jersey policy of reimbursing parents of Catholic school students for the costs of busing their children to school.
- *Engel v. Vitale (1962)*—The Court ruled school-sanctioned prayer in public schools is unconstitutional.
- *Abington School District v. Schempp (1963)*—The Court struck down a Pennsylvania law requiring the reading of a Bible passage at the beginning of each day.
- *Lemon v. Kurtzman (1971)*—The Court struck down a Pennsylvania law reimbursing parochial schools for textbooks and teacher salaries and established the **Lemon Test**. To pass the test (1) a law must have a primarily secular purpose; (2) its principal effect must neither aid nor inhibit religion; and (3) it must not create excessive entanglement between government and religion.

- *Lynch v. Donnelly (1984)*—The Court upheld the right of governmental entities to celebrate the Christmas holiday with Christmas displays that might include nativity scenes, if secular displays are also sufficiently included.
- *Wallace v. Jaffree (1985)*—The Court overturned a state law setting aside time for "voluntary prayer" in public schools.
- *Edwards v. Aguillard (1987)*—The Court ruled that Louisiana could not force public schools that taught evolution to also teach creationism.
- *Board of Education of Westside Community Schools v. Mergens (1990)*—The Court upheld the Equal Access Act of 1984, which required public secondary schools to provide religious groups the same access to facilities that other extracurricular groups had.
- *Lee v. Weisman (1992)*—The Court ruled against clergy-led prayer at high school graduation ceremonies.
- *Santa Fe Independent School District v. Doe (2002)*—The Court overturned a Texas law allowing high school students to read a prayer at athletic events such as football games.

The Free Exercise Clause

The Free Exercise Clause guarantees the right to practice any religion or no religion at all. In its interpretations of the Free Exercise Clause, the Supreme Court has made distinctions between belief and practice. The Court has ruled that while religious belief is absolute, the practice of those beliefs may be restricted, especially if those practices conflict with criminal laws. For example:

- *Reynolds v. United States (1879)*—The Court upheld the federal law that prohibited polygamy even though Reynolds, a Mormon from Utah, claimed that the law limited his religious freedom.
- *Wisconsin v. Yoder (1972)*—The Court ruled that Wisconsin could not require Amish parents to send their children to public school beyond the eighth grade because it would violate long-held religious beliefs.
- *Employment Division of Oregon v. Smith (1990)*—The Court ruled that Oregon could deny unemployment benefits to workers fired for using drugs (peyote) as part of a religious ceremony.
- *Church of the Lukumi Babalu Aye v. City of Hialeah (1993)*—The Court ruled that laws banning animal sacrifice were unconstitutional because they targeted the Santeria religion.

In 1993 Congress passed the Religious Freedom Restoration Act, giving people the right to practice religious activities unless prohibited by laws that are narrowly tailored and the government can show a "compelling interest." In 1997 the Supreme Court ruled this law unconstitutional in *City of Boerne, Texas v. Flores*.

Freedom of Speech

Types of Speech

There are several different classifications of speech:

- *pure speech*—the most common form of speech, verbal speech; given the most protection by the courts
- *speech plus*—verbal and symbolic speech used together, such as a rally and then picketing; may also be limited

- *symbolic speech*—using actions and symbols to convey an idea rather than words (burning a draft card or flag, wearing an armband in protest); may be subject to government restrictions if it endangers public safety

Regulating Speech

KEY IDEA

Limitations on free speech have generally existed in the area of providing for national security. In 1798 Congress passed the Alien and Sedition Acts, making it illegal to say anything "false, scandalous and malicious against the government or its officials." Although these acts were aimed at the opponents of President John Adams and his Federalist supporters, others were convicted under these laws. The Alien and Sedition Acts were never challenged in court, and they expired in 1801.

After the assassination of President McKinley by an anarchist in 1901 and the entrance of the United States into World War I, Congress again passed sedition laws forbidding verbal attacks on the government, and the states began following suit. These and subsequent laws were challenged in the courts.

- *Schenck v. United States (1919)*—Schenck mailed fliers to draftees during World War I urging them to protest the draft peacefully; he was convicted of violating a federal law against encouraging the disobedience of military orders. Oliver Wendell Holmes wrote in the opinion that such speech was not protected during wartime because it would create a clear and present danger, establishing a standard for measuring what would and would not be protected speech.
- *Gitlow v. New York (1925)*—The Court applied the protections of free speech to the states under the due process clause of the Fourteenth Amendment.
- *Chaplinsky v. New Hampshire (1942)*—The Court ruled that the first amendment did not protect "fighting words."
- *Tinker v. Des Moines (1969)*—The Court ruled that wearing black armbands in protest of the Vietnam War was symbolic speech, protected by the First Amendment.
- *Brandenburg v. Ohio (1969)*—The Court made the "clear and present" danger test less restrictive by ruling that using inflammatory speech would be punished only if there was imminent danger that this speech would incite an illegal act.
- *Miller v. California (1973)*—The Court established the Miller test, which sets standards for measuring obscenity: (1) major theme appeals to indecent sexual desires applying contemporary community standards; (2) shows in clearly offensive way sexual behavior outlawed by state law; and (3) "lacks serious literary, artistic, political, or scientific value."
- *Texas v. Johnson (1989)*—The Court ruled that flag burning is a protected form of symbolic speech.
- *Reno v. ACLU (1997)*—The Court ruled the Communications Decency Act unconstitutional because it was "overly broad and vague" in regulating Internet speech.

Since the 1940s the Court has supported the preferred position doctrine: First Amendment freedoms are more fundamental than other freedoms because they provide a basis for other liberties; therefore, they hold a preferred position and laws regulating these freedoms must be shown to be absolutely necessary to be declared constitutional.

Freedom of the Press

Freedom of the press is often protected because it is closely related to freedom of speech; the press is used as a form of expression. Today the press includes newspapers, magazines, radio, television, and the Internet.

- *Near v. Minnesota (1931)*—The Court applied the protections of free press to the states under the Due Process Clause of the Fourteenth Amendment and prohibited **prior restraint**.
- *New York Times v. Sullivan (1964)*—The Court protected statements about public officials.
- *New York Times v. United States (1971)*—The Court reaffirmed its position of prior restraint, refusing to stop the publication of the Pentagon Papers.
- *Hazelwood School District v. Kuhlmeier (1988)*—The Court ruled in favor of school district censorship of student newspapers as long as censorship is related to legitimate concerns.

Freedom of Assembly and Petition

The First Amendment guarantees the "right of the people peacefully to assemble, and to petition the Government for a redress of grievances." Freedom of assembly and petition applies to both private and public places, allowing citizens to make their views known to government officials through petitions, letters, picketing, demonstrations, parades, and marches. The courts have protected these rights while allowing the government to set limits to protect the rights and safety of others.

- *Dejonge v. Oregon (1937)*—The Court established that the right of association (assembly) was as important as other First Amendment rights and used the Due Process Clause of the Fourteenth Amendment to apply freedom of assembly to the states.

The courts have generally ruled that:

- To protect public order, government may require groups wanting to parade or demonstrate to first obtain a permit.
- Certain public facilities (schools, airports, jails) not generally open to the public may be restricted from demonstrations.
- Restrictions on assembly must be worded precisely and must apply to all groups equally.
- The right to assemble does not allow groups to use private property for its own uses (creates buffer zones around abortion clinics).
- Police may disperse demonstrations in order to keep the peace or protect the public's safety (if demonstrations become violent or dangerous to public safety).

Property Rights

The Due Process Clause of the Fifth and Fourteenth Amendments provide for the protection of private property by guaranteeing that the government cannot deprive a person of "life, liberty, or property, without due process of law." Although the Supreme Court has not defined the term due process, it has generally accepted the concept of government acting in a fair manner according to established rules. **Substantive due process** involves the policies of government or the subject matter of the laws, determining whether the law is fair or if it violates constitutional protections. **Procedural due process** is the method of government action or how the law is carried out, according to established rules and procedures. Although the Due Process Clause has often been applied to those accused of crimes (the guarantee of a fair trial would be due process), due process has also been used to protect property rights. The Fifth Amendment states that government cannot take private property for public use without paying a fair price for it. This right of **eminent domain** allows government to take property for public use but also requires that government provide just compensation for that property.

Right to Privacy

The Constitution makes no mention of a "right to privacy." The Supreme Court, however, has interpreted several rights that might fall under the category of privacy.

- *Griswold v. Connecticut (1965)*—The Court ruled that the First, Third, Fourth, Ninth, and Fourteenth Amendments created "zones of privacy" and enhanced the concept of enumerated rights.
- *Roe v. Wade (1973)*—The outcome was a continuation of the recognition of a constitutional right of privacy for a woman to determine whether to terminate a pregnancy.

Rights of the Accused

Several amendments of the Bill of Rights address the rights of those accused of crimes. The Fourteenth Amendment extends those protections to apply to the states.

Fourth Amendment: Search and Seizure
- *Wolf v. Colorado (1949)*—The Court applied protections against unreasonable search and seizure to the states under the Due Process Clause of the Fourteenth Amendment.
- *Mapp v. Ohio (1961)*—The Court ruled that evidence obtained without a search warrant was excluded from trial in state courts. *Mapp v. Ohio* involved the application of the **exclusionary rule** to the states. The exclusionary rule is the Court's effort to deter illegal police conduct by barring from court evidence that has been obtained in violation of the Fourth Amendment.
- *Terry v. Ohio (1968)*—The Court ruled that searches of criminal suspects are constitutional and police may search suspects for safety purposes.
- *Nix v. Williams (1984)*—The Court established the inevitable discovery rule, allowing evidence discovered as the result of an illegal search to be introduced if it can be shown that the evidence would have been found anyway.
- *United States v. Leon (1984)*—The Court established the good faith exception to the exclusionary rule.

Fifth Amendment: Self-Incrimination

- *Miranda v. Arizona (1966)*—The Court ruled that suspects in police custody have certain rights and that they must be informed of those rights (right to remain silent; right to an attorney).

Sixth Amendment: Right to an Attorney
- *Powell v. Alabama (1932)*—The Court established that the Due Process Clause of the Fourteenth Amendment guarantees defendants in death penalty cases the right to an attorney.
- *Betts v. Brady (1942)*—The Court ruled that poor defendants in noncapital cases are not entitled to an attorney at government expense.

- *Gideon v. Wainwright (1963)*—The Court ruled that in state trials, those who cannot afford an attorney will have one provided by the state, overturning *Betts v. Brady.*

- *Escobedo v. Illinois (1964)*—The Supreme Court extended the exclusionary rule to illegal confessions in state court cases. The Court also defined the "Escobedo rule," which stated that persons have the right to an attorney when an investigation begins "to focus on a particular suspect." If the suspect has been arrested, has requested an attorney, and has not been warned of his or her right to remain silent, the suspect has been "denied council in violation of the Sixth Amendment."

Eighth Amendment: Cruel and Unusual Punishment

- *Furman v. Georgia (1972)*—The Court ruled the death penalty unconstitutional under existing state law because it was imposed arbitrarily.
- *Gregg v. Georgia (1976)*—In this case, the death penalty was constitutional because it was imposed based on the circumstances of the case.

Civil Rights

KEY IDEA

Civil rights are guaranteed by the Equal Protection Clause of the Fourteenth Amendment, which was added to the Constitution after the Civil War to prevent states from discriminating against former slaves and to protect former slaves' rights. The courts recognize that some forms of discrimination may be valid (preventing those under 21 from consuming alcohol) and have therefore devised the rational basis test to determine if the discrimination has a legitimate purpose. The courts have also developed the strict scrutiny test, a much stricter standard. If the discrimination reflects prejudice, the courts automatically classify it as suspect and require the government to prove a compelling reason for the discrimination. For example, if a city had separate schools for different races, the city would have to prove how this serves a compelling public interest.

The Civil Rights Movement

After the Civil War three amendments were passed to ensure the rights of the former slaves.

- The Thirteenth Amendment abolished slavery.
- The Fourteenth Amendment defined citizenship to include the former slaves and provided for due process and equal protection, which were used by the Supreme Court to apply the Bill of Rights to the state and local governments.
- The Fifteenth Amendment provided that individuals could not be denied the right to vote based on race or the fact that they were once a slave.

Until the 1950s and 1960s states continued to use discriminatory practices to prevent African Americans from participating in the political processes.

- Black codes were state laws passed to keep former slaves in a state of political bondage. The laws included literacy tests, poll taxes, registration laws, and white primaries.
- The Civil Rights Act of 1875 outlawed racial discrimination in public places such as hotels, theaters, and railroads but required African Americans to take their cases to federal court, a time-consuming and costly endeavor. The Act was ruled unconstitutional in 1883.
- Jim Crow laws were laws designed to segregate the races in schools, public transportation, and hotels.

- In *Plessy v. Ferguson* (1896) the Supreme Court upheld the Jim Crow laws by allowing separate facilities for the different races if those facilities were equal. This created the separate but equal doctrine.
- With Executive Order 8802 (1941) Franklin Roosevelt banned racial discrimination in the defense industry and government offices.
- With Executive Order 9981 (1948) Harry Truman ordered the desegregation of the armed forces.
- In *Brown v. Board of Education* (1954) the Supreme Court overturned the *Plessy* decision, ruling that separate but equal is unconstitutional.
- In *Brown v. Board of Education II* (1955) the Supreme Court ordered the desegregation of schools "with all deliberate speed."
- The Civil Rights Act of 1957 created the Civil Rights Division within the Justice Department and made it a crime to prevent a person from voting in federal elections.
- The Civil Rights Act of 1964 prohibited discrimination in employment and in places of public accommodation, outlawed bias in federally funded programs, and created the Equal Employment Opportunity Commission (EEOC).
- The Twenty-Fourth Amendment (1964) outlawed poll taxes in federal elections.
- The Voting Rights Act of 1965 allowed federal registrars to register voters and outlawed literacy tests and other discriminatory tests in voter registration.
- The Civil Rights Act of 1991 made it easier for job applicants and employees to bring suit against employers with discriminatory hiring practices.

Other Minorities

With the successes of the African American civil rights movement, other minorities have also pressed to end discrimination. Hispanics, American Indians, Asian Americans, women, and people with disabilities have all joined in the quest for protections from discriminatory actions.

Hispanic Americans

Hispanic Americans is a term often used to describe people in the United States who have a Spanish-speaking heritage, including Mexican Americans, Cuban Americans, Puerto Ricans, and Central and South Americans. Today, the Hispanic population is the fastest growing minority in America.

Although the number of Hispanics elected to public office has increased since the 1970s, their progress continues to be hampered by unequal educational opportunities and language barriers. Civil rights action on behalf of Hispanics has concentrated on health care for undocumented immigrants, affirmative action, admission of more Hispanic students to state colleges and universities, and redistricting plans that do not discriminate against Hispanic Americans.

Native Americans

More than two million Native Americans live on reservations in the United States. As a result of discrimination, poverty, unemployment, alcoholism, and drug abuse are common problems. Lack of organization has hampered Native American attempts to gain political power. With the formation of militant organizations (National Indian Youth Council and American Indian Movement) and protests (siege at Wounded Knee), Native Americans have brought attention to their concerns. A 1985 Supreme Court ruling upheld treaty rights of Native American tribes.

The Indian Gaming Regulatory Act (1988) allowed Native Americans to have gaming operations (casinos) on their reservations, creating an economic boom in many tribes. In 1990 Congress passed the Native American Languages Act, encouraging the continuation of native languages and culture.

Asian Americans

Discrimination against Asians arriving in the United States began almost immediately as Asian workers began competing for jobs. Beginning in 1882, the Chinese Exclusion Act (and other similar acts) limited the number of Asians permitted to enter the United States. After the bombing of Pearl Harbor, people of Japanese descent were forced into relocation camps. The Supreme Court upheld these actions when they declared the internments to be legal in *Korematsu v. U.S.* In 1988 Congress appropriated funds to compensate former camp detainees or their survivors.

The Women's Movement

Throughout much of American history, women have not been given the same rights as men.

- The Nineteenth Amendment (1920) gave women the right to vote.
- The Equal Pay Act (1963) made it illegal to base an employee's pay on race, gender, religion, or national origin. This also affected the African American civil rights movement.
- The Civil Rights Act of 1964 banned job discrimination on the basis of gender.
- In *Reed v. Reed* (1971) the Supreme Court ruled against a law that discriminated against women, deciding that the Equal Protection Clause of the Fourteenth Amendment denied unreasonable classifications based on gender.
- The Equal Employment Opportunity Act (1972) prohibited gender discrimination in hiring, firing, promotions, pay, and working conditions.
- The Omnibus Education Act (1972) required schools to give all boys and girls an equal opportunity to participate in sports programs.
- The Equal Credit Opportunity Act (1974) prohibited discrimination against women seeking credit from banks, finance agencies, or the government and made it illegal to ask about a person's gender or marital status on a credit application.
- The Women's Equity in Employment Act (1991) required employers to justify gender discriminations in hiring and job performance.

People with Disabilities

- The Rehabilitation Act (1973) prohibited discrimination against people with disabilities in federal programs.
- The Education for All Handicapped Children Act (1975) guarantees that children with disabilities will receive an "appropriate" education.
- The Americans with Disabilities Act (1990) forbids employers and owners of public accommodations from discriminating against people with disabilities (must make facilities wheelchair accessible, etc.). The Act created the Telecommunications Relay Service, which allows hearing- and speech-impaired people access to telephone communications.

The Gay Rights Movement

Prior to the 1960s and 1970s few people were willing to discuss their sexual preferences in relation to same-sex relationships. After a riot following a police raid of a gay and lesbian bar in 1969, the gay power movement gained momentum. Organizations such as the Gay Activist Alliance and the Gay Liberation Front began exerting pressure and influence on state legislatures to repeal laws prohibiting homosexual conduct. As a result of the growth of the gay rights movement, the Democratic Party has included protection of gay rights as part of its platform, and several states have passed laws prohibiting discrimination against homosexuals in employment, housing, education, and public accommodations. In *Romer v. Evans* (1996) the Supreme Court ruled that a Colorado constitutional amendment invalidating state and local laws that protected gays and lesbians from discrimination was unconstitutional because it violated the **Equal Protection Clause** of the Fourteenth Amendment.

The Elderly

Discrimination has also been an issue with the elderly. Job discrimination made it difficult for older people to find work. As a result, in 1967 Congress passed the Age Discrimination in Employment Act, prohibiting employers from discriminating against individuals over the age of 40 on the basis of age.

Affirmative Action

Affirmative action is a policy designed to correct the effects of past discrimination. Most issues of affirmative action are race or gender based. In 1978 the Supreme Court ruled in *Regents of the University of California v. Bakke* that the affirmative action quotas used by the University of California in their admissions policies were unconstitutional, and that Bakke had been denied equal protection because the university used race as the sole criterion for admissions. In the more recent *Hopwood v. Texas* (1996) the Court struck down the University of Texas Law School's admissions program, stating that race could not be used as a factor in deciding which applicants to admit to achieve student body diversity, to prevent a hostile environment at the law school, to counteract the law school's reputation among minorities, or to end the effects of past discrimination by institutions other than the law school. In 2003 the Supreme Court ruled that universities within the jurisdiction of the Fifth Circuit can use race as a factor in admissions as long as quotas are not used. In recent Court decisions the Court seems to be taking a more conservative view of affirmative action programs and many fear that affirmative action is on the decline.

› Review Questions

1. Which Constitutional amendment provides for the expansion of individual rights found in the Bill of Rights?
   (A) Fourteenth Amendment
   (B) Fifteenth Amendment
   (C) Nineteenth Amendment
   (D) Twenty-Second Amendment
   (E) Twenty-Fifth Amendment

2. The Constitution creates a "wall of separation between Church and State" in the words of the
   (A) elastic clause
   (B) establishment clause
   (C) exclusionary clause
   (D) judiciary clause
   (E) expansion clause

3. The Supreme Court case that overturned a state law setting aside time for "voluntary prayer" in public schools was
   (A) *Santa Fe Independent School District v. Doe*
   (B) *Lee v. Weisman*
   (C) *Edwards v. Aguillard*
   (D) *Lemon v. Kurtzman*
   (E) *Wallace v. Jaffree*

4. Using actions rather than words to convey an idea would be an example of
   (A) speech plus
   (B) pure speech
   (C) free speech
   (D) symbolic speech
   (E) limited speech

5. Which Supreme Court case ruled that flag burning is a protected form of symbolic speech?
   (A) *Reno v. ACLU*
   (B) *Miller v. California*
   (C) *Texas v. Johnson*
   (D) *Tinker v. Des Moines*
   (E) *Texas v. White*

6. The right of the government to take property for public use as long as the government provides just compensation for the property is called
   (A) substantive due process
   (B) eminent domain
   (C) public domain
   (D) procedural due process
   (E) emigrant domain

7. The Supreme Court, in *Mapp v. Ohio*, ruled that evidence obtained without a search warrant could be excluded from trial in state courts. This finding upholds the Constitutional guarantee of no unreasonable search and seizure found in the
   (A) Fourth Amendment
   (B) Fifth Amendment
   (C) Fourteenth Amendment
   (D) First Amendment
   (E) Fifteenth Amendment

8. What government action brought an end to Jim Crow laws and legal segregation in America?
   (A) the Civil Rights Act of 1875
   (B) Presidential Executive Order 8802
   (C) the Supreme Court ruling in *Plessy v. Ferguson*
   (D) the Supreme Court ruling in *Brown v. Board of Education*
   (E) the Twenty-Fourth Amendment

9. What has been the most recent government action taken to end discrimination against Native Americans in the United States?
   (A) the American Indian Movement Act
   (B) the Native American Tribal Act
   (C) the Native American Language Act
   (D) the Indian Gaming Regulatory Act
   (E) the Native American Reservation Act

10. Which of the following prohibits gender discrimination in the workplace?
    (A) Equal Pay Act
    (B) Equal Unemployment Opportunity Act
    (C) Women's Civil Rights Act of 1964
    (D) Nineteenth Amendment
    (E) Equal Employment Opportunity Act

› Answers and Explanations

1. **A.** The Fourteenth Amendment has been used to apply the freedoms listed in the Bill of Rights to the states. The Fifteenth Amendment (B) prevents the states from denying the right to vote to any person on the basis of race, color, or servitude. The Nineteenth Amendment (C) prohibits the denial of suffrage on the basis of sex. The Twenty-Second Amendment (D) addresses presidential tenure, while the Twenty-Fifth Amendment (E) deals with presidential succession.

2. **B.** The First Amendment's Establishment Clause creates a wall of separation between Church and State.

3. **E.** *Wallace v. Jaffree* overturned a state law setting aside time for voluntary prayer in public schools. *Santa Fe Independent School District v. Doe* (A) overturned a Texas law allowing high school students to read a prayer at athletic events. *Lee v. Weisman* (B) ruled against clergy-led prayer at high school graduation ceremonies. In *Edwards v. Aguillard* (C) the Court ruled that Louisiana could not force public schools that taught evolution to also teach creationism. In *Lemon v. Kurtzman* (D) the Court struck down a Pennsylvania law reimbursing parochial schools for textbooks and salaries and established the Lemon Test.

4. **D.** Symbolic speech is the use of actions and symbols to convey ideas. Speech plus (A) is the use of verbal and symbolic speech together. Pure speech (B) means verbal speech.

5. **C.** *Texas v. Johnson* was the case in which the Supreme Court ruled that flag burning is a protected form of symbolic speech. In *Reno v. ACLU* (A) the Court ruled the Communications Decency Act unconstitutional because it was vague in its regulation of Internet speech. *Miller v. California* (B) established the Miller test, which sets standards for measuring obscenity. In *Tinker v. Des Moines* (D) the Court ruled that wearing black armbands in protest of the Vietnam War was symbolic speech protected by the First Amendment. In *Texas v. White* (E) the Court held that Texas had remained a state since it first joined the Union.

6. **B.** Eminent domain is the right of the government to take property for public use provided the government compensates for the property. Substantive due process (A) refers to the requirement that the government must create fair laws and policies. Procedural due process (D) refers to the requirement that the government must use fair methods and procedures.

7. **A.** Constitutional guarantees of protections against unreasonable searches and seizures are found in the Fourth Amendment.

8. **D.** The Supreme Court ruling in *Brown v. Board of Education* brought an end to Jim Crow laws and legal segregation in the United States. The Civil Rights Act of 1875 (A) outlawed racial discrimination in public places, but required African Americans to take their cases to federal court. Executive Order 8802 (B) banned racial discrimination in the defense industry and government offices. In *Plessy v. Ferguson* (C) the Court upheld Jim Crow laws and created the "separate but equal" doctrine. The Twenty-Fourth Amendment (E) ended the poll tax.

9. **C.** The Native American Language Act (1990), which encouraged the continuation of native languages and culture, is the most recent of the acts listed.

10. **E.** The Equal Employment Opportunity Act prohibits gender discrimination in the workplace. The Equal Pay Act (A) made it illegal to base an employee's pay on race, gender, religion, or national origin. The Nineteenth Amendment (D) prohibits the denial of suffrage on the basis of gender. There are no acts titled the Women's Civil Rights Act (C) or the Equal Unemployment Opportunity Act (B).

› Rapid Review

- Civil liberties are those rights that belong to everyone and are guaranteed by the Constitution, Bill of Rights, Fourteenth Amendment, legislative actions, and court decisions.
- The Establishment Clause of the First Amendment has been interpreted to mean that there is a separation between Church and State, preventing the government from supporting religion or one religion over another.
- The Lemon Test established standards for measuring separation of church and state.
- The Free Exercise Clause guarantees the right to practice any religion or no religion at all.
- There are three classifications of speech: pure speech, symbolic speech, and speech plus.
- The right to free speech is not absolute. Speech may be regulated if national security is at stake; fighting words and obscenity are not protected forms of free speech. The Internet has not been regulated.
- Freedom of the press is often protected because it is closely related to free speech. Press includes newspapers, magazines, radio, television, and the Internet.
- The First Amendment also guarantees freedom of assembly and petition.
- The Due Process Clauses of the Fifth and Fourteenth Amendments provide for the protection of private property.
- The Constitution makes no mention of the right to privacy; however, the Supreme Court ruled that such a right exists under the Constitution.
- Several amendments of the Bill of Rights address the rights of those accused of crimes, including the Fourth, Fifth, Sixth, and Eighth Amendments. The Fourteenth Amendment extends those protections to apply to the states.
- Civil rights are the positive acts of government designed to prevent discrimination and provide equality before the law.
- The civil rights movement began after the Civil War, with African Americans striving to gain political, social, and economic equality.
- Discriminatory practices were used by the states to prevent political participation by African Americans. These practices included black codes and Jim Crow laws.
- A positive step for African Americans came with the *Brown v. Board of Education* ruling in which the Supreme Court overturned the *Plessy* "separate but equal" ruling.
- The successes of the African American civil rights movement have encouraged other minorities, such as Hispanics, Native Americans, and Asian Americans, to call for an end to discrimination.
- Women have also worked to end discrimination. Their successes include gaining the right to vote and protections against employment discrimination.
- The Americans with Disabilities Act of 1990 forbids discrimination against people with disabilities.
- Affirmative action is a controversial policy designed to correct the effects of past discrimination.

CHAPTER 16

Politics and Public Policymaking

IN THIS CHAPTER

Summary: Public policy is the method by which government attempts to solve the problems of a nation. Governments are constantly making public policy. Even the decision to keep the status quo is a public policy decision. Public policy is made at all levels of government. Policymaking may be a slow process with only small changes (**incrementalism**) or a major shift from previous policies.

Key Terms

incrementalism	environmental impact	fiscal year
agenda setting	statements	appropriations
political agenda	discretionary spending	North American Free
policy formulation	national debt	Trade Agreement
policy adoption	federal budget	(NAFTA)
policy implementation	social welfare programs	mandatory spending
policy evaluation	entitlement programs	constitutional law

The Policymaking Process

The policymaking process involves several steps:

- *agenda setting*—Recognizing an issue as a problem that must be addressed as a part of the political agenda. Problems are often brought to the **political agenda** by citizens, interest groups, the media, or governmental entities.
- *policy formulation*—Finding ways to solve the problem; exploring alternative plans of action and developing proposals to solve the problem.

- *policy adoption*—Adopting a plan of action to solve the problem; may require the passage of legislation.
- *policy implementation*—Executing the plan of action by the appropriate agency or agencies.
- *policy evaluation*—Analysis of policy and its impact upon the problem; judging the effectiveness of the policy and making adjustments if necessary.

Domestic Policy

Domestic policy often refers to the social policies of the United States in the areas of crime prevention, education, energy, the environment, health care, and social welfare.

Crime Prevention

Although crime prevention has traditionally been a state and local matter, as crime and violence have increased, the federal government has become more involved in crime prevention. Lyndon Johnson declared a "war on crime," creating a commission to study the causes of crime and suggest solutions. Today, more crimes are classified as federal crimes, with punishments often more harsh than those for state crimes. Since the shooting of President Ronald Reagan, debate has centered on gun control legislation. President Bill Clinton signed the Brady Bill, requiring a five-day waiting period and background checks before the purchase of a handgun. Clinton also won congressional support of a ban on the sale of some types of semiautomatic assault weapons and legislation authorizing new federal spending on crime initiatives, including the hiring of new police officers and building new prisons and "boot camps" for juvenile offenders. Clinton's crime bill also listed federal crimes punishable by the death penalty and the "three strikes laws," mandating certain sentences if convicted of a third felony. As the federal government has become more involved in crime prevention, federal agencies have played a larger role.

- The Federal Bureau of Investigation (FBI) collects and reports evidence in matters relating to federal law or the crossing of state borders; provides investigative and lab services to local law enforcement agencies.
- The Drug Enforcement Administration (DEA) prohibits the flow of illegal narcotics into the United States and patrols U.S. borders.
- The Bureau of Alcohol, Tobacco, and Firearms (ATF) administers laws dealing with explosives and firearms and regulates the production and distribution of alcohol and tobacco products.

Education

Although public education falls under the authority of the state governments, the federal government has played an increasing role in education. Since the 1950s (*Brown v. Board of Education,* 1954, and the Soviet Union's launch of *Sputnik*) the major goal of education policy has been to ensure equal access to educational opportunities. Under Lyndon Johnson's Great Society, Congress passed the Elementary and Secondary Education Act in 1965, providing federal funding to public school districts with low-income populations. In 1979 Congress created the Department of Education to coordinate education policy. Congress has also provided programs for higher education, including loans and grant programs for college students. Recent proposals in education have concerned the use of school vouchers that would allow parents to choose the schools their children attend at public expense, and the national testing of students.

In 2002 President George W. Bush signed a bill called No Child Left Behind. This Act requires all states to administer proficiency tests in public schools in order to monitor student progress. Though the Act has created some improvement in many of America's public schools, many provisions of the legislation remain controversial. President Barack Obama made education a central part of his domestic agenda.

Energy

Energy policy has traditionally been one of conservation and the study of alternative and renewable sources of fuel. Newer energy policies have addressed issues such as global warming and toxic waste disposal. In 1980 a superfund was established for cleanup of toxic waste sites, and current law provides for the tracking of hazardous chemicals and the disposal of toxic waste. Energy policy often involves highly technical issues about which the average citizen may have limited knowledge. Energy will be an important issue in the coming years.

The Environment

In the late eighteenth century, the federal government began setting aside public lands as national parks, monuments, and forests. Not until the 1950s, however, did Congress begin passing legislation aimed at protecting the environment and cleaning up polluted air and water. In the 1970s Congress created the Environmental Protection Agency (EPA) to enforce environmental legislation. The Clean Air Acts of 1970 and 1990 were implemented to reduce air pollution. The Water Pollution Control Act of 1972 was designed to clean up the nation's lakes and rivers. Wilderness areas were established, the Endangered Species Act provided government protection of species listed as endangered, and **environmental impact statements** required studies and reports of likely environmental impacts be filed with the Environmental Protection Agency. President Obama repeatedly promised in the 2008 campaign that this would be a key issue for his administration.

Health Care

Unlike Canada or Great Britain, the United States has no national health care system, yet the largest percentage of government spending goes to the Medicare and Medicaid programs. Medicare provides hospitalization insurance for the elderly, and Medicaid provides public assistance in health care for the poor. The government operates several programs aimed at promoting and protecting public health in the United States. The Public Health Service, Centers for Disease Control (CDC), Veterans Affairs (VA), and Food and Drug Administration (FDA) are among the agencies involved in promoting public health. Health care was a major campaign issue in the 1992 presidential election, when Bill Clinton campaigned on a plan to address both the high cost of health care and limited access. Clinton's proposals to reform health care in the United States died in Congress. A controversial national health care program was passed by Congress late in 2009.

Social Welfare

Social welfare began during the New Deal era. The Great Depression led citizens to want more government help against economic downturns and poverty. The Social Security Act (1935) was a first step in this fight. Lyndon Johnson's Great Society continued the war on poverty by creating new programs (Medicare, school aid, job training) designed to prevent poverty. Housing programs and urban renewal have been implemented with the goal of providing adequate housing for all citizens. In the 1980s Ronald Reagan reduced benefits and removed people from eligibility in an effort to reform the social welfare system amid claims of increasing government. Bill Clinton continued to bring reform to the social welfare system by limiting how long a person could receive benefits and giving money to the states to run their own programs. In 1996, the entitlement program Aid to Families with Dependent Children (AFDC) was replaced by a new program, Temporary Assistance for Needy Families (TANF). Unlike AFDC, TANF is a block grant that limits recipients to no more than five years of assistance. TANF also requires recipients to work, receive vocational training, or participate in community service.

Economic Policy

Economic policy can have a profound effect on national elections. The president and Congress are held responsible for the economic "health" of the nation. Economic policy involves improving the overall economic health of the nation through government spending and taxation policies.

Raising Revenue

The government raises revenue through the collection of taxes. The federal government collects individual income taxes, corporate income taxes, social insurance taxes, excise taxes, customs duties, and estate and gift taxes. The government also raises revenue through the sale of government securities by the Federal Reserve and through the collection of fees for services provided, such as patents.

Government Spending

Government spending may be discretionary or nondiscretionary (mandatory). **Discretionary spending** is spending about which government planners may make choices, while nondiscretionary spending is required by existing laws for current programs. In recent years the percentage of nondiscretionary spending has grown while the percentage of discretionary spending has decreased. Discretionary spending includes defense spending, education, student loans, scientific research, environmental cleanup, law enforcement, disaster aid, and foreign aid. Nondiscretionary spending includes interest on the **national debt** and **social welfare** and **entitlement programs** such as Social Security, Medicare, Medicaid, veterans' pensions, and unemployment insurance. A large stimulus package was enacted in the first months of the Obama presidency.

The Federal Budget

The **federal budget** indicates the amount of money the federal government expects to receive and authorizes government spending for a fiscal (12-month period) year. The **fiscal year** for the federal government is from October 1 to September 30. The process of preparing the federal budget takes about 18 months and involves several steps:

- *proposals*—Each federal agency submits a detailed estimate of its needs for the coming fiscal year to the Office of Management and Budget (OMB).
- *executive branch*—The OMB holds meetings at which representatives from the various agencies may explain their proposal and try to convince the OMB that their needs are

justified. The OMB works with the president's staff to combine all requests into a single budget package, which the president submits to Congress in January or February.

- *Congress*—Congress debates and often modifies the president's proposal. The Congressional Budget Office (CBO) provides Congress with economic data. Congressional committees hold hearings, analyze the budget proposals, and by September offer budget resolutions to their respective houses (which must be passed by September 15). The Appropriations Committee for each house submits bills to authorize spending.
- *president*—Congress sends **appropriations** bills to the president for approval. If no budget is approved, Congress must pass temporary emergency funding or the government will shut down.

Foreign and Defense Policy

Foreign policy involves all the strategies and procedures for dealing with other nations. One of the purposes of foreign policy is to maintain peaceful relations with other countries through diplomatic, military, or trade relations. The process of carrying out foreign policy is accomplished through foreign relations. Defense policy is the role that the military establishment plays in providing for the defense of the nation.

KEY IDEA

The President and Foreign Policy

The president is often considered the leader in the development of foreign policy. Presidential authority for foreign policy originates from the constitutional powers, historical precedent, and institutional advantages of the executive. The president is commander-in-chief of the armed forces, negotiates treaties and executive agreements, and appoints foreign ambassadors, ministers, and consuls. Historically, presidents have often issued foreign policy statements (for example, the Monroe Doctrine and the Truman Doctrine) that have not passed through the legislative process but which set the tone for foreign policy. Executive agreements, or pacts between the president and heads of state of foreign countries, do not require Senate ratification. Also, the president can often respond more quickly than Congress when a national crisis requires quick action (for example, the attack on Pearl Harbor or the events of September 11, 2001).

The Department of State

The Department of State is the major organization for carrying out foreign policy. The secretary of state reports directly to the president with advice about foreign policy matters. The secretary of state also supervises the diplomatic corps of ambassadors, ministers, and consuls. The State Department is organized into bureaus, each specializing in a region of the world.

The Department of Defense (DoD)

The Department of Defense provides military information to the president. The secretary of defense advises the president on troop movements, military installations, and weapons development. Because the secretary of defense is a civilian, the Joint Chiefs of Staff, composed of a chairman and the highest-ranking military officer in the Army, Navy, Air Force, and Marines, also provide advice on military matters.

The National Security Council (NSC)

The National Security Council is part of the Executive Office of the President. Membership includes the president, vice president, the secretaries of state and defense, chairman of the Joint Chiefs of Staff, director of the Central Intelligence Agency, and the president's national security advisor.

The United States Information Agency

The United States Information Agency helps keep the world informed about America, the American way of life, and American views on world problems through information centers around the world. It also sponsors the "Voice of America" radio programs that are broadcast around the world.

The Central Intelligence Agency

The Central Intelligence Agency is responsible for gathering secret information essential to national defense. Although the CIA is an independent agency, it operates within the executive branch to gather information, analyze that information, and brief the president and the National Security Council.

Congress and Foreign Policy

Congress also plays a major role in the development of foreign policy. It is the responsibility of the Senate Foreign Relations Committee and the House Committee on Foreign Affairs to make recommendations to Congress and the president on foreign relations. The Senate must approve all treaties between the United States and foreign nations by a two-thirds vote, and all nominations for ambassadors by majority vote. Congress has the power to declare war and must approve spending for national defense.

Current Issues in Foreign Policy

Current foreign policy issues include:

- *nuclear proliferation*—With only a few nations having nuclear capabilities, how do we prevent possible enemies from gaining access to nuclear technology that might someday be used against the United States or our allies?
- *terrorism*—How does the United States defend itself against possible terrorist attacks? What role will the Department of Homeland Security play in intelligence gathering, border security, immigration, and holding, questioning, and prosecuting suspected terrorists?
- *international trade*—Trade can be used as a tool of foreign policy by providing military or economic aid or by reducing or eliminating tariffs through trade agreements such as the **North American Free Trade Agreement (NAFTA)** and the World Trade Organization (WTO).
- *how to manage conflicts abroad*—During the presidency of George W. Bush many criticized the United States for its "go it alone" policy. Should President Obama and subsequent presidents do more to create alliances and agreements with other nations?

› Review Questions

1. During the policymaking process, when a plan of action is executed by an agency or agencies, what important step has taken place?
   (A) policy formulation
   (B) policy implementation
   (C) policy adoption
   (D) agenda setting
   (E) policy evaluation

2. What has been the major goal of the government's education policy?
   (A) give more power to the states
   (B) increase the power of the Department of Education
   (C) provide more money to low-income schools
   (D) provide more programs for higher education
   (E) ensure equal access to educational opportunity

3. Which of the following is NOT associated with U.S. domestic policy?
   (A) The Federal Bureau of Investigation
   (B) The Environmental Protection Agency
   (C) The Drug Enforcement Administration
   (D) The National Security Council
   (E) The Centers for Disease Control

4. In the United States the largest percentage of government spending goes to
   (A) Medicare and Medicaid programs
   (B) public health services
   (C) the Food and Drug Administration
   (D) Centers for Disease Control
   (E) Veterans Affairs

5. Which of the following was the first major government act of economic support?
   (A) the Great Society Act
   (B) the Medicare and Medicaid Act
   (C) the Social Security Act
   (D) the Welfare Act
   (E) the Reduction in Poverty Act

6. Which of the following is true regarding U.S. economic policy?
   (A) Government planners may make choices about nondiscretionary spending.
   (B) The Department of the Treasury is held responsible for the economic health of the nation.
   (C) The government raises revenue primarily through the collection of taxes.
   (D) Discretionary spending includes interest on the national debt.
   (E) Disaster aid is included under **mandatory spending**.

7. Which of the following is NOT a part of the federal budget process?
   (A) The Supreme Court reviews budget requests that are outside the realm of **constitutional law**.
   (B) The executive branch (OMB) holds meetings to review budget proposals.
   (C) Each federal agency submits an estimate of needs to the OMB.
   (D) Congress debates budget proposals.
   (E) Congress sends appropriations bills to the president.

8. Which of the following is NOT a true statement?
   (A) The purpose of foreign policy is to maintain peaceful relations with foreign nations.
   (B) Foreign policy is the responsibility of the Congress through the secretary of state.
   (C) The process of carrying out foreign policy is accomplished through foreign relations.
   (D) Defense policy is the role that the military establishment plays in providing for the defense of the nation.
   (E) Foreign policy involves all the strategies and procedures for dealing with other nations.

9. Which of the following departments is most responsible for providing the president with military information that would be useful in dealing with foreign nations?
   (A) the Department of State
   (B) the Department of Defense
   (C) the National Security Council
   (D) the United States Information Agency
   (E) the Central Intelligence Agency

10. Current foreign policy issues include all of the following EXCEPT
    (A) nuclear proliferation
    (B) national defense
    (C) terrorism
    (D) international trade
    (E) national education

› Answers and Explanations

1. **B**. Policy implementation is the process of enactment of policy. Policy formulation (A) involves finding ways to solve the problem. Policy adoption (C) is adopting a plan of action. Agenda setting (D) is the recognition of an issue as a problem that must be addressed. Policy evaluation (E) is analysis of the policy and its impact.

2. **E**. The major educational policy goal of the federal government has been to ensure equal access to educational opportunities. Recently the federal government has played an increasing role in education (A). Although choices (B), (C), and (D) are goals of the government's educational policy, these goals are subordinate to the greater goal of equal access to education.

3. **D**. The National Security Council deals with foreign and defense policy and includes the chairman of the Joint Chiefs of Staff, the president's national security advisor, and the director of the CIA. The other answer choices deal with U.S. domestic policy.

4. **A**. Medicare and Medicaid receive the largest percentage of government spending. The other answer choices are programs and agencies that involve somewhat less government spending.

5. **C**. The first major governmental act to aid citizens was the Social Security Act. Answers D and E are nonexistent organizations. Medicare and Medicaid (B) are programs that began under President Johnson's Great Society (A) in the 1960s.

6. **C**. The primary source of government revenue is taxation. Government planners make choices about discretionary spending (A). The president and the Congress are held responsible for the nation's economic health (B). Interest on the national debt is discretionary spending (D). Disaster aid (E) is included under discretionary spending. Mandatory spending is another term for nondiscretionary spending.

7. **A**. The Supreme Court does not participate in the federal budget process. The remaining answer choices are steps in the process of creating the federal budget.

8. **B**. The president, not Congress, works with the secretary of state to develop foreign policy. The other answer choices describe the nature of foreign policy.

9. **B**. The Department of Defense is responsible for providing military information to the president. The Department of State (A), the National Security Council (C), and the Central Intelligence Agency (E) deal with foreign policy. The United States Information Agency (D) runs radio stations, libraries, and educational programs in foreign countries.

10. **E**. National education is a domestic policy issue. The remaining answer choices deal with foreign policy issues.

> Rapid Review

- Public policymaking occurs at all levels of government.
- Policymaking is a slow process involving several steps: agenda setting, policy formulation, policy adoption, policy implementation, and policy evaluation.
- Domestic policies are the social policies of the United States: crime prevention, education, energy, environment, health care, and social welfare.
- Crime prevention at the national level is the responsibility of the Federal Bureau of Investigation, the Drug Enforcement Administration, and the Bureau of Alcohol, Tobacco, and Firearms.
- Education falls under the authority of state governments; however, the federal government has played an increasing role in education.
- The Environmental Protection Agency was created in the 1970s to enforce environmental legislation.
- The government operates several programs aimed at promoting and protecting public health: the Public Health Service, Centers for Disease Control, Veterans Affairs, and the Food and Drug Administration.
- Social welfare programs include Medicare, Medicaid, and Social Security.
- Economic policy can have an impact on national elections.
- Economic policy includes raising revenue, government spending, and formulation of the federal budget.
- The federal budget indicates the amount of money the federal government expects to receive and spend during a fiscal year.
- The Office of Management and Budget (OMB) plays a major role in creating the budget.
- Foreign policy involves all the strategies and procedures for dealing with foreign nations. The president is considered the leader in the development of foreign policy.
- The Department of State, headed by the secretary of state, is responsible for the execution of foreign policy.
- The Department of Defense provides military information to the president.
- Congress plays a role in the development of foreign policy by making recommendations to the president on foreign relations, approving treaties, and approving nominations of ambassadors.
- Current issues in foreign policy include nuclear proliferation, terrorism, international trade, and how to manage conflicts abroad.

STEP 5 ➜

Build Your Test-Taking Confidence

AP U.S. Government and Politics Practice Exam 1
AP U.S. Government and Politics Practice Exam 2
AP U.S. Government and Politics Practice Exam 3

AP U.S. Government and Politics
Practice Exam 1—Section I

ANSWER SHEET

1 (A) (B) (C) (D) (E)   21 (A) (B) (C) (D) (E)   41 (A) (B) (C) (D) (E)
2 (A) (B) (C) (D) (E)   22 (A) (B) (C) (D) (E)   42 (A) (B) (C) (D) (E)
3 (A) (B) (C) (D) (E)   23 (A) (B) (C) (D) (E)   43 (A) (B) (C) (D) (E)
4 (A) (B) (C) (D) (E)   24 (A) (B) (C) (D) (E)   44 (A) (B) (C) (D) (E)
5 (A) (B) (C) (D) (E)   25 (A) (B) (C) (D) (E)   45 (A) (B) (C) (D) (E)
6 (A) (B) (C) (D) (E)   26 (A) (B) (C) (D) (E)   46 (A) (B) (C) (D) (E)
7 (A) (B) (C) (D) (E)   27 (A) (B) (C) (D) (E)   47 (A) (B) (C) (D) (E)
8 (A) (B) (C) (D) (E)   28 (A) (B) (C) (D) (E)   48 (A) (B) (C) (D) (E)
9 (A) (B) (C) (D) (E)   29 (A) (B) (C) (D) (E)   49 (A) (B) (C) (D) (E)
10 (A) (B) (C) (D) (E)   30 (A) (B) (C) (D) (E)   50 (A) (B) (C) (D) (E)
11 (A) (B) (C) (D) (E)   31 (A) (B) (C) (D) (E)   51 (A) (B) (C) (D) (E)
12 (A) (B) (C) (D) (E)   32 (A) (B) (C) (D) (E)   52 (A) (B) (C) (D) (E)
13 (A) (B) (C) (D) (E)   33 (A) (B) (C) (D) (E)   53 (A) (B) (C) (D) (E)
14 (A) (B) (C) (D) (E)   34 (A) (B) (C) (D) (E)   54 (A) (B) (C) (D) (E)
15 (A) (B) (C) (D) (E)   35 (A) (B) (C) (D) (E)   55 (A) (B) (C) (D) (E)
16 (A) (B) (C) (D) (E)   36 (A) (B) (C) (D) (E)   56 (A) (B) (C) (D) (E)
17 (A) (B) (C) (D) (E)   37 (A) (B) (C) (D) (E)   57 (A) (B) (C) (D) (E)
18 (A) (B) (C) (D) (E)   38 (A) (B) (C) (D) (E)   58 (A) (B) (C) (D) (E)
19 (A) (B) (C) (D) (E)   39 (A) (B) (C) (D) (E)   59 (A) (B) (C) (D) (E)
20 (A) (B) (C) (D) (E)   40 (A) (B) (C) (D) (E)   60 (A) (B) (C) (D) (E)

I _____ did _____ did not finish all the questions in the allotted 45 minutes.

I had _____ correct answers. I had _____ incorrect answers, including questions I left blank.

Scoring Formula:

_____ = _____
     number right   raw score

I have carefully reviewed the explanations of the answers. I need to work on the following types of questions:

AP U.S. Government and Politics
Practice Exam 1

Section I

Total Time—45 minutes

60 Questions

omplete statements below is followed by five suggested answers or
each case and then fill in the corresponding oval on the answer sheet.

. Ohio, the

ith a legal
n court
Fourteenth
arches
ects are

rt if the
inevitably

ly to cases

o be sued,
; damages

method of floor vote is used in the passage
of a bill in both houses of Congress?

I.   voice vote
II. standing vote
III. roll-call vote
IV. teller vote
V.   electronic vote
   (A) I only
   (B) II only
   (C) III only
   (D) I, II, III
   (E) IV and V only

4. A constitutional duty of the vice president is to
   (A) work with the Supreme Court on constitutional issues
   (B) preside over the Senate and break tie votes
   (C) balance the ticket
   (D) preside over the House of Representatives and break tie votes
   (E) issue directives, on the president's order, to the political parties

5. The United States Constitution has been amended
   (A) 27 times
   (B) 26 times
   (C) 17 times
   (D) originally only 10 times including the Bill of Rights
   (E) 28 times

6. The first woman appointed to the Supreme Court of the United States was
   (A) Sandra Day O'Connor
   (B) Ruth Bader Ginsburg
   (C) Barbara Jordan
   (D) Jeannette Rankin
   (E) Geraldine Ferraro

7. Which of the following is a function that political parties are expected to perform?
   I.   nominate candidates for office
   II. politically educate the electorate
   III. create a sense of centralized responsibility
   IV. maintain the separation of powers in government
   (A) I and III only
   (B) I, II, III, and IV
   (C) III and IV only
   (D) I, II, and III only
   (E) I only

GO ON TO THE NEXT PAGE

8. Regulating securities, financial markets, and investment companies, and prohibiting fraud and dishonest investment practices would be the major functions of which of the following independent regulatory agencies?
    (A) the Federal Reserve
    (B) Federal Trade Commission
    (C) Commodity Futures Trading Commission
    (D) Securities and Exchange Commission
    (E) Consumer Product Safety Commission

9. Which of the following would be a true statement if a presidential election had to be decided by the House of Representatives?
    (A) Each member of the House is allowed one vote.
    (B) Each state's delegation casts one vote.
    (C) Only the speaker votes.
    (D) The House votes as a single unit.
    (E) The House Rules Committee makes the decision.

10. Which of the following is most accurate regarding interest groups?
    (A) Interest groups always provide accurate and concise information.
    (B) Some interest groups have influence that is not proportional to their size.
    (C) Interest groups attempt to control government.
    (D) Interest groups are well financed.
    (E) Interest groups undermine the goals of the American political system.

11. The Necessary and Proper Clause found in Article I, Section 8 of the United States Constitution is also known as the
    (A) elastic clause
    (B) expressed clause
    (C) implied clause
    (D) the general practice clause of Congress
    (E) congressional clause

12. Which of the following is a qualification required in order to be president of the United States?
    (A) naturalized citizen
    (B) 30 years of age
    (C) natural-born citizen
    (D) previous experience in government
    (E) resident of the United States for at least nine years

13. Which of the following is the best definition of political socialization?
    (A) individuals playing different political roles in society
    (B) individuals with diverse beliefs about public policy
    (C) individuals with diverse sets of values and beliefs about public policy
    (D) individuals acquiring their differing beliefs and political orientation
    (E) individuals defining their political society in relation to their form of government

14. Which of the following is a right that would not be guaranteed to a noncitizen?
    (A) freedom of speech
    (B) freedom of religion
    (C) freedom of press
    (D) right to an attorney
    (E) freedom to move about the country

15. In order for a case to be heard in the Supreme Court of the United States, a consensus must be reached among the justices. This agreement is known as:
    (A) a *writ of certiorari*
    (B) a precedent
    (C) *amicus curiae*
    (D) "the rule of four"
    (E) a certificate

16. Which of the following would be a true statement regarding judicial review and the power of the court to declare an act of government unconstitutional?
    (A) Only federal courts hold this power.
    (B) All federal courts and most state courts hold this power.
    (C) All federal courts and all state courts hold this power.
    (D) Most federal courts and most state courts hold this power.
    (E) Only the Supreme Court of the United States holds this power.

17. The executive department charged with the administration of the largest entitlement program in the United States is
    (A) Health and Human Services
    (B) Homeland Security
    (C) Veterans Affairs
    (D) Labor
    (E) Education

GO ON TO THE NEXT PAGE

18. Presidential impeachment
    (A) requires a majority vote of the Senate for conviction
    (B) exemplifies the concept of checks and balances
    (C) is the removal of a president from office
    (D) is presided over by the vice president
    (E) allows the Senate to bring charges against the president

19. A group of individuals seeking to control government by winning an election and placing a candidate in office would best be described as a(n)
    (A) caucus
    (B) political party
    (C) interest group
    (D) political action committee
    (E) constituency

20. In order to get elected to the Congress, the most significant advantage is
    (A) incumbency
    (B) an endorsement by a major business or community leader
    (C) financial support
    (D) knowledge of the workings of government
    (E) military service

21. Constitutional amendments may be ratified by
    (A) state conventions called by Congress
    (B) a national convention
    (C) a two-thirds vote of each house of the Congress
    (D) legislatures of three-fourths of the states
    (E) legislatures of two-thirds of the states

22. Justices of the Supreme Court and the lower federal courts serve for a period of
    (A) 25 years
    (B) time determined by the president
    (C) life, during good behavior
    (D) time determined by Congress
    (E) 4 years

23. James Madison applied the term "faction" to
    (A) political parties and interest groups
    (B) negative members of Congress
    (C) splinter groups of the executive
    (D) political parties
    (E) states not willing to be a part of the federal union

24. The general beliefs that the American public has about politics and policy issues can best be defined as
    (A) political socialization
    (B) public policy
    (C) policy formulation
    (D) political ideology
    (E) public opinion

25. Which of the following is NOT a check on the power of the executive branch?
    (A) executive agreements
    (B) the power of the purse
    (C) judicial review of executive actions
    (D) public opinion
    (E) approval powers over appointments

26. After a proposed bill has had its first reading, what is generally the next step that a bill might encounter?
    (A) The proposed bill is reviewed by an investigating committee.
    (B) The proposed bill is sent to the president.
    (C) The proposed bill is sent to a standing committee.
    (D) The proposed bill is vetoed by the president.
    (E) The proposed bill is voted on by the entire Congress.

27. Which of the following is true of the constitutional provision regarding the electoral college?
    (A) Each presidential electoral casts two ballots.
    (B) State legislatures with the help of the electoral college choose the president.
    (C) Electoral ballots are cast along political party lines.
    (D) Electors are bound by federal law to vote for their party's candidate.
    (E) Electors are bound by state law to vote for their party's candidate.

28. Which of the following is NOT a correct statement regarding interest groups?
    (A) Interest groups sometimes form coalitions to strengthen their influence.
    (B) Federal law requires political action committees to donate to several candidates.
    (C) Interest groups seek to improve their image by appealing to the public.
    (D) Interest groups concentrate on influencing Congress without involving the courts.
    (E) In recent years lobbying has become increasingly more regulated.

GO ON TO THE NEXT PAGE

29. Sometimes litigants that are not part of the formal proceeding of Supreme Court oral arguments wish to have their points of view presented. They may file what is known as a(n)
    (A) *per curiam* decision
    (B) certificate
    (C) *writ of certiorari*
    (D) *amicus curiae* brief
    (E) *stare decisis*

30. Which of the following is NOT a basic principle of government found in the Constitution?
    (A) popular sovereignty
    (B) conservatism
    (C) limited government
    (D) judicial review
    (E) federalism

31. Which of the following would best describe gerrymandering?
    (A) a group of Congress members teaming together in order to get legislation passed
    (B) the breakdown of a political party within the Congress
    (C) dividing the states into regional electoral districts
    (D) dividing states along party lines in order to determine party strategy
    (E) drawing electoral districts within a state in order to favor a political party or candidate

32. The political theory proposed by John Locke, calling for a nation to be developed as a voluntary agreement between citizens and government, is known as the
    (A) divine right theory
    (B) hyperpluralist theory
    (C) social contract theory
    (D) state theory
    (E) elite theory

33. The power of the Supreme Court to determine the constitutionality of a law passed by Congress is called
    (A) judicial review
    (B) Supreme Court review
    (C) constitutional review
    (D) congressional review
    (E) special review

34. Independent agencies that are usually beyond the reach of presidential control are called
    (A) independent regulatory commissions
    (B) executive agencies
    (C) independent executive agencies
    (D) government corporations
    (E) independent government agencies

35. Which of the following is NOT an expressed presidential power found in the United States Constitution?
    (A) making appointments
    (B) commander of the military
    (C) treaty making
    (D) budget management
    (E) granting pardons

36. Which of the following stages generally occurs earliest in the presidential election contest?
    (A) national party conventions
    (B) the popular election
    (C) state primaries and caucuses
    (D) the electoral college election
    (E) choosing a running mate

37. Which of the following are types of opinions that may be submitted by the justices when the Supreme Court reaches a decision in a case?
    I. majority opinion
    II. concurring opinion
    III. dissenting opinion
    IV. concluding opinion
    (A) I only
    (B) I, II, and III only
    (C) II and IV only
    (D) II and III only
    (E) I, II, III, and IV

38. The most effective tool of any interest group wishing to influence the workings of government is
    (A) the political party
    (B) the American voter
    (C) the lobbyist
    (D) propaganda
    (E) grassroots organizations

GO ON TO THE NEXT PAGE

39. All of the following are strategies typically used by successful interest groups EXCEPT
    (A) engaging in acts of civil disobedience and violence
    (B) litigation
    (C) creating coalitions with other interest groups
    (D) contributing to political candidates through political action committees
    (E) bringing grassroots pressures on legislators

40. Poll taxes were fees paid by individuals in order to vote. Which amendment in the United States Constitution outlaws this practice?
    (A) Twentieth Amendment
    (B) Eighteenth Amendment
    (C) Twenty-First Amendment
    (D) Twenty-Fifth Amendment
    (E) Twenty-Fourth Amendment

41. Which of the following is NOT a role of the members of Congress?
    (A) constituent servant
    (B) gatekeeper
    (C) policymaker
    (D) delegate
    (E) trustee

42. Amnesty would fall under which power of the president?
    (A) ordinance power
    (B) executive power
    (C) judicial power
    (D) immigration power
    (E) naturalization power

43. In the United States government the creation of every bureaucratic agency may be traced back to
    (A) Congress
    (B) the president
    (C) the Constitution
    (D) state governments
    (E) the Articles of Confederation

44. What is the correct term for an organizational department of the government that has been created by the Congress but is still not located within the jurisdiction of one of the cabinet departments?
    (A) legislative agency
    (B) congressional agency
    (C) independent agency
    (D) government agency
    (E) executive agency

45. During the 1930s, President Franklin Roosevelt attempted to increase the size of the Supreme Court by an unusual scheme. If he had been successful, six new positions would have been added. What was this scheme called?
    (A) *stare decisis*
    (B) *amicus* addendum
    (C) court packing
    (D) partisan control
    (E) constitutional court controlling

46. Which of the following best describes the speaker of the House?
    (A) presiding officer of the House
    (B) shares power with the president pro tem
    (C) appointed by the president
    (D) appointed by members of his political party within the House
    (E) controls Congress with the help of the president

47. Which of the following is NOT a function of an interest group?
    (A) creates interest in public affairs
    (B) provides for a system of checks and balances on government officials
    (C) stimulates political participation by the people
    (D) provides information to government officials
    (E) provides an avenue for political parties to obtain the vote and confidence of the people

48. Which amendment of the United States Constitution altered the manner of voting in the electoral college?
    (A) Twenty-Second Amendment
    (B) Twenty-Fifth Amendment
    (C) Twelfth Amendment
    (D) Twentieth Amendment
    (E) Twenty-Sixth Amendment

49. Which of the following is NOT mentioned in the United States Constitution?
    (A) political parties
    (B) taxation
    (C) impeachment
    (D) treason
    (E) ex post facto laws

GO ON TO THE NEXT PAGE

50. The primary purpose of a conference committee is to
    (A) provide an investigative step in the passage of a bill
    (B) provide the president with an update on vetoed bills
    (C) compromise proposed bills between the two houses of the Congress
    (D) review revenue bills
    (E) determine if proposed bills are worthy of continuing the legislative process

51. Which of the following is considered to be the main trial court within the federal court system?
    (A) the Supreme Court
    (B) a district court
    (C) an appellate court
    (D) a federal circuit court
    (E) a court of appeals

52. Which of the following best describes the action taken by the Congress when the president vetoes a bill?
    (A) The bill is tabled.
    (B) The bill is sent to a conference committee.
    (C) The Speaker of the House is sent to discuss the bill with the president.
    (D) The bill may become a law if both houses override the presidential veto by a two-thirds vote.
    (E) The bill may become a law if both houses override the presidential veto by a simple majority in each house.

53. Which of the following is a false statement about the United States Constitution?
    (A) It is the guideline for fundamental law in the United States.
    (B) It provides for a system of checks and balances among the branches of government.
    (C) It limits the individual liberties of the American people.
    (D) It provides for the protection of individual freedoms.
    (E) It provides for the separation of power among the three branches of government.

54. Which of the following is a characteristic of cooperative federalism?
    I.   block grants
    II. revenue sharing
    III. federal grants-in-aid
    IV. devolution
    (A) I, II, and IV only
    (B) I, II, and III only
    (C) II, III, and IV only
    (D) I only
    (E) II only

55. In the absence of the vice president, who is the presiding officer in the United States Senate?
    (A) the president of the Senate
    (B) the president pro tem
    (C) the majority leader
    (D) the minority leader
    (E) the speaker

56. Where in the Constitution is the establishment of a federal court system found?
    (A) Article I
    (B) Article II
    (C) Articles I and II
    (D) Articles II and IV
    (E) Article III

57. Which of the Supreme Courts was the most active in the area of increasing the rights of the accused?
    (A) Warren Court
    (B) Rehnquist Court
    (C) Marshall Court
    (D) Nixon Court
    (E) Taft Court

58. Which of the following is part of the legislative process in the House of Representatives but NOT in the Senate?
    (A) debate on the floor
    (B) a filibuster
    (C) referral to committee
    (D) roll-call vote
    (E) assignment of rules

GO ON TO THE NEXT PAGE

59. If a state is using a party-column ballot, what type of voting strategy is a voter more likely to use?
    (A) split-ticket voting
    (B) party-line voting
    (C) nonpartisan voting
    (D) straight-ticket voting
    (E) partisan voting

60. According to James David Barber, which of the following is not a classification of presidential character?
    (A) positive-assertive
    (B) passive-negative
    (C) active-negative
    (D) passive-positive
    (E) active-positive

END OF SECTION I

"*Taking practice released-exams gave me confidence on the real exam.*"
—JG, AP student

Section II

Total Time—100 minutes

Directions: You have 100 minutes to answer all four of the following questions. Unless the directions indicate otherwise, respond to all parts of all four questions. It is suggested that you take a few minutes to plan and outline each answer. *Spend approximately one-fourth of your time (25 minutes) on each question.* Illustrate your essay with substantive examples where appropriate. Make certain to number each of your answers as the question is numbered below. Use a separate sheet of paper if you need more space.

1. (a) Identify and discuss how each of the following interacts with the bureaucracy.

   - the president

   - Congress

   - the federal courts

(b) Give one specific example of how each of the following interacts with the bureaucracy.

- special interests

- media

2. One of the most important methods of political participation is voting in elections. Over the years, the right to vote has been expanded. Choose two of the methods listed below. Explain how the right to vote has been expanded by this method in the United States. Provide one example for each explanation.

(a) constitutional amendment

GO ON TO THE NEXT PAGE

(b) congressional legislation

(c) judicial decision

Presidential Vetoes and Congressional Overrides 1960–1999

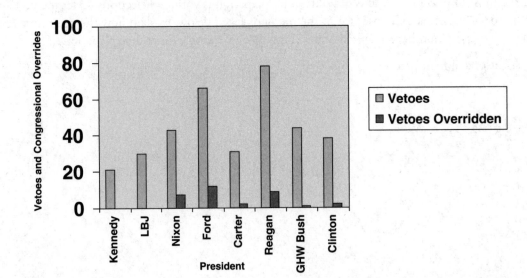

GO ON TO THE NEXT PAGE

3. Using the data in the graph above and your knowledge of U.S. government and politics, perform the following tasks:

(a) Identify two patterns shown in the graph.

(b) Discuss the relationships between presidential vetoes, congressional overrides, and the patterns you identified.

(c) Discuss two factors that might account for the two patterns you described in part (a).

4. The national government's use of incentives and sanctions accounts for the largest shift in the relationship between the federal and state governments in recent years.

- legislation
- judicial interpretation
- grants-in-aid

(a) Select two of the incentives or sanctions identified above. For each, identify and discuss its functions as an incentive or sanction.

(b) Explain how each incentive or sanction chosen has created a shift in the relationship between the federal and state governments.

END OF SECTION II

Answers to Multiple-Choice Questions

ANSWER KEY

1. C	16. B	31. E	46. A
2. E	17. A	32. C	47. E
3. D	18. B	33. A	48. C
4. B	19. B	34. A	49. A
5. A	20. A	35. D	50. C
6. A	21. D	36. C	51. B
7. D	22. C	37. B	52. D
8. D	23. A	38. C	53. C
9. B	24. E	39. A	54. B
10. B	25. A	40. E	55. B
11. A	26. C	41. B	56. E
12. C	27. A	42. C	57. A
13. D	28. D	43. A	58. E
14. E	29. D	44. C	59. D
15. D	30. B	45. C	60. A

❯ Answers and Explanations

1. **C.** The case of *Mapp v. Ohio* is among several cases that established the exclusionary rule of evidence (evidence seized in an illegal search may not be used in a court of law). *Mapp v. Ohio* also applied the exclusionary rule to state courts (E). Choice (A) refers to *United States v. Leon*. In *Wolf v. Colorado*, the Court applied protections against unreasonable search and seizure to the states under the Due Process Clause of the Fourteenth Amendment (B). Also, in *Terry v. Ohio* the Court ruled that searches of criminal suspects are constitutional (B). The Court established the inevitable discovery rule in *Nix v. Williams* (D).

2. **E.** Cases against the U.S. government are heard in the U.S. Court of Claims. The U.S. District Courts (A) have original jurisdiction and serve as trial courts at the federal level. The Supreme Court (B) is the final authority dealing with all questions arising from the Constitution, federal laws, and treaties. The U.S. Courts of Appeals (C) decide appeals from U.S. district courts and review decisions of federal administrative agencies. The U.S. Tax Court (D) is a special court within the federal judicial system.

3. **D.** Voting on legislation in both houses of Congress may be by voice, standing, or roll-call vote. The House of Representatives also uses teller and electronic voting; the Senate does not.

4. **B.** According to the Constitution, the duty of the vice president is to preside over the Senate and vote only in the case of a tie (D). The vice president does not work with the Supreme Court (A), nor does he or she issue directives to the political parties (E). The president often chooses the vice presidential running mate to balance the ticket. Balancing the ticket, however, is not a constitutional role of the vice president (C).

5. **A.** There are 27 formal amendments to the U.S. Constitution.

6. **A.** Sandra Day O'Connor was appointed in 1981 by President Ronald Reagan as the first woman on the Supreme Court. Ruth Bader Ginsburg (B) is the Court's second woman Supreme Court justice. Barbara Jordan (C) was a member of the U.S. House of Representatives from Texas. Jeannette Rankin (D) was the first woman elected to the U.S. Congress. Geraldine Ferraro (E) is a former member of the U.S. House of Representatives and the first woman to run for vice president from a major political party.

7. **D.** Political parties nominate candidates for office, politically educate the electorate, and help create a sense of centralized responsibility. The U.S. Constitution provided for the separation of powers before the entrance of parties onto the U.S. political scene.

8. **D.** The Securities and Exchange Commission was created as an independent regulatory agency to regulate securities, financial markets, and investment companies, and to prohibit fraud and dishonest investment practices. The Federal Reserve (A) regulates the lending practices of banks and the nation's money supply. The Federal Trade Commission (B) regulates misleading and false trade practices. The Commodity Futures Trading Commission (C) is an independent agency that monitors the trading of futures contracts. The Consumer Product Safety Commission (E) is an independent regulatory agency that regulates the sale and manufacture of consumer products.

9. **B.** If the House of Representatives were to act upon the failure of the electoral college to elect a president, each state delegation would receive one vote. A majority of 26 votes would be necessary for a candidate to win election.

10. **B.** Some interest groups have influence that is not proportional to the group's number of members. Some interest groups are small in membership and exert considerable influence, while other groups with large memberships may exert very little influence. Interest groups sometimes distort facts to sway the public toward their cause (A). They seek to influence the policies of government, while political parties attempt to control government (C). Interest groups vary in their degree of financial support (D). They provide channels for political participation that enable citizens to work together to achieve a common goal (E).

11. **A.** The Necessary and Proper Clause is often termed the "elastic clause" because it stretches the powers of Congress.

12. **C.** In order to be eligible to be elected president of the United States, a candidate must be a natural-born citizen. Other qualifications include being at least 35 years of age and having lived in the United States for at least 14 years.

13. **D.** Political socialization involves personal acquisition of differing beliefs and political ideology.

14. **E.** Noncitizens are not guaranteed the freedom to move about the country, while citizens of the United States have this right under the Privileges and Immunities Clause of Article IV of the Constitution. The freedoms of speech (A), religion (B), and the press (C) are guaranteed to all persons by the First Amendment. The right to an attorney (D) is granted to accused persons through Supreme Court decisions in *Powell v. Alabama*, *Betts v. Brady*, *Escobedo v. Illinois*, and *Gideon v. Wainwright*.

15. **D.** In order for cases to be heard by the Supreme Court, the "rule of four" requires that at least four of the justices agree to place the case on the Court's docket. A *writ of certiorari* (A) is an order issued by the Supreme Court directing a lower court to send up a record of a case for review. A precedent (B) is an example set by a court decision for future court cases. An *amicus curiae* (C) is a "friend of the court" brief. A certificate (E) is a query from a lower court to the Supreme Court regarding a rule of law or a procedure.

16. **B.** All federal and most state courts have the power of judicial review. Municipal courts are one type of court that does not have the power of judicial review.

17. **A.** The Department of Health and Human Services administers the Social Security program, which is the most extensive entitlement program in the United States. Homeland Security (B) prevents terrorist attacks in the United States. It includes the Coast Guard, Secret Service, Border Patrol, Immigration and Visa Services, and FEMA. The Department of Veterans Affairs (C) promotes the welfare of veterans of the armed forces. The Department of Labor (D) enforces federal labor laws and administers unemployment programs. The Department of Education (E) administers federal aid programs to schools.

18. **B.** In the impeachment process the House checks the power of the executive branch by bringing charges of impeachment against the president (E). The chief justice of the Supreme Court sits as the presiding judge in the impeachment trial, thus checking the power of the legislative branch over the executive branch (D). A two-thirds vote of the Senate is required for conviction (A). Impeachment is the act of bringing charges against the president; it may or may not result in conviction and the subsequent removal of the president from office (C).

19. **B.** In the United States, a political party is a group of individuals that seeks to control government by winning elections. A caucus (A) is a state meeting to select delegates who, in turn, nominate candidates to political offices. An interest group (C) has no legal status in the election process. Political action committees (D) are the political arms of interest groups. A constituency (E) is the group of people in a state or district that a member of Congress represents.

20. **A.** Although choices (B), (C), (D), and (E) may contribute to the success of a congressional candidate, the most significant advantage is incumbency. Name recognition, claiming credit for projects, providing casework for constituents, greater media exposure, and fundraising abilities are all advantages of incumbents during an election.

21. **D.** One method of ratification of constitutional amendments is by the state legislatures in three-fourths of the states (E). A second method of ratification is by special conventions held in three-fourths of the states. These conventions are called by the states, not by Congress (A). Amendments may be proposed by a national convention (B) or by a two-thirds vote of both houses of Congress (C).

22. **C.** Federal judges, including Supreme Court justices, serve for a period of life, during good behavior. They may be removed from office only through the impeachment process.

23. **A.** In *Federalist #10*, James Madison referred to factions, meaning political parties and interest groups.

24. **E.** Public opinion is the belief that the general public has about politics and public policy issues. Political socialization (A) is the complex process by which people get their sense of political identity, beliefs, and values. Public policy (B) is the exercise of governmental power in doing those things necessary to maintain legitimate authority and control over society. Policy formulation (C) is the crafting of a policy to resolve public problems. Political ideology (D) is a consistent set of beliefs about politics and public policy that sets the framework for evaluating government and public policy.

25. **A.** Executive agreements are pacts made between the president and other heads of state. Unlike treaties, executive agreements do not require Senate approval. The power of the purse (B) is the fact that agency budgets must be authorized and appropriated by Congress. Judicial review of executive actions (C) is the power to declare executive actions unconstitutional. Public opinion may act as a check on presidential actions (D). Presidential appointments must be approved by a two-thirds vote of the Senate (E).

26. **C.** After a bill is introduced, which is considered the first reading, it is then sent to the appropriate standing committee for review. The correct order for the remaining choices is A (if further information on the bill is necessary), E, B, and D.

27. **A.** According to the Twelfth Amendment, each elector casts two ballots, one for president and another for vice president. State legislatures do not have a role in the choice of the president (B). Although not a constitutional provision, electoral votes are cast according to the state popular vote (C). Although electors are not bound by federal law to vote for their party's candidate (D), the laws of a few states bind electors to vote according to the popular vote (E).

28. **D.** Interest groups often take an issue to court if they are unsuccessful in gaining the support of Congress. The remaining answer choices are true regarding interest groups.

29. **D.** *Amicus curiae* briefs are filed by "friends of the court," interested parties who have no standing in the case but who wish to provide information and opinions to the court for consideration. A *per curiam* decision (A) is one delivered by the court as a whole. A certificate (B) is a method of bringing a case before the Supreme Court. A *writ of certiorari* (C) is an order by a higher court directing a lower court to provide the record in a case for review. *Stare decisis* (E) is the doctrine that a trial court is bound by the decisions of appellate courts.

30. **B.** Conservatism, or the belief that big government infringes on personal liberties, is not a principle found in the Constitution. Popular sovereignty (A) is the concept that government exists with the consent of the governed. Limited government (C) is the principle that governmental power is restricted. Judicial review (D), one aspect of the principle of checks and balances, is the power of courts to determine the constitutionality of legislative and executive actions. Federalism (E) is the division of powers between a national government and several regional governments.

31. **E.** The drawing of electoral districts within a state in order to favor one political party or candidate is known as gerrymandering. The other answer choices do not describe gerrymandering.

32. **C.** The social contract theory, based on the writings of John Locke and supported by Thomas Jefferson in the Declaration of Independence, calls for a voluntary agreement between citizens and government. The divine right theory (A) was the traditional European belief that monarchs derived their power to govern from God. Hyperpluralism (B) views democracy as a system of many groups pulling government in many directions at the same time. The elite theory (E) holds that governmental power is in the hands of a small powerful elite. There is no state theory (D).

33. **A.** Judicial review allows a court to act on the constitutionality of a law passed by Congress. The Supreme Court established this principle in *Marbury v. Madison* (1803).

34. **A.** Independent regulatory commissions are created to act independently of presidential control.

35. **D.** The Constitution does not delegate management of the federal budget to the president. The Constitution does grant the president the powers of making appointments (A) and treaties (C), both with the consent of the Senate. The president is the commander-in-chief of the armed forces (B). The Constitution also gives the president the power to grant pardons (E).

36. **C.** State primaries and caucuses generally occur earliest in the presidential election contest. The next stage is usually the national party convention (A) and selection of the running mate (E). The next stage is the popular election (B) followed by the electoral college election (D).

37. **B.** The majority opinion is submitted by those justices who agree with the Court's majority decision. A concurring opinion is submitted by a justice or justices who agree with the majority decision but have different reasons for doing so. A dissenting opinion is submitted by a justice or justices who disagree with the majority opinion. All three may be submitted to explain the decisions of the Court.

38. **C.** Lobbyists serve interest groups by trying to bring influence on the workings of government.

39. **A.** Successful interest groups usually employ tactics and strategies other than civil disobedience or violence. The remaining answer choices are methods frequently used by interest groups.

40. **E.** The Twenty-Fourth Amendment abolished the poll tax. The Twentieth Amendment (A) set the dates of the terms of the president and vice president and of the sessions of Congress. The Eighteenth Amendment (B) established prohibition, while the Twenty-First Amendment (C) repealed prohibition. The Twenty-Fifth Amendment (D) dealt with presidential succession.

41. **B.** Gatekeepers are media executives, news editors, and prominent reporters who decide what news to present and how it will be presented. The remaining answer choices represent roles of the members of Congress.

A constituent servant (A) is a representative who is interested in assisting constituents with problems. As a policymaker (C), a member of Congress makes public policy through the passage of legislation. A delegate (D) is a representative whose vote is based on the wishes of constituents. A trustee (E) is a representative who, after listening to constituents, votes based on his or her own opinions.

42. **C.** One of the judicial powers of the president is the power to grant amnesty, the offer of a pardon to a group of people who have committed offenses against the government. President Gerald Ford granted amnesty to men who left the United States during the Vietnam Conflict to avoid the draft.

43. **A.** The Constitution gives Congress the power to establish agencies of the federal bureaucracy.

44. **C.** An independent agency is an agency of the executive branch that does not fall within the jurisdiction of a cabinet-level department. Examples include the Equal Opportunity Employment Commission and the Environmental Protection Agency.

45. **C.** "Court packing" is the term used to describe President Franklin Roosevelt's plan to increase the size of the Supreme Court by allowing the appointment of justices who were more likely to support Roosevelt's New Deal legislation. The plan was never implemented.

46. **A.** The Speaker of the House is the presiding officer of the House of Representatives. The Speaker does not share power with the president *pro tempore* of the Senate (B). The Speaker is elected by the members of the majority party in the House (C, D). The majority leader and the majority whip, not the president, assist the Speaker (E).

47. **E.** Interest groups do not provide ways for political parties to obtain votes. Interest groups do create interest in public affairs (A), stimulate political participation by the people (C), provide information to the government on issues they represent (D), and help provide for the system of checks and balance through their monitoring functions (B).

---

48. **C.** The Twelfth Amendment provides for electors to choose the president and vice president by casting separate ballots for each office. Before the ratification of this amendment, each elector would cast two ballots. The candidate with the largest number of electoral votes became president, while the candidate receiving the second highest number of votes became vice president. The Twelfth Amendment was added in 1804 after the election of 1800 failed to produce a winner in the electoral college. Thomas Jefferson became president in 1801 after a long battle in the House of Representatives.

49. **A.** Since political parties did not begin to form until George Washington's second administration, the Constitution does not refer to political parties.

50. **C.** Conference committees are created to iron out the differences in the House and Senate versions of a bill. Their goal is to create a compromise bill that, once passed by the House and Senate, can be sent to the president for signature or veto.

51. **B.** District courts serve as the trial courts within the federal court system. The remaining answer choices do not refer to trial courts.

52. **D.** When the president vetoes a bill it is sent back to Congress, where it may become law if it is overridden by a two-thirds vote of both houses.

53. **C.** The Constitution does not limit the individual liberties of the American people. The Constitution, including the Bill of Rights, guarantees numerous rights to the people.

54. **B.** Block grants, revenue sharing, and federal grants-in-aid are all characteristic of cooperative federalism. Devolution requires greater state responsibility about how grant money should be spent and is, therefore, a step away from cooperative federalism.

55. **B.** If the vice president, who serves as president of the Senate, is not present, the president *pro tempore* serves in the vice president's absence. The majority party selects the president *pro tempore*.

56. **E.** Article III of the Constitution establishes the federal court system. Article I describes the organization and powers of the legislative branch, while Article II establishes the executive branch. Article IV deals with relations among the states.

57. **A.** The Supreme Court under Chief Justice Earl Warren (1953–1969) was the most active in increasing the rights of the accused. (Sample cases include *Miranda v. Arizona*, 1966; *Gideon v. Wainwright*, 1963; and *Mapp v. Ohio*, 1961.)

58. **E.** The assignment of rules occurs in the Rules Committee in the House of Representatives, but no such committee exists in the Senate. Filibusters (B) may occur in the Senate but not in the House of Representatives. Floor debate (A), referral to committee (C), and the roll-call vote (D) occur in both the House of Representatives and the Senate.

59. **D.** Since the party-column ballot lists only the party members running for each office on the ballot, the party-column ballot attracts voters to the ease of straight-ticket voting.

60. **A.** James David Barber classified types of presidential character as active-positive, active-negative, passive-positive, and passive-negative. Positive-assertive was not a classification used by Barber.

› Rubrics for the Free-Response Essay

1. Total Value: 8 points
   Part (a): 1 point for each correct identification of interaction = 3 points
       1 point for each correct discussion of interaction = 3 points
   Part (b): 1 point for each correct example of interaction = 2 points

2. Total Value: 4 points

   1 point for each correct explanation of the right to vote = 2 points
   1 point for each correct example = 2 points

3. Total Value: 5 points

   Part (a): 1 point for two correctly identified patterns = 1 point
   Part (b): 1 point for each correct discussion tied to a pattern = 2 points
   Part (c): 1 point for each correct discussion of factors tied to a pattern = 2 points

4. Total Value: 6 points

   Part (a): 1 point for each correct identification of incentive or sanction = 2 points
       1 point for each correct discussion of incentive or sanction = 2 points
   Part (b): 1 point for each correct explanation of shifts in relationship = 2 points

"Practice taking timed tests and writing timed free-response essays."
—LL, AP teacher

AP U.S. Government and Politics
Practice Exam 2—Section I

ANSWER SHEET

1 Ⓐ Ⓑ Ⓒ Ⓓ Ⓔ
2 Ⓐ Ⓑ Ⓒ Ⓓ Ⓔ
3 Ⓐ Ⓑ Ⓒ Ⓓ Ⓔ
4 Ⓐ Ⓑ Ⓒ Ⓓ Ⓔ
5 Ⓐ Ⓑ Ⓒ Ⓓ Ⓔ
6 Ⓐ Ⓑ Ⓒ Ⓓ Ⓔ
7 Ⓐ Ⓑ Ⓒ Ⓓ Ⓔ
8 Ⓐ Ⓑ Ⓒ Ⓓ Ⓔ
9 Ⓐ Ⓑ Ⓒ Ⓓ Ⓔ
10 Ⓐ Ⓑ Ⓒ Ⓓ Ⓔ
11 Ⓐ Ⓑ Ⓒ Ⓓ Ⓔ
12 Ⓐ Ⓑ Ⓒ Ⓓ Ⓔ
13 Ⓐ Ⓑ Ⓒ Ⓓ Ⓔ
14 Ⓐ Ⓑ Ⓒ Ⓓ Ⓔ
15 Ⓐ Ⓑ Ⓒ Ⓓ Ⓔ
16 Ⓐ Ⓑ Ⓒ Ⓓ Ⓔ
17 Ⓐ Ⓑ Ⓒ Ⓓ Ⓔ
18 Ⓐ Ⓑ Ⓒ Ⓓ Ⓔ
19 Ⓐ Ⓑ Ⓒ Ⓓ Ⓔ
20 Ⓐ Ⓑ Ⓒ Ⓓ Ⓔ

21 Ⓐ Ⓑ Ⓒ Ⓓ Ⓔ
22 Ⓐ Ⓑ Ⓒ Ⓓ Ⓔ
23 Ⓐ Ⓑ Ⓒ Ⓓ Ⓔ
24 Ⓐ Ⓑ Ⓒ Ⓓ Ⓔ
25 Ⓐ Ⓑ Ⓒ Ⓓ Ⓔ
26 Ⓐ Ⓑ Ⓒ Ⓓ Ⓔ
27 Ⓐ Ⓑ Ⓒ Ⓓ Ⓔ
28 Ⓐ Ⓑ Ⓒ Ⓓ Ⓔ
29 Ⓐ Ⓑ Ⓒ Ⓓ Ⓔ
30 Ⓐ Ⓑ Ⓒ Ⓓ Ⓔ
31 Ⓐ Ⓑ Ⓒ Ⓓ Ⓔ
32 Ⓐ Ⓑ Ⓒ Ⓓ Ⓔ
33 Ⓐ Ⓑ Ⓒ Ⓓ Ⓔ
34 Ⓐ Ⓑ Ⓒ Ⓓ Ⓔ
35 Ⓐ Ⓑ Ⓒ Ⓓ Ⓔ
36 Ⓐ Ⓑ Ⓒ Ⓓ Ⓔ
37 Ⓐ Ⓑ Ⓒ Ⓓ Ⓔ
38 Ⓐ Ⓑ Ⓒ Ⓓ Ⓔ
39 Ⓐ Ⓑ Ⓒ Ⓓ Ⓔ
40 Ⓐ Ⓑ Ⓒ Ⓓ Ⓔ

41 Ⓐ Ⓑ Ⓒ Ⓓ Ⓔ
42 Ⓐ Ⓑ Ⓒ Ⓓ Ⓔ
43 Ⓐ Ⓑ Ⓒ Ⓓ Ⓔ
44 Ⓐ Ⓑ Ⓒ Ⓓ Ⓔ
45 Ⓐ Ⓑ Ⓒ Ⓓ Ⓔ
46 Ⓐ Ⓑ Ⓒ Ⓓ Ⓔ
47 Ⓐ Ⓑ Ⓒ Ⓓ Ⓔ
48 Ⓐ Ⓑ Ⓒ Ⓓ Ⓔ
49 Ⓐ Ⓑ Ⓒ Ⓓ Ⓔ
50 Ⓐ Ⓑ Ⓒ Ⓓ Ⓔ
51 Ⓐ Ⓑ Ⓒ Ⓓ Ⓔ
52 Ⓐ Ⓑ Ⓒ Ⓓ Ⓔ
53 Ⓐ Ⓑ Ⓒ Ⓓ Ⓔ
54 Ⓐ Ⓑ Ⓒ Ⓓ Ⓔ
55 Ⓐ Ⓑ Ⓒ Ⓓ Ⓔ
56 Ⓐ Ⓑ Ⓒ Ⓓ Ⓔ
57 Ⓐ Ⓑ Ⓒ Ⓓ Ⓔ
58 Ⓐ Ⓑ Ⓒ Ⓓ Ⓔ
59 Ⓐ Ⓑ Ⓒ Ⓓ Ⓔ
60 Ⓐ Ⓑ Ⓒ Ⓓ Ⓔ

I _____ did _____ did not finish all the questions in the allotted 45 minutes.

I had _____ correct answers. I had _____ incorrect answers, including questions I left blank.

Scoring Formula:

_____ = _____

number right   raw score

I have carefully reviewed the explanations of the answers. I need to work on the following types of questions:

AP U.S. Government and Politics
Practice Exam 2

Section I

Total Time—45 minutes

60 Questions

Directions: Each of the questions or incomplete statements below is followed by five suggested answers or completions. Select the one that is best in each case and then fill in the corresponding oval on the answer sheet.

1. The burning of a United States flag would best be described as
   (A) unintended speech
   (B) an obscenity
   (C) a right that would be prohibited by the First Amendment
   (D) symbolic speech
   (E) a criminal activity

2. Richard Neustadt, a noted political theorist, has stated that a president's power comes from
   (A) having the president's political party control both houses of the Congress during the presidential term
   (B) the president's ability to persuade others to do what he or she wants
   (C) being outside of politics
   (D) not being sensitive to the political surroundings
   (E) implementing his or her policies over the party's policies

3. The first African American to serve on the Supreme Court of the United States was
   (A) Thurgood Marshall
   (B) John Marshall
   (C) Clarence Thomas
   (D) Oliver Wendell Holmes
   (E) William O. Douglas

4. How often are members of the House of Representatives elected?
   (A) every six years
   (B) every five years
   (C) every four years
   (D) every three years
   (E) every two years

5. Which of the following was an expansion of suffrage that occurred before the Civil War?
   (A) elimination of gender disqualifications
   (B) elimination of poll taxes
   (C) elimination of religious qualifications
   (D) elimination of race disqualifications
   (E) elimination of literacy tests

6. If the president must nominate a new vice president due to the office being vacated, the nomination must be approved and confirmed by
   (A) the Senate
   (B) the House of Representatives
   (C) both houses of Congress
   (D) the Supreme Court
   (E) the Senate and the Supreme Court

7. Interest groups are different from political parties because they
   (A) only attempt to influence the president
   (B) do not nominate candidates for office
   (C) are only concerned with the winning of elections
   (D) deal with a wide range of policy issues
   (E) are more concerned with the making of policy than influencing policy

8. In the United States Constitution, where is the congressional power of taxation found?
   (A) Article III
   (B) Article II
   (C) Article I
   (D) Article VI
   (E) Article IV

GO ON TO THE NEXT PAGE

9. When Congress passed the Brady Bill, which required a five-day waiting period before the purchase of a handgun, it was following which step of the policymaking process?
   (A) agenda setting
   (B) policy formulation
   (C) policy evaluation
   (D) policy adoption
   (E) policy implementation

10. The Full Faith and Credit Clause of the Constitution is the requirement that each state accept the public acts, records, and judicial proceedings of every other state, found in the Constitution in
    (A) Article I
    (B) Article VI
    (C) Article IV
    (D) Article III
    (E) Article II

11. Which amendment of the United States Constitution applies to unreasonable searches and seizure?
    (A) Fourth Amendment
    (B) Tenth Amendment
    (C) Fifth Amendment
    (D) Ninth Amendment
    (E) Second Amendment

12. What is a possible result of an "off-year" election?
    (A) The president may be forced to resign.
    (B) The political power of Congress increases.
    (C) The power base of Congress may change.
    (D) The Constitution may change.
    (E) An entirely new Senate is elected.

13. Executive agreements
    (A) are nonbinding agreements
    (B) require the approval of both houses of Congress
    (C) do not have the force of law
    (D) must be approved by the Supreme Court
    (E) do not require Senate approval

14. An order from the Supreme Court requesting that a lower court send up its records on a particular case is known as a(n)
    (A) certificate
    (B) *writ of certiorari*
    (C) appeal
    (D) brief proposal
    (E) writ of power

15. Which of the following was NOT an aspect of the political culture of most of the Founding Fathers present at the Constitutional Convention?
    (A) Enlightenment philosophy
    (B) divine right theory
    (C) traditional democratic theory
    (D) natural rights
    (E) limited government

16. Which of the following is a proposed plan of reform for the electoral college when electing the president?
    I. the district plan
    II. the proportional plan
    III. direct population election
    IV. the national bonus plan
    (A) I only
    (B) II and IV only
    (C) I, II, III, and IV
    (D) III only
    (E) III and IV only

17. Political action committees are extensions of interest groups that
    (A) raise money for campaigns
    (B) call for the resignation of fraudulent office holders
    (C) encourage massive use of propaganda
    (D) define public opinion
    (E) determine public opinion

18. Which of the following is true about most presidential elections in modern history?
    (A) Candidates from all parties usually receive some electoral votes.
    (B) They result in major party realignments.
    (C) They often center around one important issue.
    (D) The winner of the popular vote usually wins the majority of the electoral vote.
    (E) They are nonpartisan elections.

19. The power of television in U.S. politics was best illustrated in which of the following presidential elections?
    (A) the Bush-Gore election of 2000
    (B) the Truman-Dewey election of 1948
    (C) the Nixon-Kennedy election of 1960
    (D) the Carter-Ford election of 1976
    (E) the Reagan-Carter election of 1980

GO ON TO THE NEXT PAGE

20. An important result of *McCulloch v. Maryland* (1819) was to
    (A) establish the supremacy of the federal government over the states
    (B) place limits on the powers of Congress
    (C) establish the doctrine of judicial review
    (D) establish the doctrine of dual federalism
    (E) give greater power to the states

21. Which of the following occurs latest in the passage of a bill in Congress?
    (A) conference committee
    (B) referral to committee
    (C) investigation and hearings
    (D) debate on the floor
    (E) amendment committee

22. Voters casting their ballots for candidates of a presidential candidate's political party because of the popularity of the presidential candidate is best described as
    (A) same-party voting
    (B) the presidential-coattail effect
    (C) the party-electoral effect
    (D) the electoral effect
    (E) presidential-party voting

23. Which is true of the Supreme Court of the United States?
    (A) Judges are nominated by the president and confirmed by the House of Representatives.
    (B) Judges serve at the will of the president.
    (C) Judges are appointed for life and can only be removed by impeachment.
    (D) Judges set their own salaries and benefits.
    (E) Judges are always from the same political party as the president.

24. A low percentage of voter turnout is often caused by
    I. mobility of the electorate
    II. the perception of obvious differences between candidates or parties
    III. lack of political efficacy
    IV. dissatisfaction with things as they are
    (A) II only
    (B) I and IV only
    (C) III only
    (D) I and II only
    (E) I and III only

25. Cabinet-level executive departments are created by
    (A) Congress
    (B) the Constitution
    (C) the president
    (D) the Supreme Court
    (E) recommendation of other cabinet-level offices

26. When the House of Representatives sits as one large committee, it is sitting as
    (A) the full house
    (B) a quorum
    (C) a standing committee
    (D) the Committee of the Whole
    (E) the Committee at Large

27. Which of the following is a false statement regarding minor parties?
    (A) Third parties have been useful in introducing new ideas in American politics.
    (B) Minor parties have played an important role in reforming American politics.
    (C) Minor parties have usually been successful in getting candidates elected to office.
    (D) Minor parties may also be classified as ideological parties.
    (E) Minor parties tend to focus on single issues.

28. Checking with party members on party policy and helping the floor leader to determine if there are enough votes to pass a particular issue is part of the job description of which of the following members of Congress?
    (A) minority floor leaders
    (B) whips
    (C) the Speaker of the House
    (D) the president *pro tempore*
    (E) committee chairpersons

29. When the United States government is party to a case, who represents the United States before the Supreme Court?
    (A) the attorney general
    (B) the chief justice of the Supreme Court
    (C) the solicitor general
    (D) the secretary of justice
    (E) the general counsel for the president

GO ON TO THE NEXT PAGE

30. With reference to the executive branch, the Twenty-Fifth Amendment establishes
    (A) a system of checks and balances
    (B) direct election of the president
    (C) a direct change in the electoral college
    (D) more power to be given to the vice president
    (E) presidential succession and disability procedures

31. Which of the following is a reason for the decline in voting?
    (A) decrease in the number of eligible voters
    (B) decline in parties' ability to mobilize voters
    (C) same-day registration in a larger number of states
    (D) penalties for nonvoting
    (E) increase in party loyalty

32. Which of the following is true of the incumbency effect?
    (A) Members of the House of Representatives benefit more than members of the Senate.
    (B) Members of the Senate benefit more than members of the House of Representatives.
    (C) Members of the House of Representatives and Senate benefit equally.
    (D) Incumbency does not benefit either members of the House of Representatives or Senate.
    (E) The president benefits from the incumbency effect.

33. Which of the following would probably be least likely to vote?
    (A) a high school dropout
    (B) a wealthy white businessman
    (C) a woman professional
    (D) a labor union member
    (E) an active Roman Catholic

34. The issuance of an executive order falls under the president's
    (A) legislative powers
    (B) diplomatic powers
    (C) executive powers
    (D) judicial powers
    (E) military powers

35. After 1950, the success of the civil rights movement was aided most by
    (A) African Americans lowering their expectations
    (B) the passage of the Fourteenth Amendment
    (C) a shift of the movement to the courts
    (D) African Americans winning election to public office
    (E) decreased participation by interest groups in the civil rights movement

36. As a special interest group, the National Organization for Women was organized for the purpose of
    (A) ratifying an equal rights amendment for women
    (B) creating more jobs for women
    (C) dealing with the abortion issue in America
    (D) advocating for legislation to protect women's rights
    (E) promoting a national women's party devoted to the purpose of electing the first woman president

37. Which of the following is NOT true of federalism?
    (A) A state may not unreasonably discriminate against the resident of another state.
    (B) The federal government handles matters of national concern.
    (C) States may extradite fugitives from one state to another.
    (D) States must honor another state's public acts, laws, and records.
    (E) The powers of the federal government are less than the powers of the state governments.

38. The Supreme Court case of *Gideon v. Wainwright* was a significant case in that it
    (A) caused law enforcement officers to advise the criminally accused of their rights
    (B) called for attorney rights to be applied at the state level as well as at the federal level
    (C) called for the accused to be confronted by witnesses against them
    (D) stated that search warrants were constitutionally required under all circumstances
    (E) allowed judges to determine what constitutes double jeopardy in a case

GO ON TO THE NEXT PAGE

39. A bill that has been held up in a committee may be forced out of that committee by which of the following methods?
    (A) joint resolution
    (B) House call by the Speaker
    (C) discharge petition
    (D) cloture petition
    (E) cannot be forced out of a committee in either house of Congress

40. Party dealignment might be occurring if
    (A) government tends to be "divided"
    (B) one party tends to win control of government more often
    (C) support for minor parties is declining
    (D) political parties are becoming more centralized
    (E) people are voting Republican more often than they are voting Democrat

41. Which of the following is NOT a check on the power of the federal courts by Congress?
    (A) changing the tenure of justices
    (B) confirmation of appointments
    (C) changing the court's jurisdiction
    (D) altering the number of justices
    (E) amending the Constitution

42. The War Powers Resolution of 1973 requires
    I.   the president to inform Congress within 48 hours of any commitment of American troops abroad
    II.   the president to keep troops abroad for at least 60 days
    III. the president to follow the guidelines of the Constitution regarding war
    (A) I only
    (B) II only
    (C) III only
    (D) I and II only
    (E) I, II, and III

43. Which of the following historic Supreme Court cases called for apportionment of representative seats in Congress to be as equal as possible?
    (A) *Marbury v. Madison*
    (B) *McCulloch v. Maryland*
    (C) *Mapp v. Ohio*
    (D) *Wesberry v. Sanders*
    (E) *Miranda v. Arizona*

44. A list of cases to be heard is called a(n)
    (A) *decisis* of cases
    (B) agenda of cases
    (C) docket
    (D) court agenda
    (E) *amicus* docket

45. Compared to a political conservative, a political liberal generally
    (A) favors limited governmental involvement in civil rights issues
    (B) supports active governmental involvement in the promotion of individual welfare
    (C) favors a limited governmental role in the promotion of national security
    (D) supports more traditional values and lifestyles
    (E) promotes a limited governmental role in aiding individuals economically

46. The Constitution of the United States was written as a direct result of
    (A) the American Revolution
    (B) orders issued by the Second Continental Congress
    (C) the failure of state governments under the new federal union
    (D) the decisions reached at the Annapolis Convention
    (E) the failure of the Articles of Confederation to provide adequate direction for the union

47. When voters elect a representative from a district within a state, and that representative is selected from several candidates, what type of election system is that state using?
    (A) a general ticket system
    (B) a single-member district system
    (C) at-large voting
    (D) a one-person one-vote system
    (E) gerrymandering

48. Which of the following include the president's key foreign and military advisors?
    (A) State Department
    (B) Central Intelligence Agency
    (C) Federal Bureau of Investigation
    (D) Department of Homeland Security
    (E) National Security Council

GO ON TO THE NEXT PAGE

49. How many presidents of the United States have been impeached?
    (A) two
    (B) three
    (C) one
    (D) four
    (E) none

50. Which constitutional amendment provided for the direct election of senators?
    (A) Twelfth Amendment
    (B) Sixteenth Amendment
    (C) Twentieth Amendment
    (D) Fourteenth Amendment
    (E) Seventeenth Amendment

51. Which of the following is not considered to be one of the special or legislative courts in the federal court system?
    (A) the Territorial Courts
    (B) the United States Tax Court
    (C) the United States Claims Court
    (D) the Courts of Appeals
    (E) the Court of Military Appeals

52. What is the minimum age requirement for a member of the United States Senate?
    (A) 35
    (B) 25
    (C) 30
    (D) 21
    (E) There is no minimum age requirement.

53. The first political parties in America were the Federalist and the Democratic-Republicans. The leaders of these two parties were
    (A) John Adams and Andrew Jackson
    (B) George Washington and John Adams
    (C) Alexander Hamilton and Thomas Jefferson
    (D) Alexander Hamilton and Aaron Burr
    (E) James Madison and Dewitt Clinton

54. When appointing justices to the Supreme Court, the president considers all of the following EXCEPT
    (A) political ideology
    (B) senatorial courtesy
    (C) judicial experience
    (D) political party of nominee
    (E) race, age, and gender of nominee

55. Which of the following is NOT a constitutional power of the president?
    (A) the president invoking the practice of executive privilege
    (B) the president creating cabinet-level departments of the executive branch
    (C) delivery of the State of the Union Address
    (D) the president serving as commander of the military
    (E) the president signing or vetoing legislation

56. Which of the following is a specific power of the Senate?
    I.   tries and convicts in impeachment cases
    II. elects the vice president when the electoral college fails
    III. approves presidential appointments and treaties
    (A) I only
    (B) II only
    (C) I and II
    (D) II and III
    (E) I, II, and III

57. Which office of the executive branch is responsible for helping the president prepare the national budget?
    (A) Office of Budget Affairs
    (B) Department of the Treasury
    (C) Department of Commerce
    (D) Office of Management and Budget
    (E) United States Tax Office

58. What type of jurisdiction does the Supreme Court have?
    (A) only original
    (B) only appellate
    (C) only exclusive
    (D) original and mutual
    (E) original and appellate

59. Which of the following is the most powerful person in the United States Senate?
    (A) speaker
    (B) vice president
    (C) president of the Senate
    (D) minority leader
    (E) majority leader

GO ON TO THE NEXT PAGE

60. A major factor influencing whether or not a person approves of a president's job performance is
    (A) political party identification
    (B) geographic location
    (C) race
    (D) level of income
    (E) gender

END OF SECTION I

Section II

Total Time—100 minutes

Directions: You have 100 minutes to answer all four of the following questions. Unless the directions indicate otherwise, respond to all parts of all four questions. It is suggested that you take a few minutes to plan and outline each answer. *Spend approximately one-fourth of your time (25 minutes) on each question.* Illustrate your essay with substantive examples where appropriate. Make certain to number each of your answers as the question is numbered below. Use a separate sheet of paper if you need more space.

1. Interest groups often exert vast influences over public policymaking.

   (a) Identify three major activities used by interest groups to influence public policymaking.

   (b) Explain how each activity identified affects each of the following:
   - legislative branch

   - executive branch

   - judicial branch

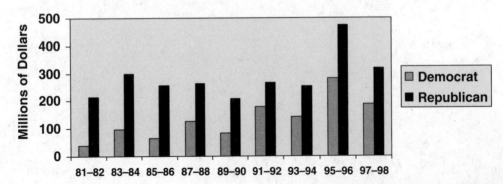

Political Campaign Receipts: 1981–1998

GO ON TO THE NEXT PAGE

2. Using the data in the graph above and your knowledge of U.S. government and politics, perform the following tasks:

(a) Identify one significant pattern shown in the graph.

(b) Discuss two factors that might contribute to the trends you identified.

(c) Discuss one consequence of this trend for the U.S. political process.

3. Relationships between the president and both Congress and the courts involve the use of strategies designed to achieve the president's public policy goals.

(a) Identify and discuss two strategies the president may use with Congress to achieve public policy goals.

(b) Identify and discuss two strategies the president may use with the courts to achieve public policy goals.

(c) Identify one method Congress has and one method the courts have that might prevent the president from achieving public policy goals.

GO ON TO THE NEXT PAGE

4. In both presidential and congressional campaigns, the candidates must get nominated and then elected. Major differences exist between presidential and congressional campaigns.

    (a) Discuss the process of being nominated to run for presidential or congressional office.

    (b) Identify and discuss two major differences that exist between presidential and congressional campaigns.

    (c) Identify two methods that have been used in recent presidential elections to encourage voter participation. Explain how each method has been used to encourage voter participation.

END OF SECTION II

Answers to Multiple-Choice Questions

ANSWER KEY

1. D	16. C	31. B	46. E
2. B	17. A	32. A	47. B
3. A	18. D	33. A	48. E
4. E	19. C	34. C	49. A
5. C	20. A	35. C	50. E
6. C	21. A	36. D	51. D
7. B	22. B	37. E	52. C
8. C	23. C	38. B	53. C
9. D	24. E	39. C	54. B
10. C	25. A	40. A	55. B
11. A	26. D	41. A	56. E
12. C	27. C	42. A	57. D
13. E	28. B	43. D	58. E
14. B	29. C	44. C	59. E
15. B	30. E	45. B	60. A

> Answers and Explanations

1. **D.** In *Texas v. Johnson* the Supreme Court stated that burning the U.S. flag was a form of symbolic speech protected under the First Amendment.

2. **B.** Richard Neustadt stated that a president's power comes from the ability to persuade others to do what he or she wants.

3. **A.** The first African American appointed to the Supreme Court was Thurgood Marshall, appointed by Lyndon Johnson. John Marshall (B) was the first Chief Justice of the Supreme Court. Oliver Wendell Holmes (D) and William O. Douglas (E) were Supreme Court justices. Clarence Thomas (C) currently serves as a justice on the Supreme Court.

4. **E.** Members of the House of Representatives are elected every two years.

5. **C.** Religious qualifications for voting were eliminated in the early years of the nineteenth century. Gender disqualifications (A) were eliminated in 1920 with the passage of the Nineteenth Amendment. Poll taxes in federal elections (B) were eliminated in 1964 with the passage of the Twenty-Fourth Amendment. Race disqualifications (D) were eliminated in 1870 with the passage of the Fifteenth Amendment. Literary tests (E) were eliminated in the Voting Rights Act of 1965.

6. **C.** If the president nominates a vice president because of a vacancy in the office, the Twenty-Fifth Amendment calls for both houses of Congress to approve the nomination.

7. **B.** Interest groups do not nominate candidates for office. Choices (C), (D), and (E) describe the activities of political parties. Neither interest groups nor political parties attempt to influence only the president (A).

8. **C.** Article I, which establishes the legislative branch, gives Congress the power to tax. Article II (B) establishes the executive branch, while Article III (A) establishes the judicial branch. Article IV (E) deals with relationships among the states, while Article VI (D) establishes the supremacy of the Constitution.

9. **D.** Congress was involved in the policy adoption step, in which government adopts a plan of action, including the passage of legislation, to solve a problem. Agenda setting (A) is the recognition of an issue as a problem that must be addressed. Policy formulation (B) involves finding ways to solve the problem. Policy implementation (E) is the execution of the plan of action by the appropriate agencies, while policy evaluation (C) is the analysis of policy and its impact upon the problem.

10. **C.** The Full Faith and Credit Clause is found in Article IV of the Constitution, which addresses the relationship among the states.

11. **A.** The Fourth Amendment protects against unreasonable searches and seizures. The Tenth Amendment (B) speaks of the powers reserved to the states or to the people. The Fifth Amendment (C) deals with criminal proceedings and due process. The Ninth Amendment (D) addresses rights retained by the people, while the Second Amendment (E) guarantees the right to bear arms.

12. **C.** Frequently during off-year elections the party of the president may lose seats in Congress, changing the base of power. Off-year elections do not force the president to resign (A), nor does the political power of Congress increase (B). The Constitution changes only by amendment (D). In any congressional election, only one-third of the Senate is elected (E).

13. **E.** Executive agreements do not require Senate approval (B). They are pacts between the president and the head of state of a foreign country and are binding on the parties who make the agreement (A). They do not require the consent of the Supreme Court (D), nor do they remove governmental authority from Congress (C).

14. **B.** A *writ of certiorari* (cert) is an order from the Supreme Court requesting that a lower court send up its records on a particular case.

15. **B.** Political culture is the set of basic beliefs and values about government that is shared by most

citizens. The divine right theory was the traditional European belief that monarchs ruled by direct authority from God. By the time in which the Constitution was written, the divine right theory had been challenged by Enlightenment philosophy (A), which included a belief in natural rights (D) ensured by limited government (E). The Founding Fathers embraced traditional democratic theory (C), or the concept that government depends on the consent of the governed.

16. **C**. Proposed reforms of the electoral college include the district plan, proportional plan, national bonus plan, and direct popular election. In the district plan, two electors would be chosen at large from each state, while the other electors would be chosen within the state's congressional districts. Under the proportional plan, each presidential candidate would receive a share of the electoral vote proportional to the state's popular vote. The national bonus plan keeps the basic structure of the electoral college, but awards an additional 102 electoral votes to the winner of the popular vote. Direct popular election is the concept of abolishing the electoral college.

17. **A**. Political action committees are extensions of interest groups that raise money for political candidates and campaigns.

18. **D**. In most modern presidential elections, the winner of the popular vote also wins the majority of the electoral vote. Usually only candidates of major parties receive electoral votes (A). Most modern elections center around a variety of issues (C), but seldom result in realignment of the major parties (B). Elections involve the active participation of political parties (E).

19. **C**. The power of the media, especially television, is best illustrated by the Kennedy-Nixon campaign in 1960, when a presidential debate was televised for the first time. Television coverage of the debates is credited as one of the factors in Kennedy's victory over Nixon. Television continued to play a major role in the coverage of future presidential campaigns (A, D, E). The role of the media in the Truman-Dewey campaign (B) is best noted by faulty polling methods that incorrectly predicted Dewey as the winner of the election.

20. **A**. An important result of *McCulloch v. Maryland* (1819) was to establish the supremacy of the federal government over the states (E). *McCulloch* upheld the implied powers of Congress to create a Bank of the United States (B). Judicial review (C) was established in *Marbury v. Madison*. Dual federalism (D) views the national and state governments each remaining supreme within their own sphere of influence.

21. **A**. The conference committee occurs latest in this list of steps in the passage of a bill through Congress. Conference committees are organized when the House and the Senate pass a bill in different forms. The steps in the passage of a bill are B, C, E, D, and A.

22. **B**. The presidential coattail effect refers to the phenomenon whereby voters support members of the president's party running for other offices, because of the president's popularity.

23. **C**. Justices to the Supreme Court are appointed for life terms, during good behavior, and can be removed only through impeachment and conviction of the charges against them (B). They are nominated by the president and confirmed by the Senate (A). Although the president tends to choose justices who reflect his or her own political ideology, he or she does not always nominate a candidate from the president's party (E). Congress sets the salaries and benefits of Supreme Court justices (D).

24. **E**. Both the mobility of the electorate and lack of political efficacy are reasons for low voter turnout. Political efficacy is the belief that a person can influence politics and public policymaking. Dissatisfaction with the status quo tends to produce a higher voter turnout. If candidates or parties show distinct differences in their programs or ideologies, voters tend to feel that their vote is more significant.

25. **A**. Congress creates executive departments, including those at the cabinet level.

26. **D**. The House of Representatives sitting as one large committee is the Committee of the Whole. A standing committee (C) is a permanent committee of the House or Senate. A quorum (B) is the number of members who must be present for business to take place. The full house

(A) and the Committee at Large (E) are not types of House committees.

27. **C.** Minor parties have not been very successful in electing candidates to office. No president and only a few members of Congress have been elected from minor parties. Major parties have frequently adopted the ideas of third parties into their platform (A, B). Many minor parties are ideological, or based upon a set of social, political, or economic beliefs (D). Minor parties often tend to focus on a single public policy matter such as abolition, abortion, or prohibition (E).

28. **B.** Floor whips check on party members and assist the floor leader in gathering the votes necessary to pass or defeat a bill. The minority floor leader (A) is the major spokesperson for the minority party and organizes opposition to the majority party. The Speaker of the House (C) is the presiding officer of the House. The president *pro tempore* is the presiding officer of the Senate in the absence of the vice president (D). Committee chairpersons (E) set agendas, assign members to subcommittees, and decide whether the committee will hold public hearings.

29. **C.** The solicitor general represents the U.S. government before the Supreme Court.

30. **E.** The Twenty-Fifth Amendment calls for a method to deal with presidential succession and disability.

31. **B.** A decline in the ability of political parties to mobilize voters is a reason for the decline in voter turnout. The expansion, not a decrease, in the size of the electorate often results in a lower percentage of voter turnout. (A) For example, after the increase in the size of the electorate caused by the ratification of the Twenty-Sixth Amendment, the low turnout of new voters between the ages of 18 and 21 decreased the percentage of voter turnout. The few states that have same-day registration have shown an increase in voter turnout (C). In recent years, party loyalty has tended to decrease (E). There are no penalties for nonvoting (D).

32. **A.** Because the terms of the members of the House of Representatives last only two years, the incumbency effect benefits members of the House of Representatives more than it benefits the members of the Senate.

33. **A.** Because education is a key factor in voter participation, the high school dropout would probably be the least likely to vote. Those with higher incomes and persons involved in the professions or business are more likely to vote (B, C). Union members and persons who actively participate in their religion are also more likely to vote (D, E).

34. **C.** The president's issuance of an executive order to carry out a policy is an example of the executive powers of the presidency. An example of the president's legislative powers is the veto power (A). The president's diplomatic powers include issuing executive agreements (B). Granting reprieves and pardons is a judicial power of the presidency (D). Providing for domestic order is one of the president's military powers (E).

35. **C.** The success of the civil rights movement after 1950 was aided by the movement's shift to the courts. The Fourteenth Amendment, ratified in 1868, defined citizenship and the rights of citizens (B). The number of African Americans in public office did not increase significantly until the 1970s (D). Interest groups such as the NAACP continue to promote the goals of the civil rights movement (E).

36. **D.** The goal of the National Organization for Women is to protect women's rights through the passage of legislation.

37. **E.** Under federalism the national and state governments each have certain authority over the same territory and people. A constitution outlines the powers and prohibitions pertaining to each level of government.

38. **B.** *Gideon v. Wainwright* provided for attorney rights in state cases. This case was used by the Supreme Court to apply the Sixth Amendment to the states through the Due Process Clause of the Fourteenth Amendment. Choice (A) refers to *Miranda v. Arizona*. The Sixth Amendment guarantees the right of the accused to be confronted by witnesses against them (C) and prohibits double jeopardy (E). Several Court

cases, including *Terry v. Ohio*, place limits on the constitutional guarantee of protection against unreasonable search and seizure (D).

39. **C.** Bills held up in committee may be forced out of committee by members of the House of Representatives so that the whole house may debate the bill. A joint resolution (A) is a proposal for action that is issued by both the House and Senate acting together; it has the force of law when passed. A cloture petition (D) is a request for a Senate vote to limit or end floor debate.

40. **A.** One sign of party dealignment may be "divided government," with one party controlling the executive branch and the other party controlling one or both houses of Congress.

41. **A.** Changing the tenure of judges is not a check on the power of the federal courts by Congress. Tenure for federal judges is established by the Constitution. The remaining answer choices represent checks on the power of the judicial branch.

42. **A.** The War Powers Resolution requires the president to inform Congress within 48 hours of any commitment of U.S. troops abroad.

43. **D.** In *Wesberry v. Sanders* the Court ruled that the apportionment of representative seats in Congress must be as equal as possible. *Marbury v. Madison* established the power of judicial review (A). *McCulloch v. Maryland* established the supremacy of the national government (B). *Mapp v. Ohio* applied the exclusionary rule to state courts (C). *Miranda v. Arizona* requires that anyone arrested for a crime be advised of the right to counsel and the right to remain silent (E).

44. **C.** A docket is a list of cases to be heard by the court.

45. **B.** A political liberal tends to believe in active governmental involvement to promote individual welfare. The remaining answer choices describe a political conservative.

46. **E.** The Constitution of the United States was written as a direct result of the failure of the Articles of Confederation to provide adequate direction for the Union. The Annapolis Convention (D) failed to reach a decision regarding the weaknesses of the Articles of Confederation. The Second Continental Congress (B) was the government that oversaw the conduct of the American Revolution. The writing of the Articles of Confederation was a direct result of the American Revolution (A). The state governments were stronger than the national government under the Articles (C).

47. **B.** A single-member district allows for the election of only one winner to represent the voters. At-large voting (C) involves an election in which candidates for office compete throughout the district or state as a whole. The one-person one-vote system (D) is the concept that each legislative district within a state should contain the same number of eligible voters to assure equal representation based on population. Gerrymandering (E) is the redrawing of legislative districts to give an advantage to a political party or group.

48. **E.** As part of the Executive Office of the President, the National Security Council is composed of the president's key foreign and military advisors. The Department of Homeland Security (D) is a department with cabinet status. It is in charge of the prevention of terrorist attacks within the United States. Another cabinet-level department, the Department of State (A), advises the president on foreign policy. The CIA (B) gathers secret information essential to national defense. The FBI (C) defends the United States against terrorism and enforces U.S. criminal laws.

49. **A.** Two presidents, Andrew Johnson and Bill Clinton, were impeached by the House of Representatives; neither was convicted by the Senate. Richard Nixon resigned prior to a vote on impeachment charges by the House of Representatives; therefore, he was not impeached.

50. **E.** The Seventeenth Amendment provided for the direct election of senators. The Twelfth Amendment (A) changed the method of voting in the electoral college. The Sixteenth Amendment (B) established a federal income tax. The Twentieth Amendment (C) set the terms of office of the president and members of Congress, while the

Fourteenth Amendment (D) defined citizenship and the rights of citizens.

51. **D.** The Courts of Appeals are constitutional courts, not legislative courts.

52. **C.** The minimum age for members of the Senate is 30 years.

53. **C.** The leaders of the Federalists and Democratic-Republicans were Alexander Hamilton and Thomas Jefferson, respectively.

54. **B.** Senatorial courtesy is not used by the president when appointing justices to the Supreme Court. The other answer choices are factors a president commonly considers when appointing a justice to the Supreme Court.

55. **B.** Congress, not the president, creates cabinet-level departments of the executive branch. The remaining answer choices represent presidential powers.

56. **E.** Powers of the Senate include trying and convicting impeachment cases, electing the vice president if the electoral college fails to determine a winner, and approving presidential appointments and treaties.

57. **D.** The Office of Management and Budget is the executive branch agency responsible for helping the president prepare the annual budget. The Department of the Treasury (B) collects federal revenue, pays federal bills, and mints coins and prints paper money. The Department of Commerce (C) grants patents and trademarks and promotes international trade.

58. **E.** The Supreme Court has both original and appellate jurisdiction.

59. **E.** The most powerful person in the Senate is the majority leader. He or she is also the spokesperson for the majority party in the Senate. The vice president (B, C) serves as president of the Senate, but he or she does not debate and votes only to break a tie. The minority leader (D) organizes opposition to the majority party in the Senate. There is no speaker of the Senate (A).

60. **A.** Political party identification is a major factor that influences whether a person approves or disapproves of a president's job performance.

› Rubrics for the Free-Response Essay

1. Total Value: 6 points
   Part (a): 1 point for each correct identification of activities = 3 points
   Part (b): 1 point for each correct explanation of activities = 3 points

2. Total Value: 4 points
   Part (a): 1 point for correct identification of pattern = 1 point
   Part (b): 1 point for correct identification of each factor = 2 points
   Part (c): 1 point for correct identification of consequence of trend = 1 point

3. Total Value: 8 points
   Part (a): 1 point for correct identification of two strategies = 1 point
   1 point for each correct discussion of strategies = 2 points
   Part (b): 1 point for correct identification of two strategies = 1 point
   1 point for each correct discussion of strategies = 2 points
   Part (c): 1 point for each correct identification of methods = 2 points

4. Total Value: 9 points
   Part (a): 1 point for each correct discussion of nomination process = 1 point
   Part (b): 1 point for each correct identification of a difference = 2 points
   1 point for each correct discussion of a difference = 2 points
   Part (c): 1 point for each correct identification of recent methods = 2 points
   1 point for each correct explanation of recent methods = 2 points

"Take your time! Even though the test is timed, pace yourself, especially on the free-response essays."
—DC, AP student

AP U.S. Government and Politics
Practice Exam 3—Section I

ANSWER SHEET

1 Ⓐ Ⓑ Ⓒ Ⓓ Ⓔ	21 Ⓐ Ⓑ Ⓒ Ⓓ Ⓔ	41 Ⓐ Ⓑ Ⓒ Ⓓ Ⓔ
2 Ⓐ Ⓑ Ⓒ Ⓓ Ⓔ	22 Ⓐ Ⓑ Ⓒ Ⓓ Ⓔ	42 Ⓐ Ⓑ Ⓒ Ⓓ Ⓔ
3 Ⓐ Ⓑ Ⓒ Ⓓ Ⓔ	23 Ⓐ Ⓑ Ⓒ Ⓓ Ⓔ	43 Ⓐ Ⓑ Ⓒ Ⓓ Ⓔ
4 Ⓐ Ⓑ Ⓒ Ⓓ Ⓔ	24 Ⓐ Ⓑ Ⓒ Ⓓ Ⓔ	44 Ⓐ Ⓑ Ⓒ Ⓓ Ⓔ
5 Ⓐ Ⓑ Ⓒ Ⓓ Ⓔ	25 Ⓐ Ⓑ Ⓒ Ⓓ Ⓔ	45 Ⓐ Ⓑ Ⓒ Ⓓ Ⓔ
6 Ⓐ Ⓑ Ⓒ Ⓓ Ⓔ	26 Ⓐ Ⓑ Ⓒ Ⓓ Ⓔ	46 Ⓐ Ⓑ Ⓒ Ⓓ Ⓔ
7 Ⓐ Ⓑ Ⓒ Ⓓ Ⓔ	27 Ⓐ Ⓑ Ⓒ Ⓓ Ⓔ	47 Ⓐ Ⓑ Ⓒ Ⓓ Ⓔ
8 Ⓐ Ⓑ Ⓒ Ⓓ Ⓔ	28 Ⓐ Ⓑ Ⓒ Ⓓ Ⓔ	48 Ⓐ Ⓑ Ⓒ Ⓓ Ⓔ
9 Ⓐ Ⓑ Ⓒ Ⓓ Ⓔ	29 Ⓐ Ⓑ Ⓒ Ⓓ Ⓔ	49 Ⓐ Ⓑ Ⓒ Ⓓ Ⓔ
10 Ⓐ Ⓑ Ⓒ Ⓓ Ⓔ	30 Ⓐ Ⓑ Ⓒ Ⓓ Ⓔ	50 Ⓐ Ⓑ Ⓒ Ⓓ Ⓔ
11 Ⓐ Ⓑ Ⓒ Ⓓ Ⓔ	31 Ⓐ Ⓑ Ⓒ Ⓓ Ⓔ	51 Ⓐ Ⓑ Ⓒ Ⓓ Ⓔ
12 Ⓐ Ⓑ Ⓒ Ⓓ Ⓔ	32 Ⓐ Ⓑ Ⓒ Ⓓ Ⓔ	52 Ⓐ Ⓑ Ⓒ Ⓓ Ⓔ
13 Ⓐ Ⓑ Ⓒ Ⓓ Ⓔ	33 Ⓐ Ⓑ Ⓒ Ⓓ Ⓔ	53 Ⓐ Ⓑ Ⓒ Ⓓ Ⓔ
14 Ⓐ Ⓑ Ⓒ Ⓓ Ⓔ	34 Ⓐ Ⓑ Ⓒ Ⓓ Ⓔ	54 Ⓐ Ⓑ Ⓒ Ⓓ Ⓔ
15 Ⓐ Ⓑ Ⓒ Ⓓ Ⓔ	35 Ⓐ Ⓑ Ⓒ Ⓓ Ⓔ	55 Ⓐ Ⓑ Ⓒ Ⓓ Ⓔ
16 Ⓐ Ⓑ Ⓒ Ⓓ Ⓔ	36 Ⓐ Ⓑ Ⓒ Ⓓ Ⓔ	56 Ⓐ Ⓑ Ⓒ Ⓓ Ⓔ
17 Ⓐ Ⓑ Ⓒ Ⓓ Ⓔ	37 Ⓐ Ⓑ Ⓒ Ⓓ Ⓔ	57 Ⓐ Ⓑ Ⓒ Ⓓ Ⓔ
18 Ⓐ Ⓑ Ⓒ Ⓓ Ⓔ	38 Ⓐ Ⓑ Ⓒ Ⓓ Ⓔ	58 Ⓐ Ⓑ Ⓒ Ⓓ Ⓔ
19 Ⓐ Ⓑ Ⓒ Ⓓ Ⓔ	39 Ⓐ Ⓑ Ⓒ Ⓓ Ⓔ	59 Ⓐ Ⓑ Ⓒ Ⓓ Ⓔ
20 Ⓐ Ⓑ Ⓒ Ⓓ Ⓔ	40 Ⓐ Ⓑ Ⓒ Ⓓ Ⓔ	60 Ⓐ Ⓑ Ⓒ Ⓓ Ⓔ

I _____ did _____ did not finish all the questions in the allotted 45 minutes.

I had _____ correct answers. I had _____ incorrect answers, including questions I left blank.

Scoring Formula:

_____ = _____

number right   raw score

I have carefully reviewed the explanations of the answers. I need to work on the following types of questions:

AP U.S. Government and Politics
Practice Exam 3

Section I

Total Time—45 minutes

60 Questions

Directions: Each of the questions or incomplete statements below is followed by five suggested answers or completions. Select the one that is best in each case and then fill in the corresponding oval on the answer sheet.

1. In nearly every congressional election, the candidates talk about overhauling
   (A) the number of terms a member of Congress can stay in office
   (B) the franking privilege enjoyed by members of Congress
   (C) the cumbersome committee structure of both houses of Congress
   (D) the persistence of pork barrel legislation
   (E) the control the president has over the annual congressional agenda

2. Which of the following is NOT a result of the Electoral College system?
   (A) Voters do not actually elect the president when they go to the polls in early November.
   (B) It is possible for a candidate to win the popular vote on the national level but still lose the presidential election.
   (C) A scenario is possible where the House of Representatives chooses the president.
   (D) Candidates campaign in many small states in the days leading up to a presidential election.
   (E) A third-party candidate would have a difficult time winning a presidential election.

3. Impeachment proceedings were started against both Presidents Richard Nixon and Bill Clinton. Which statement best compares the two situations?
   (A) The House Judiciary Committee passed articles of impeachment against both presidents.
   (B) Both men were formally impeached by the House of Representatives.
   (C) Both men had a trial in the Senate; neither was convicted.
   (D) The case of Richard Nixon was very similar to the case of Andrew Johnson; the case of Bill Clinton was not.
   (E) The mass media were sympathetic to both Clinton and Nixon during their impeachment hearings.

4. Many people, including a number who have actually served as vice presidents, have observed that the vice president of the United States has little real power. The powers of the vice president include all EXCEPT which of the following?
   (A) casting tie-breaking votes in the United States Senate
   (B) presiding over presidential impeachment trials in the United States Senate
   (C) serving as an advisor to the president on many issues
   (D) taking over for a disabled president under the terms of the Twenty-Fifth Amendment
   (E) playing a pivotal role in "balancing the ticket" in a number of presidential campaigns

GO ON TO THE NEXT PAGE

5. The principle of judicial activism was most ardently practiced by which Supreme Court?
   (A) the Supreme Court of John C. Marshall
   (B) the Supreme Court of Warren Burger
   (C) the Supreme Court of the early New Deal era
   (D) the Supreme Court of John Roberts
   (E) the Supreme Court of Earl Warren

6. The pivotal Supreme Court case that ruled that the wearing of black armbands in school to protest the Vietnam War was symbolic speech and protected by the First Amendment was
   (A) *Gitlow v. New York*
   (B) *Brandenburg v. Ohio*
   (C) *Texas v. Johnson*
   (D) *Tinker v. Des Moines*
   (E) *Reno v. ACLU*

7. As a result of the Connecticut Compromise
   (A) a bicameral legislature was created
   (B) all states had equal representation in both legislative bodies
   (C) a single executive was chosen who could only serve one term
   (D) a national court structure was established
   (E) the issue of the power of the presidency was solved

8. Which of the following is NOT a check that the legislative branch has over the executive branch?
   (A) Congress can officially ask for a referendum on a specific executive act.
   (B) Congress can refuse to confirm a presidential appointment.
   (C) Congress can refuse to fund programs requested by the executive branch.
   (D) Congress can override a presidential veto.
   (E) Congress can impeach the president and remove him or her from office.

9. Which of the following is NOT a power of state government?
   (A) regulation of corporations
   (B) establishment of licensing requirements for certain professions
   (C) regulation of immigration
   (D) regulation of intrastate commerce
   (E) regulation of the public schools

10. A political candidate who states that the government should be actively involved in supporting human rights and individual welfare and who supports change within the system would be termed a
    (A) moderate
    (B) reactionary
    (C) radical
    (D) liberal
    (E) conservative

11. During the 1936 presidential election campaign, a poll taken by *Literary Digest* predicted that Alfred Landon would defeat Franklin Roosevelt. The problem with this poll was
    (A) the poll was conducted only in certain states
    (B) the manner in which the question was worded favored Landon
    (C) more men were asked the question than women
    (D) those who responded to the poll were not a true cross-section of the voting public
    (E) the names of those polled were provided by the national Democratic and Republican parties

12. The vast majority of cases appealed to the Supreme Court are never actually ruled on by the Court. Which of the following is NOT a reason the Court may decide not to rule on a case?
    (A) Through brief orders, the case may be sent back to a lower court.
    (B) The Supreme Court justices agree with the decision of the lower court.
    (C) The case has passed the "date of expiration" established by the Court.
    (D) The justices agree that the case does not involve a significant point of law.
    (E) The case does not pass the "rule of four."

GO ON TO THE NEXT PAGE

13. The heads of the executive departments are all members of the president's cabinet. The two newest executive departments are
    (A) Department of Agriculture and Department of Homeland Security
    (B) Department of Commerce and Department of Labor
    (C) Department of Education and Department of Veterans Affairs
    (D) Department of Human Services and Department of Veterans Affairs
    (E) Department of Veterans Affairs and Department of Homeland Security

14. When is a filibuster used?
    (A) when a member of the House of Representatives wants to introduce new legislation
    (B) when a member of the Senate wants to introduce legislation specifically desired by the president
    (C) when a member of the Senate wishes to persuade members of the opposition party to support a specific bill
    (D) when there is a tie vote in the Senate on a bill
    (E) when a member of the Senate wishes to delay action or a vote on a specific bill

15. To enforce federal laws or federal court decisions in extreme cases, the president can
    (A) call for congressional impeachment of elected officials from states that do not comply with federal law
    (B) order the U.S. military to see that federal law is enforced
    (C) appoint new governors in states that do not comply with federal law
    (D) disband the state legislatures in states that do not comply with federal law
    (E) direct state courts in states that do not comply with a federal law to rule on the legality of the federal law(s) in question

16. If the census determines that a state's population has declined significantly from the last census, which of the following would NOT be expected to happen as a result?
    (A) a decline in federal funding for that state
    (B) loss of committee chairmanships for senators and representatives from that state
    (C) a decline in the overall "political pull" of that state
    (D) a possible decline in the number of representatives from that state in the House of Representatives
    (E) less chance that a candidate from that state would be chosen as a vice presidential candidate to "balance the ticket"

17. According to the preamble of the United States Constitution, the goals of public policy for the United States include all EXCEPT which of the following?
    (A) protecting private property
    (B) establishing justice
    (C) providing for the common defense
    (D) promoting the general welfare
    (E) forming a more perfect union

18. According to the pluralist theory of democratic government
    (A) a small number of elites rule in their own self-interest
    (B) there are many strong groups influencing government and each pulls the government in numerous directions, creating gridlock
    (C) bureaucrats, who carry on the day-to-day workings of the government, actually control public policy
    (D) interest groups continually compete in the public arena; as a result, bargaining and compromise is a necessity
    (E) government depends on the consent of the governed

19. Who was the only president to serve more than two terms in office?
    (A) Franklin Roosevelt
    (B) Theodore Roosevelt
    (C) Grover Cleveland
    (D) Woodrow Wilson
    (E) William Henry Harrison

GO ON TO THE NEXT PAGE

20. Today, a president cannot serve more than two terms. This is because of
    (A) an executive order
    (B) congressional legislation
    (C) a Supreme Court ruling
    (D) an amendment to the Constitution
    (E) congressional legislation that was validated by a Supreme Court ruling

21. The ideas of the Enlightenment had an impact on many of those who wrote the U.S. Constitution. One political concept NOT generally associated with the Enlightenment is
    (A) the idea of a social contract between the government and the governed
    (B) the idea that the primary purpose of government is to govern the common people, who need firm control
    (C) the need for branches of government
    (D) the idea that individuals have natural rights
    (E) the idea that under certain circumstances citizens have the right to rebel against the government

22. Which of the following is one of the disadvantages of federalism?
    (A) It encourages wide diversity in local government.
    (B) It may create a duplication of offices and functions.
    (C) It keeps government very close to the people.
    (D) It strives to avoid a concentration of political power.
    (E) States are able to serve as training grounds to create eventual national leaders.

23. The first Supreme Court case to uphold the supremacy of the federal government over state governments was
    (A) *Gibbons v. Ogden*
    (B) *Mapp v. Ohio*
    (C) *Betts v. Brady*
    (D) *Escobedo v. Illinois*
    (E) *McCulloch v. Maryland*

24. Which of the following has the LEAST influence in creating the political opinions and identities of most Americans?
    (A) the mass media
    (B) political opinions of families and friends
    (C) the official party platforms of the major political parties
    (D) demographic factors (occupation, age, etc.)
    (E) school and educational activities

25. Which political party dominated American politics in the late 19th and early 20th century?
    (A) Republican Party
    (B) Populist Party
    (C) Whig Party
    (D) Democratic Party
    (E) Bull Moose Party

26. Which of the following interest groups was NOT a part of the New Deal coalition created by Franklin Roosevelt?
    (A) Midwestern farmers
    (B) urban blacks
    (C) blue-collar workers
    (D) Catholics
    (E) women

27. Which third party came in second place in the 1912 presidential election?
    (A) the Independent Party of Ross Perot
    (B) the States' Rights Party of Strom Thurmond
    (C) the Bull Moose Party of Theodore Roosevelt
    (D) the American Independent Party of George Wallace
    (E) the Socialist Party of Eugene Debs

GO ON TO THE NEXT PAGE

28. Some commentators predict a decline in the power of political parties in the United States. Which of the following is NOT a reason for this?
    (A) More and more Americans split their votes among candidates from both parties.
    (B) The number of Americans who identify themselves as Democrats far outnumber those who consider themselves Republicans, thus creating an "unfair" political system.
    (C) Many Americans feel there is no real difference between the two political parties.
    (D) Many candidates are now more independent of political parties.
    (E) Many Americans are repelled by the influence of money on the political system.

29. In primary elections, some states allow voters to vote for candidates of either party, whether they belong to the party or not. What is this type of primary election called?
    (A) blanket primary
    (B) general primary
    (C) open primary
    (D) runoff primary
    (E) special primary

30. How was the election of United States senators changed by the Seventeenth Amendment in 1913?
    (A) Senatorial terms were lengthened to six years.
    (B) Starting in 1914 not all senators were elected at the same time.
    (C) The minimum age for senators was increased.
    (D) All candidates for the Senate had to take part in a party primary.
    (E) Senators were elected by popular vote instead of by state legislatures.

31. The process of specifically redrawing the boundaries of congressional districts to favor one political party or group over another is called
    (A) congressional districting
    (B) gerrymandering
    (C) apportionment
    (D) reapportionment
    (E) political restructuring

32. Traditionally, the chairpersons of congressional committees have been chosen on the basis of
    (A) their expertise on the issues dealt with by the committee
    (B) geographic factors (rewarding specific states or regions)
    (C) general expertise on congressional matters
    (D) seniority
    (E) careful consultation with the executive branch

33. Which of the following is necessary for a treaty to be ratified?
    (A) It must be signed by the president after approval by the Senate.
    (B) It must be passed by both houses of Congress by a majority vote.
    (C) It must be passed by both houses of Congress by a two-thirds majority vote.
    (D) It must be passed by the Senate by a majority vote.
    (E) It must be passed by the Senate by a two-thirds majority vote.

34. Between 2002 and 2008 President George W. Bush and Vice President Richard Cheney argued that
    (A) the powers of the presidency should be greatly expanded
    (B) the Supreme Court should take a greater role in determining national policy
    (C) during the Clinton years the Congress had gradually lost too much power
    (D) the entire executive branch had become too powerful in the Clinton years
    (E) the power of the state governments should be greatly expanded

GO ON TO THE NEXT PAGE

35. Political commentators who compared Barack Obama and Franklin Roosevelt often commented that
   (A) both saw the importance of allowing market forces to dictate the nation's economic future
   (B) both saw the importance of allowing state governments to control economic development
   (C) both emphasized the role of government in "jump-starting" the economy
   (D) both consulted extensively with leaders from the business world (CEOs) before making economic decisions
   (E) neither ever seemed really comfortable in the role of the president

36. The 1939 Hatch Act
   (A) prohibited federal government employees from practicing their religion while on duty
   (B) ordered the imprisonment of government officials who were proved to be members of the Communist Party
   (C) stated that federal government employees could receive benefits from the newly created Social Security system
   (D) stated that federal government employees could not engage in partisan political activities while on duty
   (E) stated that federal government employees would be hired on the basis of merit

37. "Iron triangles" are alliances that involve all of the following groups EXCEPT
   (A) congressional committees
   (B) congressional subcommittees
   (C) interest groups
   (D) interested members of the media
   (E) bureaucratic agencies

38. Which department of the executive branch plays the most important role in administering government programs and policies related to Native Americans?
   (A) Department of Justice
   (B) Department of the Interior
   (C) Department of Health and Human Services
   (D) Department of State
   (E) Department of Homeland Security

39. The federal courts that are actual trial courts are the
   (A) Circuit courts
   (B) Courts of Appeals
   (C) District courts
   (D) Supreme Court
   (E) Probate courts

40. An issue that has recently been a "litmus test" for potential Supreme Court justices has been his or her views on
   (A) the power of the Supreme Court
   (B) gays in the military
   (C) abortion
   (D) the power of the presidency
   (E) the right of an individual to own weapons

41. Which Supreme Court decision has had the greatest effect on public school education in the United States in the past sixty years?
   (A) *Regents of the University of California v. Bakke*
   (B) *Planned Parenthood v. Casey*
   (C) *Brown v. Board of Education*
   (D) *Johnson v. Selma School District*
   (E) *Davis & Leach v. State of Mississippi*

42. In 1967 Lyndon Johnson appointed the first African American to the Supreme Court. Who was this justice?
   (A) Andrew Young
   (B) Thurgood Marshall
   (C) John Lewis
   (D) Clarence Thomas
   (E) Charles Diggs

43. Recent Supreme Court rulings concerning religion have emphasized which of the following?
   (A) It is constitutional for a public school to have informal prayer periods in its daily schedule.
   (B) It is constitutional for a state to reimburse parochial schools for religious textbooks.
   (C) Public schools that teach evolution must also teach creationism.
   (D) Student-led prayers at public-school events are constitutional.
   (E) School-sanctioned prayers in public schools during the school day are unconstitutional.

GO ON TO THE NEXT PAGE

44. What pivotal 1966 Supreme Court case held that suspects in police custody must be informed of their rights?
    (A) *Terry v. Ohio*
    (B) *Wolf v. Colorado*
    (C) *Nix v. Williams*
    (D) *Miranda v. Arizona*
    (E) *United States v. Leon*

45. What pivotal 1963 Supreme Court case held that the state must provide the defendant with an attorney in state courts if he or she cannot afford one?
    (A) *Gideon v. Wainwright*
    (B) *Betts v. Brady*
    (C) *Powell v. Alabama*
    (D) *Escobedo v. Illinois*
    (E) *Furman v. Georgia*

46. Which of the following is a reason why some conservatives criticize recent federal legislation to improve student test scores (the No Child Left Behind Act)?
    (A) The Act contradicts previous federal legislation on education.
    (B) The Act is not fully supported by the Department of Education.
    (C) The Act is not fully supported by teacher unions.
    (D) They believe that the control of education should be left to the states.
    (E) They believe that the Act doesn't go far enough to impose federal control over education.

47. Which president did the most to extend the social welfare programs that began in the New Deal era?
    (A) Dwight Eisenhower
    (B) Gerald Ford
    (C) Lyndon Johnson
    (D) Ronald Reagan
    (E) Bill Clinton

48. Criticism of American foreign policy during the presidency of George W. Bush (2001–2008) included all EXCEPT which of the following?
    (A) American efforts in Iraq cost billions of dollars and would have long-term economic consequences.
    (B) American efforts alienated many potential allies in Europe and elsewhere.
    (C) American policymakers were too concerned with America's image in the eyes of the world.
    (D) American efforts created as many enemies as friends in the Middle East.
    (E) Stories of human rights abuses in American prisons in Iraq did much to harm the image of the United States in the Middle East.

49. Which of the following has the least significant role in the creation of American foreign policy?
    (A) United States Information Agency
    (B) Department of State
    (C) Central Intelligence Agency
    (D) Department of Defense
    (E) National Security Council

50. Who are the main authors of the initial budget proposal presented to Congress by the president?
    (A) officials from the Department of the Treasury
    (B) staff members of the congressional appropriations committees
    (C) staff members from the Congressional Budget Office
    (D) staff members from the Office of Management and Budget
    (E) staff members from the president's National Economic Council

51. During which presidential campaign was televised political advertising widely used for the first time?
    (A) the campaign of Franklin Roosevelt in 1944
    (B) the campaign of Dwight D. Eisenhower in 1952
    (C) the campaign of John F. Kennedy in 1960
    (D) the campaign of Richard Nixon in 1968
    (E) the campaign of Richard Nixon in 1972

GO ON TO THE NEXT PAGE

52. What was the major political party that developed in the United States in opposition to the Democratic Party of Andrew Jackson?
    (A) Anti-Masonic Party
    (B) Free-Soil Party
    (C) Whig Party
    (D) Republican Party
    (E) Know-Nothing Party

53. What was the first document that limited the power of the British monarch?
    (A) Petition of Right
    (B) *Two Treatises on Civil Government*
    (C) Magna Carta
    (D) English Bill of Rights
    (E) *The Social Contract*

54. Shays Rebellion and other acts of violence in 1787–1788 demonstrated to many in the new nation that
    (A) farmers had too much power
    (B) the economic well-being of the country was still tied to Great Britain
    (C) the nation had expanded too quickly
    (D) the government of Massachusetts was ineffective
    (E) the Articles of Confederation had to be revised to create a stronger national government

55. Which of the following is one advantage of the multi-party elections that characterize many European political systems?
    (A) Often one party does not emerge victorious.
    (B) Coalition governments often have to be formed.
    (C) Voters are given meaningful choices in elections.
    (D) Citizens generally give more money to candidates in multi-party elections than they do to candidates in a two-party system.
    (E) Multi-party elections tend to promote stability in government.

56. What was the major reason that some states formerly had poll taxes and literacy requirements for voting?
    (A) to maintain Republican Party control
    (B) to prevent third parties from gaining influence
    (C) to prevent African Americans and other minorities from voting
    (D) to ensure that incumbents remain in power
    (E) to carry on the legacy of progressives in those states

57. Which of the following was an effect of the Watergate scandal?
    (A) a rise in membership of the Republican Party
    (B) a new interest in government service among many young Americans
    (C) a strong sense that the power of the executive branch should be increased
    (D) an increasing skepticism and cynicism towards government
    (E) a strong national sense that the laws concerning impeachment should be altered

58. When critics complain about how the media cover politics, they are speaking of all EXCEPT which of the following?
    (A) the tendency of the media to follow sensational stories at the expense of more serious ones
    (B) the tendency of the media to "create" news stories out of insignificant or unintended comments or actions by politicians
    (C) the tendency of the media to lean to the liberal side when covering the news
    (D) the tendency of the media to lean to the conservative side when covering the news
    (E) the tendency toward "pack journalism"

GO ON TO THE NEXT PAGE

59. In the 1989 *Texas v. Johnson* decision, the Supreme Court ruled that burning of an American flag was constitutionally protected. According to the Court, this decision was based on which of the following reasons?
    (A) There was precedent in previous rulings.
    (B) Flag burning is a symbolic form of speech.
    (C) The flag burning had taken place on a military base.
    (D) Protestors had gotten a permit for the rally where the flag was burned.
    (E) Congress had passed a bill legalizing the burning of the American flag in political rallies.

60. After the bombing of Pearl Harbor in 1941, Japanese Americans living on the West Coast were placed in internment camps. The Supreme Court
    (A) stated that internment was a matter that should be left to individual states
    (B) immediately ruled the internment to be unconstitutional
    (C) in 1944 ruled the internment to be constitutional
    (D) made no ruling on this issue until 1954
    (E) deferred to the executive branch on this policy

END OF SECTION I

Section II

Total Time—100 minutes

Directions: You have 100 minutes to answer all four of the following questions. Unless the directions indicate otherwise, respond to all parts of all four questions. It is suggested that you take a few minutes to plan and outline each answer. *Spend approximately one-fourth of your time (25 minutes) on each question.* Illustrate your essay with substantive examples where appropriate. Make certain to number each of your answers as the question is numbered below. Use a separate sheet of paper if you need more space.

1. Today many Americans receive their news in radically new ways.

   (a) List two new formats through which many Americans now receive their news. Discuss specific examples.

   (b) List two older ways of receiving news that are being bypassed by these new formats. Discuss specific examples.

   (c) What are the major advantages of Americans receiving their news in these new formats? What will be the positive impact of this on our political system in the long run?

   (d) What are the major disadvantages of these developments? What will be the negative impact of this on our political system in the long run?

GO ON TO THE NEXT PAGE

2. There are many commentators who say that it is time to get rid of the Electoral College and change the way presidents are selected.

   (a) Explain how the United States elects a president through the Electoral College system. Include examples in which the Electoral College system has produced a president who did not get the most popular votes.

   (b) What are the advantages of this system? In other words, what are the arguments against changing the system?

   (c) What are the major disadvantages of the Electoral College system? If we eliminate the Electoral College, what system should we put in its place and why?

3. In the first part of the 21st century, there are a number of policy dilemmas that any U.S. president confronts.

   (a) What are three major policy areas that a president in our era must grapple with? In EACH of these policy areas, identify the big issues that must be debated and decided.

GO ON TO THE NEXT PAGE

(b) For EACH of the three policy areas you chose, what departments, committees, and interest groups from the executive branch, the legislative branch, and outside of government would the president and the executive staff work with to craft a policy for that area?

4. There has been considerable debate over the years on what the role of the Supreme Court should be. Some courts have practiced judicial activism, while others have not.

(a) Describe the principle of judicial activism.

(b) What are arguments in favor of a Supreme Court that practices judicial activism?

(c) What are the arguments against a Supreme Court that practices judicial activism?

(d) Pick one specific time period from the past and analyze the level of judicial activism. Be sure to discuss specific rulings the Court made to support your position.

END OF SECTION II

Answers to Multiple-Choice Questions

ANSWER KEY

1. D	16. B	31. B	46. D
2. D	17. A	32. D	47. C
3. A	18. D	33. E	48. C
4. B	19. A	34. A	49. A
5. E	20. D	35. C	50. D
6. D	21. B	36. D	51. B
7. A	22. B	37. D	52. C
8. A	23. E	38. B	53. C
9. C	24. C	39. C	54. E
10. D	25. A	40. C	55. C
11. D	26. A	41. C	56. C
12. C	27. C	42. B	57. D
13. E	28. B	43. E	58. D
14. E	29. C	44. D	59. B
15. B	30. E	45. A	60. C

› Answers and Explanations

1. **D.** Although term limits can sometimes be an issue, the one issue that is continually critiqued in congressional elections is pork barrel spending, by which members of Congress bring projects and programs back to their own districts, sometimes with the use of earmarks in appropriations bills. Predictably, many citizens oppose pork barrel spending in principle but are not upset when their own member of Congress brings projects "home." The president does have some influence over the annual congressional agenda, but that is not an issue in congressional elections. The franking privilege (which is also not an election issue) allows members of Congress to send mail to constituents without paying postage; members of Congress are thus able to brag about all they have done for free!

2. **D.** Since all of a state's electoral votes are generally cast as a block, the result is that, in practice, the Electoral College system requires presidential candidates to try to win as many large states as possible. As a result, small states rarely see presidential candidates during the campaign.

3. **A.** The House Judiciary Committee passed articles of impeachment against both Presidents Clinton and Nixon. Richard Nixon resigned before the entire House of Representatives voted on these. Bill Clinton and Andrew Johnson were both impeached by the House of Representatives but acquitted by the Senate. The press sensationalized the impeachment hearings of Bill Clinton, particularly in its coverage of Clinton's affair with a White House intern. The press was very critical of Richard Nixon throughout his impeachment process.

4. **B.** Presidential impeachment trials in the Senate are presided over by the Chief Justice of the United States. All of the other answer choices accurately describe the vice president's duties.

5. **E.** The Warren Court was deeply involved in promoting school integration and the rights of prisoners in custody and, as a result, is the most activist of the courts listed. The Supreme Court of John C. Marshall began the principle of judicial review but was not activist; government played a much smaller role in society then than it does today. The Burger Court followed the Warren Court and was much more conservative, limiting the rights of defendants in several cases, although the Burger Court did make the famous *Roe v. Wade* abortion decision in 1973. The Supreme Court of the early New Deal era blocked a number of measures that Franklin Roosevelt attempted to enact during the New Deal, stating that they were unconstitutional. Although it is too early to pass judgment on the present Supreme Court of John Roberts, several of its members persistently call for judicial restraint.

6. **D.** The Court ruled on this case in 1969. *Gitlow v. New York* was a 1925 case in which the Court upheld the conviction of a defendant for advocating the overthrow of the United States government by passing out communist pamphlets. *Brandenburg v. Ohio* was a 1969 ruling in which the Court stated that inflammatory speech cannot be punished unless it is found to cause immediate lawless action. In *Texas v. Johnson* the Court ruled that flag-burning was a form of protected speech under the First Amendment. *Reno v. ACLU* was a 1997 Court ruling that was the first to deal with subject matter found on the Internet; the Court struck down anti-indecency provisions of the Communications Decency Act, stating that they violated free speech provisions of the First Amendment.

7. **A.** While larger states wanted a legislature that would give the bigger states more representatives and the smaller states wanted a legislature in which all states would have equal representation, the Connecticut Compromise established two legislative bodies, the House of Representatives and the Senate.

8. **A.** There is no provision for ever calling for a referendum at the federal level. Referendums commonly take place at the state and local levels. All of the other answer choices correctly describe checks Congress has on the power of the president.

9. **C.** Immigration policy, which involves the admission into the United States of individuals from other nations, is controlled by the federal government. All of the other powers listed are reserved for the states.

10. **D.** Liberals would argue that changes in society should take place within the system; radicals would say that it may be necessary to go outside of the system to create real change. A moderate would be less likely to be an advocate of fundamental changes in government involvement. A conservative is unlikely to support greater government involvement in individual welfare.

11. **D.** Those polled were chosen from automobile registrations and telephone directories, so this was not a representative sample. Many supporters of Franklin Roosevelt did not have cars or telephones.

12. **C.** There is no formal "date of expiration" for Supreme Court cases. All of the other answer choices are accurate statements that help explain why only a small percentage of cases are actually considered by the Supreme Court. The "Rule of Four" refers to the requirement that four of the nine Supreme Court justices need to agree that a case should be heard by the Supreme Court; if at least four justices do not agree to hear the case, the case is not considered by the Court.

13. **E.** The size of the cabinet has steadily expanded as more executive departments have been created. The Department of Veterans Affairs and the Department of Homeland Security were the most recent two executive departments created. The Department of Agriculture was formed in 1889, the Department of Commerce was created in 1903, the Department of Labor was formed in 1913, and the Department of Health and Human Services (originally called the Department of Health, Education, and Welfare) was formed in 1953. The Department of Education was split off from that department in 1979. The Veterans Administration (VA) was turned into a cabinet-level Department of Veterans Affairs in 1989. The Department of Homeland Security was created in 2002 in response to the September 11, 2001, attacks on the World Trade Center and the Pentagon.

14. **E.** A filibuster is used by a member or members of the Senate to delay action on a bill they oppose that is expected to be approved by the body as a whole.

15. **B.** As commander in chief, the president can use the military to enforce U.S. laws and maintain order. Presidents Eisenhower and Kennedy used the military to enforce federal court orders relating to civil rights in the South. The federal government, including the president, does not have the legal ability to directly intervene in the affairs of state government; thus, the federal government has no ability to call for the impeachment of state officials, appoint new governors, disband state legislatures, or direct state courts to make any specific rulings.

16. **B.** The selection of committee chairpersons in Congress is not related to the population of their states; chairpersons are still chosen largely by seniority, although other factors are beginning to play a part too. A decline in population might cause a state to lose representatives in the House of Representatives; with fewer representatives, the "political pull" of the state can be expected to decline as well. Thus, a drop in population can be expected to lead to a decline in federal funding for that state and a lower possibility that anyone from that state would develop into a national presidential or vice-presidential candidate.

17. **A.** There is nothing about protecting private property in the preamble to the U.S. Constitution. All of the other answer choices are specifically included in the preamble.

18. **D.** The pluralist theory holds that vigorous competition among interest groups to achieve their goals necessitates a government of compromise and a continual reevaluation of priorities. Response (A) represents the elite theory of government, and choice (B) is representative of the theory of hyperpluralism. Response (C) reflects the bureaucratic theory of government, while response (E) represents traditional democratic theory.

19. **A.** Franklin Roosevelt was elected to office four times, although he died early in his fourth term.

20. **D.** The Twenty-Second Amendment limited presidential terms of office to two.

21. **B.** Enlightenment thinkers wrote about the natural rights of persons and believed the power of government should be limited; the idea that people "need firm control" is inconsistent with most Enlightenment thought. The idea of the "social contract" was emphasized by Rousseau, the concept of branches of government was discussed by Montesquieu, and the belief that citizens have the right to rebel against a government that doesn't protect their rights was espoused by John Locke.

22. **B.** The possibility that federalism may create a duplication of offices and function is a disadvantage of the system. All of the other responses are definite advantages of the federalist system.

23. **E.** The 1819 ruling in *McCulloch v. Maryland* established the implied powers of the national government; the authority of the federal government to act, the Court ruled, could come from the Necessary and Proper Clause of the Constitution. *Gibbons v. Ogden* was an 1824 Court decision giving the power to regulate interstate commerce to Congress. *Mapp v. Ohio* was a 1961 decision stating that evidence found during "unreasonable searches and seizures" could not be used against a defendant. *Betts v. Brady* was a 1942 decision that stated the government didn't have to provide a lawyer in a state trial to a defendant who couldn't afford one (this was later overturned). *Escobedo v. Illinois* was a 1964 decision stating that suspects have a right to an attorney during interrogation.

24. **C.** What the official platforms of political parties state has little influence on anyone, including on candidates running for office from that political party; there are many cases of candidates repudiating parts of the platform of their own party during the campaign. The other answer choices all list factors that often influence the political opinions and identities of Americans.

25. **A.** The Republican Party completely dominated politics at the national level during this era. Democrat Grover Cleveland was elected president in the elections of 1884 and 1892 but the presidential elections of 1872, 1876, 1880, 1888, 1896, 1900, 1904, and 1908 were all won by Republican presidential candidates.

26. **A.** The New Deal coalition, which held together from the 1930s all the way through the 1980s, generally did not include farmers from the Midwest; as a result, many supported Republican candidates. Factory workers, urban blacks, and Catholics were all part of the Roosevelt coalition (many Catholics strongly identified with the Democratic party at least since 1928 when the Democrats nominated Al Smith, a Catholic, as their presidential candidate). Women were part of this coalition; many identified with First Lady Eleanor Roosevelt. In addition, Franklin Roosevelt named a woman, Frances Perkins, as Secretary of Labor. Many commentators said this coalition was finally and officially defeated in the 1994 congressional elections, when the Republicans gained control of the House of Representatives for the first time since 1954.

27. **C.** Theodore Roosevelt received more votes in this election than did Republican William Howard Taft; Roosevelt carried six states, while Taft carried only two. In the 1992 election Ross Perot received nearly 19% of the total votes but no electoral votes. In the 1948 election the States' Rights Party of Strom Thurmond won only 2.4% of the total votes in the United States but carried four southern states and received 39 electoral votes. In 1968 George Wallace received 13.5% of the total vote and won five southern states for a total of 46 electoral votes. Eugene Debs ran for president five times; the highest vote total he and the Socialist Party ever received was in 1920, when the party gathered 6.4% of the popular vote (at the time of the election Debs was in jail for having spoken out against American entry into World War I). No third-party candidate other than Roosevelt in 1912 ever came in higher than third place in a presidential election.

28. **B.** More Americans have registered as Democrats than Republicans, but few are calling this "unfair." And while more Americans (especially young voters) are registering as Democrats, this

fact is not considered a reason for a decline in the influence of political parties—including the Democratic Party—in our political system. All of the other four choices are factors that commentators often point to as reasons for predicting a decline in the power and influence of political parties in the United States.

29. **C.** There was some controversy concerning open primaries during the 2008 election season. Critics claimed that in the 2008 primary season Republicans took advantage of the open primary system in several states by intentionally "crossing over" and voting for the Democratic candidate they perceived to be weaker; the intent of this was to help the cause of the Republican candidate in the general election.

30. **E.** This was one of the goals of many supporters of the Progressive movement. Six-year terms for senators, staggered elections, and the age requirement to be a senator were not changed by the Seventeenth Amendment. There has never been a federal requirement that Senate candidates be chosen by a party primary, although today nearly all are.

31. **B.** Redrawing the boundaries of a congressional district in a way to favor one political party or group is called gerrymandering. Several examples of gerrymandered districts have to be seen to be believed. There are also countless examples of districts being reapportioned fairly without being gerrymandered. For examples and further discussion of gerrymandering, go to www.mscd .edu/~eas/Goedecke/GEG1220/1220session6 /Gerrymandering.ppt or www.fraudfactor.com /ffgerrymander.html.

32. **D.** Traditionally, committee chairmanships have been awarded on the basis of seniority. Seniority is simply how long someone has served in the House or the Senate; those who have served the longest have become the chairs (if a member of the House becomes a Senator his or her seniority is lost). Today, however, when assigning committee chairmanships, House and Senate leadership also look at other factors, such as the ability to lead and knowledge of the matters that the committee deals with.

33. **E.** After a president (or his or her representatives) has negotiated a treaty, it must be ratified by the Senate before it takes effect. Ratification requires that the Senate approve the treaty by a two-thirds majority. The most famous example of a treaty NOT ratified by the Senate was the treaty negotiated by Woodrow Wilson ending World War I.

34. **A.** Vice President Richard Cheney vigorously argued that the power of the presidency had been weakened since the time of Watergate and that to fight the War on Terror a presidency with much stronger powers was needed.

35. **C.** Both Roosevelt and Obama felt that the federal government had to play a major role in overcoming the economic crises the nation faced when they assumed office rather than letting market forces alone dictate the nation's economic future. Neither denied the importance of economic growth at the state level, but both saw the necessity of the federal government "jump-starting" the economic growth of the country. Business leaders were consulted by the Roosevelt administration; however, the Obama administration, at least initially, was hesitant to work too closely with CEOs of companies that had lost millions and were being blamed by some for the economic crisis. Both Roosevelt and Obama appeared to be very comfortable in the role of president.

36. **D.** The Hatch Act prohibited federal government employees from using their government position to benefit a particular candidate or political party and from taking part in partisan political activities while on duty or while wearing an official uniform. The Hatch Act also made it illegal for government employees to belong to an organization that advocated the overthrow of our system of government, a provision that was used to threaten alleged Communists with loss of their federal jobs but was never used to imprison government officials.

37. **D.** Iron triangles are formed between interest groups and members of the executive and legislative branches of government. Because of common goals, all elements of the iron triangle may work together to help each other achieve their goals.

For example, a staffer from the executive branch may seek out members of the environmental lobby for ideas when crafting environmental legislation to send on to Congress; those same lobbyists might work with members of Congress to fine-tune the details of the legislation and to gain congressional support for it; congressional and executive branch staffers might work together on compromise legislation that could be supported by both branches.

38. **B.** In the Department of the Interior, the Bureau of Indian Affairs administers federal programs and policies relating to Indian reservations and thus plays the most important role in the federal government's handling of Native American affairs.

39. **C.** District courts are the federal trial courts; each state has one, while larger states may have several. Courts of Appeals were established to help lessen the load of the Supreme Court; these courts decide appeals on decisions reached by U.S. district courts and review decisions of federal administrative agencies. In very rare cases (when there is a lawsuit between two states) the Supreme Court can also be a trial court.

40. **C.** For many vocal interest groups in U.S. politics in the 1990s and early 21st century, the debate over Supreme Court nominees was dominated by the single issue of abortion. Thus the position many people (including many senators) took to support or oppose a Supreme Court nominee depended on their perception of whether or not the candidate would support or overturn *Roe v. Wade*. In chemistry, a litmus test is a simple test used to determine whether or not a solution is acidic. The term was applied to politics to refer to the simple test (in this case, whether or not the nominee supports *Roe v. Wade*) that many used to determine if a nominee should become a Supreme Court justice.

41. **C.** *Brown v. Board of Education* was the 1954 Supreme Court decision stating that "separate but equal" school facilities are unconstitutional. Enforcement of this ruling played an important and controversial role in education through the 1960s, the 1970s, and beyond. The other real

cases in this response are *Regents of the University of California v. Bakke*, a 1978 Supreme Court decision on affirmative action that stated that quota systems for college admission are unconstitutional (although affirmative action as a principle was not), and *Planned Parenthood v. Casey*, a 1992 decision that upheld the constitutional right to an abortion but which allowed certain possible restrictions of that right.

42. **B.** Thurgood Marshall had been an attorney in many important civil rights cases before he was appointed to the Court. Andrew Young was a former leader of the civil rights movement who later served as ambassador to the United Nations, congressman, and mayor of Atlanta. John Lewis was a former civil rights leader who later became a congressman from Georgia. Clarence Thomas is currently a Supreme Court justice. Charles Diggs was the first African American elected to the House of Representatives from Michigan, serving from 1955–1980.

43. **E.** The Court has been consistent in ruling that either formal or informal school prayer is unconstitutional in public schools.

44. **D.** As a result of this decision, a court may very well rule that the defendant was unlawfully detained if the defendant was not informed of his or her rights. *Terry v. Ohio* was a 1968 ruling stating that a police officer can search a suspect without a warrant if the officer thinks the suspect is committing or is about to commit a crime. *Wolf v. Colorado* was a 1949 ruling (later overturned) stating that illegally obtained evidence can be used, under certain circumstances, in a trial. *Nix v. Williams* was a 1984 decision stating that evidence gathered without a proper warrant can still be used if the authorities would have discovered that evidence anyway. The *United States v. Leon* was a 1984 decision stating that if authorities obtain a search warrant in good faith and the warrant is later proved to be faulty, the evidence recovered as a result of that warrant can be used against a defendant.

45. **A.** *Gideon v. Wainwright*, which overturned a previous ruling, held that the state must provide an attorney for a defendant who cannot afford

one. *Betts v. Brady* was a 1942 Court decision (later overturned) stating that the state does not have to provide an attorney to a defendant who cannot afford one if the defendant is being prosecuted by that state. *Powell v. Alabama* was a 1932 decision stating that in a capital trial a defendant has the right to an attorney (this decision resulted from the case of the Scottsboro boys). *Escobedo v. Illinois* was a 1964 decision in which the Court stated that a defendant has the right to an attorney when being interrogated. *Furman v. Georgia* was a 1972 decision stating that the arbitrary and inconsistent way that the death penalty was being utilized made the death penalty a form of cruel and unusual punishment and thus unconstitutional (as a result, states had to craft new death penalty laws).

46. **D.** Many conservatives believe that the federal government has taken too much power away from state and local officials and maintain that education should not be controlled by the federal government. While there have been others who have criticized the legislation saying it doesn't go far enough to impose federal control over education, this position is associated with liberals, not conservatives.

47. **C.** Most historians maintain that the Great Society programs enacted by Lyndon Johnson in the 1960s did much to extend and expand the New Deal programs of Franklin Roosevelt.

48. **C.** Seldom was the foreign policy of President George W. Bush (2001–2008) criticized for being too concerned with America's image in the eyes of the world; in fact, the Bush administration was often criticized for not giving enough consideration to world opinion when formulating foreign policy. All of the other four responses were frequently heard criticisms of American foreign policy during the Bush administration.

49. **A.** The other four departments and agencies have a major role in the formulation of American foreign policy, while the United States Information Agency is responsible not for formulating foreign policy, but for informing the world about the United States and American beliefs.

50. **D.** Using the president's priorities and guidelines, the Office of Management and Budget authors the initial budget proposal that the president presents to Congress. This budget is then vigorously scrutinized by members of Congress and the Congressional Budget Office. The Department of the Treasury and the National Economic Council play no direct role in the creation of the annual budget.

51. **B.** The first widespread use of televised political advertising occurred with the "I Like Ike" advertisements in the 1952 Eisenhower presidential campaign. The first televised presidential debates took place between John Kennedy and Richard Nixon during the 1960 campaign.

52. **C.** The Whig Party developed in opposition to the Democratic Party of Andrew Jackson and was a major force in American politics from 1833 to 1856. Three presidents were members of the Whig Party (William Henry Harrison, Zachary Taylor, and Millard Fillmore). The Anti-Masonic Party was a single-issue party that had some influence from 1828 to 1838; in the 1832 presidential election the Anti-Masonic candidate received 7.8% of the popular vote. The Free-Soil Party was an anti-slavery party that was active in the 1848 and 1852 presidential elections, but by 1854 most of its members had joined the Republican Party. The Republican Party was not founded until 1854, long after the era of Jacksonian democracy. The Know-Nothing Party existed from 1845 to 1860; the big issue for Know-Nothings was the fear of Catholic immigration. This party came apart over the issue of slavery.

53. **C.** The Magna Carta was issued in 1215 and guaranteed British nobles certain rights that the king could not take away. The 1628 Petition of Right extended the protections of the Magna Carta to commoners. *Two Treatises on Civil Government* was a 1689 work by the English political philosopher John Locke in which he emphasized the natural rights of men and the responsibility of governments to protect those rights. The English Bill of Rights was established after the Glorious Revolution and stated that citizens

were entitled to "life, liberty, and the pursuit of property." *The Social Contract* was a work by the French philosopher Jean-Jacques Rousseau that emphasized the importance of the "general will" in society.

54. **E.** Shays Rebellion and other acts of unrest convinced many that a new national government had to be created with many more powers than were given to the government under the Articles of Confederation. The powers given to the national government as outlined in the U.S. Constitution were much greater.

55. **C.** While some critics claim that there are few real differences between the Democratic and Republican parties in the United States, in nations with multi-party systems, the parties can vary radically in their core beliefs. The existence of many parties with divergent beliefs gives voters more choices in elections. However, there are many disadvantages to multi-party systems. As responses (A) and (B) suggest, one party seldom emerges victorious and, as a result, coalition governments have to be formed. These coalitions are often volatile and sometimes dissolve very quickly. Thus multi-party elections do not promote stability in government; there are countries with multi-party systems that sometimes have more than one election within a single year!

56. **C.** Literacy tests and poll taxes were used for decades in the South to prevent African Americans from registering to vote.

57. **D.** Most historians agree that Watergate and the Vietnam War created a skepticism toward government that lasted through the 1970s; Ronald Reagan promoted a renewal of patriotism when he ran for office in 1980, but he famously portrayed government as "a problem, not a solution." None of the other answer choices reflects events or trends that actually happened after the Watergate scandal.

58. **D.** Very few commentators take the position that the media as a whole is too conservative, although many liberal commentators do complain about the power of certain conservative networks and media figures (Fox News, Rush Limbaugh). All of the other answer choices accurately state criticisms of the media often voiced by commentators and politicians.

59. **B.** The ruling in *Texas v. Johnson* shows the importance the Supreme Court places on the concept of free expression as a First Amendment right.

60. **C.** The 1944 *Korematsu v. U.S.* Court decision ruled that Japanese internment was constitutional. This followed the 1943 Court ruling *Hirabayashi v. United States*, in which the Court ruled that curfews specifically aimed at Japanese Americans were constitutional, since the United States was at war with Japan.

› Rubrics for the Free-Response Essay

1. Total Value: 6 points
   Part (a): ½ point for each new way Americans receive news = 1 point
   Part (b): ½ point for each "old" way Americans receive news = 1 point
   Part (c): Discussion of advantages of new ways of receiving news = 2 points
   Part (d): Discussion of disadvantages of new ways of receiving news = 2 points

2. Total Value: 6 points
   Part (a): Explanation of Electoral College system = 2 points
   Part (b): Discussion of the advantages of Electoral College system = 2 points
   Part (c): Discussion of the disadvantages of Electoral College system = 2 points

3. Total Value: 6 points
   Part (a): 1 point for each policy area and issues involved = 3 points
   Part (b): 1 point for identification of policymakers in each policy area = 3 points

4. Total Value: 6 points
   Part (a): Explanation of principle of judicial activism = 2 points
   Part (b): Discussion of the benefits of judicial activism = 1 point
   Part (c): Discussion of the criticisms of judicial activism = 1 point
   Part (d): Analysis of a specific time period of the Court = 2 points

Appendixes

Websites Related to the Advanced Placement Exam
Glossary of Terms

WEBSITES RELATED TO THE ADVANCED PLACEMENT EXAM

There are thousands of sites on the web that may be related in some way to the study of government and politics. This is not a comprehensive list of all of these websites. It is a list that is most relevant to your preparation and review for the AP United States Government and Politics exam. It is up to you to log on to a site of interest to you and see for yourself what it offers and whether it will benefit you.

Since you are preparing for an Advanced Placement exam, go to the source as your first choice.

The College Board—http://www.collegeboard.com/ap/students/index.html
Here you will find:

- Welcome page with student and parent information about AP
- FAQs about AP, with frequently asked questions and answers
- Benefits of AP for students, parents, and schools
- Exam information, including a calendar of exams, fees, and exam day details
- AP prep, with College Board resources, study skills, and test-taking tips
- Subjects page, where you can view sample multiple-choice questions for each AP subject, sample free-response questions (with rubrics and student samples) for the past three years, the course description, and links to related sites

Other Government and Politics sites:

- The White House—http://www.whitehouse.gov
- The House of Representatives—http://www.house.gov
- The Senate—http://www.senate.gov
- The U.S. Supreme Court—http://www.supremecourtus.gov
- Oyez Project—http://www.oyez.org

Each of these websites will lead you to many others. There are just too many to list here; in fact, there are hundreds of thousands of sites listed on the web.

I suggest you use your favorite search engine (I like http://www.google.com) and type in ADVANCED PLACEMENT GOVERNMENT AND POLITICS. From that point you can surf the Internet for sites that suit your particular needs or interests. You will have to take the time to explore the sites and evaluate their usefulness. Some AP teachers have created great sites with links to other sites that you may find of value.

GLOSSARY OF TERMS

Affirmative action—A policy designed to correct the effects of past discrimination; requirement by law that positive steps be taken to increase the number of minorities in businesses, schools, colleges, and labor.

Agenda setting—The process of forming the list of matters that policymakers intend to address.

Amendment—A revision or change to a bill, law, or constitution.

Amicus curiae brief—Friend of the court; interested groups may be invited to file legal briefs supporting or rejecting arguments of the case.

Anti-Federalists—Opposed the adoption of the U.S. Constitution because it gave too much power to the national government at the expense of the state governments and it lacked a bill of rights.

Appellate jurisdiction—Gives the court authority to hear cases on appeal from the lower courts.

Apportionment—Distribution of representatives among the states based on the population of each state.

Appropriations—Money granted by Congress or a state legislature for a specific purpose.

Articles of Confederation—The first national constitution of the United States that created a government lasting from 1781 to 1789; replaced by the current Constitution.

At-large—All the voters of a state or county elect their representative.

Bicameral—A legislature divided into two chambers; Congress has the Senate and the House of Representatives.

Bill—A law proposed by the legislature.

Bills of attainder—Prohibits a person being found guilty of a crime without a trial.

Bill of Rights—The first 10 amendments to the Constitution guaranteeing certain rights and liberties to the people.

Blanket primary—Voters may vote for candidates of either party.

Block grant—Money given to states for general programs within a broad category.

Brief—Legal document submitted to the court setting forth the facts of a case and supporting a particular position.

Brief orders—The returning of a case to a lower court because a similar case was recently decided.

Brown v. Board of Education—Supreme Court decision that overturned *Plessy v. Ferguson*; ended legal segregation, saying school segregation is unconstitutional.

Bureaucracy—A systematic way of organizing a complex and large administrative structure with responsibility for carrying out the day-to-day tasks of the organization, departments, and agencies of the government.

Bureaucratic theory—The hierarchical structure and standardized procedures of government allow bureaucrats to hold the real power over public policy; proposed by Max Weber.

Cabinet—Government departments headed by presidential appointees to help establish public policy and operate a specific policy area of governmental activity.

Casework—Assistance given to constituents by congressional members, answering questions or doing favors.

Categorical grants—Federal grants for specific purposes defined by law.

Caucus—Locally held meeting in a state to select delegates who, in turn, will nominate candidates to political offices.

Caucus (congressional)—An association of congressional members who advocate a political ideology, regional, ethnic, or economic interest.

Certificate—A lower court asks the Supreme Court about a rule of law or procedure.

Checks and balances—Each branch of government is subject to restraints by the other two branches.

Civil liberties—Constitutional freedoms guaranteed to all citizens.

Civil rights—Positive acts of government designed to prevent discrimination and provide equality before the law.

Closed primary—Only registered party members may vote.

Cloture—Prevents filibustering and ends debate in the Senate, by a three-fifths vote of the Senate.

Coattail effect—Weaker or lesser-known candidates from the president's party profit from the president's popularity by winning votes.

Commerce and Slave Trade Compromise—Resolved differences between northern and southern states; Congress could not tax exports nor ban the slave trade for 20 years.

Comparable worth—Women should be paid salaries equal to men for equivalent job responsibilities and skills.

Concurrent jurisdiction—The authority to hear cases is shared by federal and state courts.

Concurrent powers—Powers shared by the federal and state governments.

Concurring opinion—Justice or justices who agree with the majority's opinion but not with the reason behind the decision.

Conference committee—A temporary committee to work out a compromise version of a bill that has passed the House of Representatives and Senate in different forms.

Congressional districting—State legislatures draw congressional districts for states with more than one representative.

Connecticut (Great) Compromise—Settled disputes between the states over the structure of the legislative branch.

Conservative—A person whose political views favor more local, limited government, less government regulations, conformity to social norms and values; tough on criminals.

Constituency service—Casework, assistance to constituents by congressional members.

Constituent—All residents of the state for Senators, all residents of a district for House members.

Constitution—The document setting forth the laws and principles of the government; a plan of government.

Constitutional courts—Federal courts created by Congress under Article III of the Constitution, including the district courts, Courts of Appeals, and specialized courts such as the U.S. Court of International Trade.

Constitutional law—Laws relating to the interpretation of the Constitution.

Cooperative federalism—Cooperation among federal, state, and local governments; "marble cake" federalism.

Courts of Appeals—Federal courts that review decisions of federal district courts, regulatory commissions, and other federal courts.

Critical election—Sharp changes in the existing patterns of party loyalty due to changing social and economic conditions.

Dealigning election—Party loyalty becomes less important to voters, and they vote for the other party candidate or independents.

Dealignment—When a significant number of voters choose to no longer support a particular political party.

Declaration of Independence—Drafted in 1776 by Thomas Jefferson declaring America's separation from Great Britain.

Deficit—Government spending exceeds revenue.

Delegated powers—Powers specifically granted to the national government by the Constitution.

Democracy—A system whereby the people rule either directly or by elected representation.

Deviating election—Minority party is able to win the support of majority party members, independents, and new voters.

Devolution—An effort to shift responsibility of domestic programs (welfare, health care, and job training) to the states in order to decrease the size and activities of the federal government (first-order devolution); some states have attempted to shift responsibilities further to local governments (second-order devolution).

Direct democracy—Citizens meet and make decisions about public policy issues.

Direct primary—Party members vote to nominate their candidate for the general election.

Discretionary spending—Spending set by the government through appropriations bills, including operating expenses and salaries of government employees.

Discrimination—Unfair treatment of a person based on race or group membership.

Dissenting opinion—Justice or justices who disagree with the majority opinion.

District courts—Lowest level of federal courts, where federal cases begin and trials are held.

Divided government—One party controls the executive, and the other party controls one or both houses of Congress.

Double jeopardy—Being tried twice for the same offense.

Dual federalism—Federal and state governments each have defined responsibilities within their own sphere of influence; "layer cake" federalism.

Elastic Clause—The Necessary and Proper Clause, Article I, Section 8, Clause 18 that allows Congress to pass laws to carry out its powers.

Electoral college—Representatives from each state who formally cast ballots for the president and vice president.

Electorate—People qualified to vote.

Elite theory—A small group of people identified by wealth or political power, who rule in their self-interest.

Eminent domain—Allows the government to take property for public use but also requires the government to provide just compensation for that property.

Entitlement program—Payments made to people meeting eligibility requirements, such as Social Security.

Environmental impact statement—Required studies and reports of likely environmental impacts, filed with the Environmental Protection Agency prior to the beginning of a project.

Equal Protection Clause—Constitutional guarantee that everyone be treated equally.

Establishment Clause—Prohibits the establishment of a national religion.

Exclusionary rule—Rule that evidence acquired as a result of an illegal act by police cannot be used against the person from whom it was seized.

Executive agreement—Agreement with another head of state not requiring approval from the Senate.

Executive order—The president directs an agency to carry out policies or existing laws.

Executive privilege—The right of the president to withhold information from Congress or refuse to testify; limited by the Supreme Court in *U.S. v. Nixon*.

Ex post facto law—Laws applied to acts committed before passage of the laws are unconstitutional.

Extradition—States may return fugitives to a state from which they have fled to avoid criminal prosecution at the request of the state's governor.

Federal budget—Amount of money the federal government expects to receive and authorizes government to spend for a fiscal (12-month period) year.

Federal system—Power is divided between the states and the federal government.

Federalism—A division of governmental powers between the national government and the states.

Federalist Papers—Written by Hamilton, Jay, and Madison to support ratification of the U.S. Constitution.

Federalists—Supported a strong central government and expanded legislative powers.

Filibuster—A lengthy speech designed to delay the vote on a bill; used only in the Senate.

Fiscal federalism—National government's use of fiscal policy to influence states through the granting or withholding of appropriations.

Fiscal policy—The policies of taxation and spending that comprise the nation's economic policy.

Fiscal year—A 12-month period, October through September, for planning the federal budget.

Floor leaders—Direct party strategy and decisions in the House of Representatives and Senate.

Franking privilege—Privilege that allows members of Congress to mail letters and other materials to constituents postage-free.

Free Exercise Clause—Congress may not make laws restricting or prohibiting a person's religious practices.

Freedom of expression—Freedom of speech or right to petition the government for redress as a First Amendment right.

Front-loading—Choosing an early date to hold the primary election.

Full Faith and Credit Clause—States are required to recognize the laws and legal documents of other states.

Gatekeepers—Media executives, news editors, and prominent reporters who decide what news to present and how it will be presented.

General election—Voters choose office holder from among all the candidates nominated by political parties or running as independents.

Gerrymandering—Drawing of congressional districts to favor one political party or group over another.

Get-out-the-vote—A campaign near the end of an election to get voters out to the polls.

Government—The formal and informal institutions, people, and processes used to create and conduct public policy.

Grants-in-aid—Programs, money, and resources provided by the federal government to state and local governments to be used for specific projects and programs.

Grassroots—Average voter at the local level.

Gridlock—When opposing parties and interests often block each other's proposals, creating a political stalemate or inaction between the executive and legislative branches of government.

Hatch Act—Prohibits government employees from engaging in political activities while on duty or running for office or seeking political funding while off duty; if in sensitive positions, may not be involved with political activities on or off duty.

Hyperpluralism—Democracy seen as a system of many groups pulling government in many directions at the same time, causing gridlock and ineffectiveness.

Ideology—A consistent set of beliefs by groups or individuals.

Impeachment—Bringing charges of wrongdoing against a government official by the House of Representatives.

Implied powers—Not expressed, but may be considered through the use of the Necessary and Proper (elastic) Clause.

Impoundment—Refusal of the president to spend money Congress has appropriated.

Incorporation—Application of portions of the Bill of Rights to the states under the Fourteenth Amendment.

Incorporation doctrine—The Supreme Court ruling that most guarantees in the Bill of Rights are applicable to the states through the Fourteenth Amendment.

Incrementalism—Small changes in policy over long periods of time; usually in reference to budget-making—that the best indicator of this year's budget is last year's budget plus a small increase.

Incumbency effect—Tendency of those already holding office to win reelection due to advantages because they already hold the office.

Incumbent—The person currently holding office.

Inherent powers—Powers that exist for the national government because the government is sovereign.

Initiative—Allows voters to petition to propose legislation and then submit it for a vote by qualified voters.

Interest group—A group of private citizens whose goal is to influence and shape public policy.

Interstate compacts—Agreements between states to work together on common issues.

Iron triangle—Alliances that develop between bureaucratic agencies, interest groups, and congressional committees or subcommittees.

Issue network—Individuals in Washington—located within interest groups, congressional staff, think tanks, universities, and the media—who regularly discuss and advocate public policies.

Joint committee—Committee made up of members of both houses of Congress.

Judicial activism—The Court should play an active role in determining national policies.

Judicial restraint—Holds that the Court should avoid taking the initiative on social and political questions, operating strictly within the limits of the Constitution.

Judicial review—Authority given the courts to review constitutionality of acts by the executive, states, or the legislature; established in *Marbury v. Madison*.

Jurisdiction—The authority of the courts to hear and decide issues in certain cases.

Legislative courts—Courts created by Congress for a specialized purpose with a narrow range of authority.

Legislative veto—To reject the actions of the president or executive agency by a vote of one or both houses of Congress without the consent of the president; ruled unconstitutional by the Supreme Court in *Immigration and Naturalization Service v. Chadha*.

Lemon test—Standard set by the Supreme Court in *Lemon v. Kurtzman* to measure the constitutionality of state laws in regard to freedom of religion.

Liberal—A person whose views favor more government involvement in business, social welfare, minority rights, and increased government spending.

Limited government—Basic principle of U.S. government that each person has rights that government cannot take away.

Line item veto—The president can reject a part of a bill while approving the rest; declared unconstitutional by the Supreme Court.

Lobbying—Attempting to influence policymakers through a variety of methods.

Lobbyist—Uses political persuasion to influence legislation and benefit his or her organization.

Logrolling—The exchange of political favors for support of a bill.

Loose constructionist—The belief that judges should have freedom in interpreting the Constitution.

Maintaining elections—Traditional majority power maintains power based on voters' party loyalty.

Majority leader—The elected leader of the party with the most seats in the House of Representatives or Senate.

Majority-minority districts—Drawing district boundaries to give a minority group a majority.

Majority opinion—The majority of justices agree on the decision and the reasons for the decision.

Mandates—Requirements imposed by the national government on state and local governments to comply with federal rules and regulations.

Mandatory spending—Required government spending by permanent laws.

Marbury v. Madison—Established the principle of judicial review.

Markup—Rewrite of a bill after hearings have been held on it.

Mass media—All forms of communication that reach a large portion of the population.

McCulloch v. Maryland—Supreme Court decision upholding the supremacy of the national government over the states.

Media event—A speech or photo opportunity staged to give a politician's view on an issue.

Miranda v. Arizona—Requires that anyone arrested for a crime be advised of the right to counsel and the right to remain silent.

Moderate—Person whose views are between conservative and liberal and may include some of both ideologies.

Monetary policy—Economic policy in which money is controlled through the Federal Reserve.

Motor Voter Law—Allows citizens to register to vote at welfare and motor vehicle offices.

National chairperson—Appointed by a committee as head of the party.

National debt—Amount of money owed by the government.

Natural rights—Basic rights that are guaranteed to all persons; basic rights that a government cannot deny.

Necessary and Proper Clause—Gives Congress the powers to pass all laws necessary to carry out their constitutional duties, found in Article I, Section 8, Clause 18; also called "Elastic Clause."

New Deal coalition—Alliance of southern conservatives, religious, and ethnic minorities who supported the Democratic Party for 40 years.

North American Free Trade Agreement (NAFTA)—Created to allow the free movement of goods between Canada, Mexico, and the United States by lessening and eliminating tariffs.

Off-year election—An election taking place in a year when no presidential elections are occurring; midterm election.

Open primary—Voters may choose the candidates of either party, whether they belong to the party or not.

Opinion leaders—Those individuals held in great respect because of their position, expertise, or personality, who may informally and unintentionally influence others.

Original jurisdiction—Court hears and decides a case for the first time.

Oversight—Congress monitors policies of the executive branch.

Pardon—A convicted person is exempt from the penalties of a crime.

Plessy v. Ferguson—The Supreme Court case that upheld separate-but-equal segregation in 1896.

Pluralist theory—Interest groups compete in the political arena with each promoting its own policy preferences through organized efforts.

Policy adoption—The approval of a policy by legislation.

Policy evaluation—Determines if a policy is achieving its goals.

Policy formulation—The crafting of a policy to resolve public problems.

Policy implementation—Carrying out a policy through government agencies and courts.

Political action committee (PAC)—Extension of an interest group that contributes money to political campaigns.

Political agenda—Issues that merit action, as determined by the public or those in power.

Political culture—A set of basic values and beliefs about one's country or government that is shared by most citizens and that influences political opinions and behaviors.

Political efficacy—Belief that a person can influence politics and public policymaking.

Political ideology—A consistent set of beliefs about politics and public policy that sets the framework for evaluating government and public policy.

Political party—Voluntary association of people who seek to control the government through common principles, based on peaceful and legal actions such as the winning of elections.

Political socialization—Complex process by which people get their sense of political identity, beliefs, and values.

Politics—Method of maintaining, managing, and gaining control of government.

Popular sovereignty—Basic principle of U.S. government which holds that the people are the source of all governmental power.

Pork barrel legislation—Legislation giving benefits to constituents through sometimes unnecessary or unwise projects within a state or district, to enhance a member's chance of reelection.

Precedents—Standards or guides based on prior decisions that serve as a rule for settling similar disputes.

Presidential preference primaries—Voters select delegates to the presidential nominating convention.

President *pro tempore*—Serves as president of the Senate in the absence of the vice president; chosen by the majority party.

Primary election—Nominating election held to choose party candidates who will run in the general election.

Prior restraint—Censorship of information before it is published or broadcast.

Privileges and Immunities Clause—States are prohibited from unreasonably discriminating against residents of other states.

Procedural due process—Method of government action, or how the law is carried out according to established rules and procedures.

Public opinion—A collection of shared attitudes of citizens about government, politics, and the making of public policy.

Public policy—The exercise of government power in doing those things necessary to maintain legitimate authority and control over society.

Pure speech—Verbal communication of ideas and opinions.

Radical—Ideological view that favors rapid fundamental change in the existing social, economic, or political order.

Ratification—Method of enacting a constitution or amendment into law.

Reactionary—Ideological view that favors a return to a previous state of affairs.

Realigning elections—When a minority party wins by building a new coalition of voters that continues over successive elections.

Realignment—A shift of voting patterns to form new coalitions of party support.

Reapportionment—Redistribution of the congressional seats among the states after the census determines changes in population distribution.

Recall—Special election initiated by petition to allow citizens to remove an official from office before his or her term expires.

Referendum—Procedure whereby the state submits legislation to its voters for approval, allowing citizens to vote directly on issues.

Representative democracy—Citizens choose officials (representatives) who make decisions about public policy.

Reserved powers—Powers belonging specifically to the states and the people because they were not delegated to the national government nor denied to the states.

Revenue sharing—Giving money back to state and local government with no strings attached.

Rider—An addition or amendment added to a bill that often has no relation to the bill but that may not pass on its own merits.

Rule of four—Requirement that a case can only be heard by the Supreme Court if four justices vote to hear the case.

Rules committee—Determines the rules of debate for bills in the House of Representatives.

Runoff primary—When no candidate receives a majority of votes, an election held between the two candidates who received the most votes in the primary.

Sampling—Using a representative cross-section of the general population chosen at random in the polling process.

Sampling errors—Percentage of possible errors in the polling process.

Select committee—Committee selected for a specific purpose.

Self-incrimination—Accusing oneself or giving evidence that may prove oneself guilty.

Senatorial courtesy—The practice of allowing senators from the president's party who represent the state where a judicial district is located, to approve or disapprove potential nominees for the lower federal courts.

Seniority system—System in which the chairmanship of a committee is given to the member with the longest continuous service.

Separation of powers—Practice by which power is separated among three branches of government; each branch has its own powers and duties and is independent of and equal to the other branches.

Single-member districts—Only one representative is chosen from each district.

Social contract—A voluntary agreement between the government and the governed.

Social insurance programs—Programs to help the elderly, ill, and unemployed if the claimant has paid into them.

Social welfare program—Government program to enhance quality of life.

Soft money—Money distributed from a national political party organization that was not regulated by law; restricted by the Bipartisan Campaign Finance Reform Act of 2002.

Sound bite—A brief statement on TV or radio.

Speaker of the House—Leading officer in the House of Representatives, chosen by the majority party.

Speech plus—Verbal and symbolic speech used together.

Split-ticket voting—Voting for candidates from more than one party in the same election.

Standing committee—Permanent committee.

Stare decisis—Let the decision stand; decisions are based on precedents from previous cases.

Straight-ticket voting—Voting for candidates all of the same party.

Straw poll—Early form of polling that asks the same question of a large number of people.

Strict constructionist—The view that justices should base decisions on a narrow interpretation of the Constitution.

Substantive due process—The policies of government or the particular subject matter of the laws determining what the law is about and whether the law is fair or if it violates constitutional protections.

Suffrage—The right to vote.

Superdelegates—Party officials in the Democratic Party who attend the national convention without having to run in primaries or caucuses.

Super Tuesday—Day when most southern states hold presidential primaries.

Supremacy Clause—National law supersedes all other laws passed by states; found in Article VI of the Constitution.

Symbolic speech—Using actions and symbols rather than words to convey an idea.

Three-Fifths Compromise—Agreement that each slave counted as three-fifths of a person in determining representation in the House of Representatives and for taxation.

Traditional democratic theory—Government depends upon the consent of the governed.

Trial balloon—Tests the public reaction to policy or appointments by releasing information to the media and gauging public reaction.

Trustee—After listening to constituents, elected representatives vote based on their own opinions.

Two-party system—Several political parties exist, but only two major political parties compete for power and dominate elections.

Unfunded mandates—Requires states to enforce legislation without the funding necessary.

Virginia Plan—Madison's plan for a bicameral legislature, with the executive and judiciary chosen by the legislature.

War Powers Act—Limits the ability of the president to commit troops to combat.

Watergate—Break-in at the Democratic National Committee headquarters at the Watergate building in 1972 that resulted in a cover-up and the subsequent resignation of President Nixon.

Writ of certiorari—Order by the court directing a lower court to send up the records of a case for review.

Writ of habeas corpus—Requires a judge to evaluate whether there is sufficient cause to keep a person in jail.

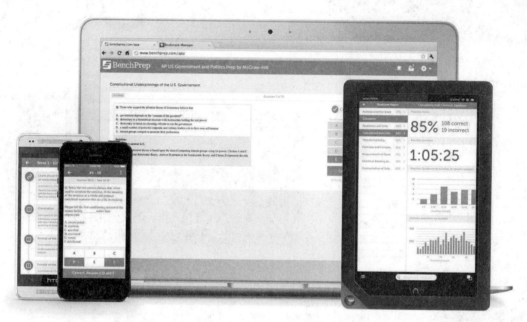

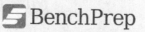

Prepare for Success at Every Step in Your AP* Journey!

AP*

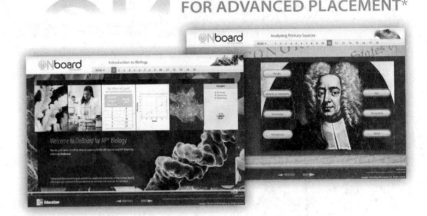